Investigating Methods

Edited by Jean McAvoy and Nicola Brace

This publication forms part of the Open University module DE100 Investigating psychology 1. Details of this and other Open University modules can be obtained from the Student Recruitment, The Open University, PO Box 197, Milton Keynes MK7 6BJ, United Kingdom (tel. +44 (0)300 303 5303; email general-enquiries@open. ac.uk).

Alternatively, you may visit the Open University website at www.open.ac.uk where you can learn more about the wide range of modules and packs offered at all levels by The Open University.

The Open University, Walton Hall, Milton Keynes MK7 6AA

First published 2014. Second edition published 2017

Edited and designed by The Open University.

Printed in the United Kingdom by Hobbs the Printers Limited, Brunel Road, Totton, Hampshire SO40 3WX.

ISBN 978 1 4730 0298 2

2.1

Contents

Introduction

Introduction

Welcome to *Investigating Methods*. How do you explore the mind? What techniques do psychologists use to research human behaviour? How do you study concepts such as thinking and thoughts? *Investigating Methods* examines these and other intriguing questions. It not only gives you an insight into how psychological research is conducted, but it prepares you to conduct your own psychological experiment.

This book is designed to be read alongside your DE100 textbook *Investigating Psychology*, and will focus on the methods that psychologists use to find answers to the questions that inspire their research. *Investigating Methods* has three main aims. First, it seeks to explain why research methods matter. This includes exploring some of the different ways in which evidence is collected, and how psychologists go about analysing their data. Second, the book looks at how psychologists present their research, and the findings, through formal research reports. In the process of reading each chapter, you will also learn how to write your own research reports. By the end of the book, you will be presented with a template that will help you to write up research that you will conduct as part of your studies on this module and beyond. Third, you will have the opportunity to engage with what are termed primary sources. Instead of reading descriptions of psychological studies written by someone not involved in carrying out the research (secondary sources), you will see parts of the original report published by those who conducted the research (primary sources). So, by the end of this book, you will not only gain a better understanding of how psychologists carry out research, but you will also have an appreciation of how research is reported.

The two books, *Investigating Psychology* and *Investigating Methods*, are designed in such a way that you should alternate your reading between them. You should read Chapter 1 of *Investigating Psychology*, followed by Chapter 1 of *Investigating Methods*; Chapter 2 of *Investigating Psychology*, followed by Chapter 2 of *Investigating Methods*, and so on. Each chapter in *Investigating Methods* will build on the studies and concepts you read about in the equivalent chapter in *Investigating Psychology*; so it is important to read them in the correct sequence.

Like *Investigating Psychology*, *Investigating Methods* is divided into three parts. Part 1 (which comprises Chapters 1, 2 and 3) introduces a selection of different methods available for conducting research, and discusses why methods matter in psychology. It looks at some of the broad differences between quantitative and qualitative methods and the benefits of each. It explains how different methods allow researchers to explore different kinds of questions. Topics include investigating belief in astrology and its links with personality, modern-day replications and new evaluations of classic studies of obedience, and alternative ways of studying children's learning.

Part 2 (Chapters 4, 5 and 6) focuses on how to organise and present data. This part of the book explains some of the different kinds of data that different methods produce, and how to describe different kinds of data once they have been collected. It looks at how to calculate and present descriptive statistics for different kinds of measurement, how to code and report complex behaviour, and how to conduct and report qualitative research using a process known as thematic analysis. Topics include the use of conditioning in advertising, attachment behaviour in dogs, working with troubled children, and understanding adolescent friendships.

The final three chapters (Chapters 7, 8 and 9) make up Part 3 of the book. Here you will learn how to evaluate research by scrutinising particular aspects of research design, and you will learn how to report and interpret formal statistical findings from research. Topics include the assessment of recovery from brain damage, the study of witness identification and misidentification, and memory and mis-remembering.

A theme running throughout the book is how researchers write up their studies so that other people can read and evaluate the findings. The carefully selected extracts from primary sources which appear in each chapter will illustrate the conventions for writing research reports and the chapters will explain why the reports are written in this way. Each chapter focuses on different sections of research reports to give you an opportunity to look in depth at what kind of information should be included in each section. Whenever the chapter authors introduce the sections of the report they will focus on, you will see a template like the one in Figure 1. The template will help you to identify what section of the report you are looking at, and where it sits in the overall sequence of the report. Figure 1, for example, indicates that the focus for that part of the chapter would be the Method section of a report.

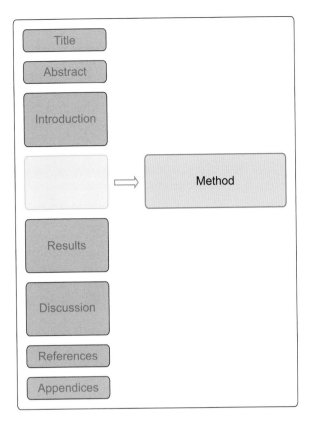

Figure 1 Throughout the book, each chapter will explain how to write specific sections of a research report

During the course of your reading, you will be introduced to a wide range of concepts and some unfamiliar terminology. Try not to be daunted by this: there will be many opportunities to check your understanding. New terms are explained when they are first introduced, and you will find a glossary of terms at the end of the book; alternatively, you can find definitions in the online glossary. You will also have opportunities to learn more about these concepts through the related online activities. You will find references to the relevant online activities throughout the chapters, so do take the opportunity to complete them.

Finally, as you read this book you may notice the style of referencing we have used. 'Referencing' refers to the practice of stating where authors have got their information from. It is an important requirement in academic writing and something you will be expected to do in your own writing during your studies. You will learn much more about the principles of referencing as you work through the module but, in the meantime, look out for the way the chapter authors write their references to primary sources (that is, where the authors cite the original research), and references for secondary sources (those where the author has read about something in somebody else's work). This will be an important distinction for you to make in your assignments. Don't worry if you are unfamiliar with these ideas to begin with. You will be given plenty of opportunity to practise.

The study of research methods in psychology can be quite challenging, but it can also be exciting as you learn how to evaluate research, understand the principles of good research design, and appreciate the way evidence is used to inform our understanding of ourselves and other people. The knowledge generated in psychological research shapes the way we live. However, any claims that psychologists make to knowledge are only as good as the methods they use to obtain it. By the end of the book, you will be in a strong position to start evaluating those methods for yourself.

Jean McAvoy and Nicola Brace

Part 1

Chapter 1
Why methods matter

Jean McAvoy

Contents

Aims and objectives

After studying this chapter you should be able to:

- describe some of the different methods common in psychological research
- explain why research methods are so important in psychology
- recognise how research reports in psychology are structured
- recognise the key features of the Title, Abstract and Introduction sections of a research report
- appreciate that different methods have different strengths.

1 Introduction to methods

The central task for psychology is to try to explain human behaviour and experience; that is, to explain all the things that people do, think, feel and say. What's more, psychology is not restricted to human behaviour. It includes non-human animals in its field of study too. But human and non-human behaviour and experience are amazingly diverse and frequently complex. Consequently, researchers in psychology have developed a wide range of different methods to help them understand this vast topic. Indeed, of all the human and social sciences, psychology probably uses a bigger variety of research methods than any other discipline. This chapter will introduce some of the methods researchers in psychology use, and explain why methods matter so much in the study of psychology. It will illustrate how researchers report their studies and, most importantly, it will begin to explain why we need to evaluate carefully the work that researchers do, the evidence they offer, and the claims they make when they try to explain all these wonderful, funny, sad, mundane or fearful things that make up the experiences of our lives.

Consider the different behaviours, feelings or thoughts involved in things like learning a language, or falling in – or out – of love, or suffering a brain injury, or experiencing prejudice and hatred. Think about the way people behave in private, and why they might behave differently in groups. What makes one person compassionate while another may appear callous? How would you help a child overcome a fear of the dark? Why are some people good at maths, or superb musicians? What makes jokes funny and memories important? There are so many very different kinds of questions that psychologists need to try to answer. Consequently, there are many different kinds of methods for doing so.

Figure 1.1   One of the great challenges in research is working out the precise questions you are attempting to answer, and which method is most likely to take you there

Research question
A research question is a carefully worded question stating precisely what a researcher is trying to find out in a study.

Deciding on the best method for solving a **research question** is a complicated business. It depends on many things, but perhaps the most important issue researchers must address is whether the methods they are considering are actually *able* to give them an answer to the question they are trying to investigate. If you want to find out how people behave when they are alone and in private there is little point bringing them into a laboratory to take part in a group experiment. If you want to explore people's unconscious behaviour there would be little point asking them to describe it in an interview; participants would struggle to describe behaviour they were unaware of. Part of the researcher's task, then, is to find creative, imaginative and **rigorous** ways to answer the research questions with which they are faced.

Rigour
A careful and thorough approach to methods and argument; to work rigorously is to work with systematic integrity.

This is a particular issue in psychology when our subject matter is ourselves and other people. As people, we often feel that we have insights into human behaviour because, of course, it is something we experience. But, being people, we are also capable of making mistakes and misjudging situations and behaviour. Therefore, in psychology, before we make any claims to knowledge, we need to carry out careful, systematic enquiries. To do that well, we have to understand the range of methods available to us. In this section we will start to look at some of the choices we have to make when we are conducting research. As research methods in psychology can be categorised into two broad groups, quantitative methods and qualitative methods, I will start there.

1.1   Choosing methods: a quantitative approach

Quantitative methods are those research methods which measure, score or count things. This might be things like *how long* it takes a person to memorise a list of words, or *how many* people believe in the paranormal, or *how often* children show aggression towards each other when they are playing. There are different methods for gathering these counts and measures. For example, McAvoy (2012) outlined the use of questionnaire scales in the authoritarian personality research conducted by Adorno et al. (1950). Questionnaires such as the scales developed by Adorno et al. (1950) are a common method for measuring attitudes and beliefs. In their study, Adorno and his colleagues asked participants to indicate how strongly they agreed with, or supported, a set of statements. The strength of participants' agreements and disagreements was measured by allocating a scoring system: 7 points for strong support, 6 for moderate support, down to 1 for strong opposition. So, this questionnaire method of matching responses to a scale allowed the researchers to take something quite complicated like the strength of a belief and assign a numerical score to it. Other types of questionnaires may be simpler, requiring only 'Yes' or 'No' in response, or 'True' or 'False'.

Another common quantitative method for researchers is the experiment. Historically, experiments have been very important in the development of psychology. Indeed, in some disciplines of psychology, such as **cognitive psychology**, for example, experiments continue to be the most common method in use. An experiment is a carefully designed, carefully controlled procedure which allows researchers to test precisely what is causing something to happen; in other words to test cause and effect. So, for example, an experiment may set out to test whether being tired has an effect on memory function. The experimenter might count the number of correct responses on a memory test taken in the morning after a good night's sleep compared with a test taken after being kept awake all night.

Quantitative methods
Methods which generate data that can be measured, counted or expressed in numerical terms; for example, scores, ratings or percentages.

You will see in the reference list at the end of this chapter that McAvoy (2012) refers to Chapter 1 of *Investigating Psychology*.

Cognitive psychology
The study of internal mental processes such as perception, attention, memory, thinking and learning.

Figure 1.2   It might seem obvious that being tired will have a negative effect on memory, but before psychologists make any claims to knowledge they must have evidence

Measurement
To apply a numerical measure according to a fixed, defined rule.

Standardisation
The process of ensuring that all participants undergo the same treatment and that all data are recorded in the same way.

Objectivity
Judgement based on observable phenomena and without the influence of personal opinion, emotion or bias.

You might think the outcome to this particular question will be quite obvious – and you may well be right! Nevertheless, in science we need evidence, and experiments are an important source of such evidence.

There are many more quantitative methods available, many of which you will meet during the course of your studies. These include methods such as observational studies, which generate numerical data by recording the number of times a particular behaviour or event occurs during a live event – laughter, smiles or frowns, for example. Content analysis is a similar method but concentrates on counting features of recorded text, such as the number of times a particular phrase or concept appears in a book, or in magazines, newspapers, letters, and so on.

1.1.1   Measurement, standardisation and objectivity

Quantitative methods can be very different in design and practice but they have some key features in common: a concern for **measurement**, **standardisation** and **objectivity**. I will use the example of personality questionnaires again to explain each of these.

First, measurement. Questionnaires made it possible for Adorno et al. (1950) to measure a particular set of personality indicators. For example, an overall score could be calculated for ethnocentrism which provided a measure of the level of prejudice towards people from other ethnic groups.

Their questionnaires met a second criterion for quantitative methods of data collection: standardisation. All participants were given the same questionnaires, with the same questions, phrased in precisely the same way, and given in the same sequence. In addition, the way participants could respond was also standardised. All participants were asked to choose their responses from the same specific and limited set of options: strong support, moderate support, slight support, slight opposition, moderate opposition and strong opposition. Moreover, each possible response was accorded a pre-set number of 'points' on the scale. This ensured that the responses were scored by the researchers in the same way. All quantitative methods must ensure data measurement and data recording is standardised.

This process of standardised collection and measurement of data helps ensure a third important aspect of quantitative methods: objectivity. Try to imagine what the data in Adorno's study might have looked like if participants were invited to describe their attitudes to the statements on the scale, rather than simply indicating a level of agreement from a limited selection of options. There would be so many possible responses that participants might give. Here are two examples. (This is an actual item from the F-scale but I made up the responses just as an illustration!)

You read about the F-scale in Chapter 1, Section 2, of *Investigating Psychology*.

F-scale item:

One main trouble today is that people talk too much and work too little.

Response from participant 1:

'Well I think it might be true but not everybody can get work these days. Some people would work really hard but can't get jobs.'

Response from participant 2:

'I don't think being talkative means someone can't do their job properly.'

If you had to categorise these responses, how would you rate them? Does the response from participant 1 show slight support for the item from the F-scale, or moderate disagreement, perhaps? Would the response from participant 2 indicate moderate disagreement or strong disagreement? Even if *you* were confident about which way to rate these responses, a second researcher might rate them in a completely different way. Developing standardised measures, with standardised responses, removes this problem and allows researchers to be objective in the way they collect and score data.

1.2   Choosing methods: a qualitative approach

Qualitative methods form the second broad category of research methods.

Qualitative methods aim to explore the rich details of people's experiences and behaviours, with a particular focus on the meanings that people give to those events. The focus on detailed meaning and personal experience means that researchers using qualitative methods generally work with small groups of participants or even individuals. This is in contrast to the large numbers of participants who can be recruited for some quantitative methods.

One very common method of generating qualitative data is through interviews. Research interviews are usually recorded so that the researcher can return to them repeatedly to examine what was said. Generally, interviews in psychological research are thought of as 'a conversation with a purpose' (Bingham and Moore, 1959). So, like a conversation, they allow participants to respond to questions in the way that participants choose rather than according to a list of possible responses fixed by the interviewer (such as in a questionnaire, for example). But, unlike most casual conversations, the research interview is very carefully planned in advance.

There are different kinds of research interviews. **Structured interviews** entail asking the same questions of all the participants, in the same order. All the questions and the sequence of questions are carefully decided in advance of the interview. This ensures that the researcher will ask each participant precisely the same questions and in the same order.

Semi-structured interviews are similar, in that a set of questions is determined in advance, but there is more freedom for both the interviewer and the interviewee to add new questions during the interview to follow up on things the participant says.

Qualitative methods
Methods which generate data that are not in numerical form, for instance interviews, written text such as newspaper articles or diaries, visual materials such as photographic records, or detailed observations of behaviour and practices.

You were introduced to interviews in Chapter 1, Section 2.3, of *Investigating Psychology*.

Structured interviews
These entail asking the same questions of all the participants, in the same order.

Semi-structured interviews
Questions are prepared in advance but the interviewer may ask additional questions during the interview in response to the interviewee's comments.

Unstructured interviews are even more open-ended. The topic of the interview is decided in advance, with a provisional list of questions, but the questions will be adapted to suit the details that unfold in the interview. This also allows the researcher to benefit from the participants contributing ideas that the researcher had not thought of.

What all these interviews have in common is that they generate rich verbal data, on pre-determined topics, and allow participants to say what they think is important, what they think matters. The distinction between these different kinds of interviews is how much or how little the interviewer might vary the questions and sequence from person to person.

Unstructured interviews
These are the most flexible interviews, beginning with a provisional list of questions which will be adapted to suit the details that unfold in the interview.

Activity 1.1

Think back to a time when you were asked to explain your thoughts about something. Perhaps you were asked for your opinion about a work colleague, or a friend, or maybe you were asked to explain why you were upset by something that someone had said to you. It doesn't matter which example you use, but try to think of an occasion when you had to think carefully about how you expressed yourself.

How easy or difficult was it to choose the right words? Have your words ever been misinterpreted?

Figure 1.3   Finding the right words to express what we mean is not always easy

It can be difficult answering questions about ourselves. This is true for research participants too. Participants have to decide what to tell the researcher. They might say what they think they *ought* to say. They may understandably be concerned about appearing sensible and reasonable. They may try to give the answer that they think is wanted. Alternatively, people might try to surprise a researcher, or even try to be intentionally provocative. What's more, if participants were asked the same question the next day or the next year, or asked questions by a different interviewer, they might well give very different answers. This is not an issue about people being difficult or uncooperative. Rather, it is a feature of working with these kinds of data. Interviews generate rich data but, because people must inevitably be selective about what they say, interview data also require careful, cautious interpretation by researchers.

Focus groups, another qualitative method of research, are rather like interviews but they take place with small groups of participants together, rather than individually as in an interview. However, an additional feature of focus groups is that they make it possible to explore how people's talk interacts, how participants shape their answers in relation to each other. Do they share meanings, are they in agreement about things, or do they raise a range of conflicting ideas, for example? The same caution that applies to analysing interview data also applies to analysing focus group data. In addition, there will be some topics that are sensitive, where it may not be appropriate to ask people to discuss them in a group. So, as with all methods, researchers have to choose not simply what works, but what is ethical. Research methods – of any kind – should not put participants at risk of harm or distress.

Figure 1.4   Researchers need to exercise care in how they manage focus groups or the groups may descend into chaos!

Of course, interviews, whether they are with individuals or groups, are not the only method of conducting qualitative research. Moreover, spoken responses are not the only kinds of data. Later in this module you will read about **ethnography**, for example.

Ethnography is a method of research where the researcher joins in with the activities of a group to carry out extensive observations in natural real-life settings over a period of time. In Section 1.1, I mentioned that observations can be a quantitative approach because a researcher might count the number of times something happens. In ethnography, observations are used to collect qualitative data in the form of rich descriptions of events rather than recording the frequency of events. An important aspect of this method is that the researcher can join in with the activities of the group being studied, to get first-hand experience of what happens, and how. So, while other methods may allow, or require, the researcher to stand back from the participants, to be objective in

Ethnography
A research approach where the researcher carries out extensive observations of a group through being involved in its activities over a period of time.

what they record and how they record it, ethnography requires researchers to get involved in the activities. Like many qualitative methods, this allows and encourages researchers to use their own **subjectivity** and their own experience as an important tool in the process of noticing, gathering and organising data.

Subjectivity
Knowledge and understanding arising from personal involvement and experience.

1.3   To count, or not to count: that is the question

Actually, what that subheading should have said is 'To count, or not to count: that *depends on* the research question'! As you have already read, there are many different methods available to researchers in psychology and here I have presented just a flavour of some of them. Whereas quantitative methods capture data by using numbers, qualitative methods capture data through rich descriptions. In addition, while quantitative methods aim to say something about people in general, qualitative methods tend to focus on meanings and experiences of a particular group or individual. While numbers make it possible to make ready comparisons between groups, such comparisons between groups in qualitative work are harder to make, but complex or unusual nuances in behaviour and understanding can be retained. Whereas quantitative methods aim for objectivity, qualitative methods are inescapably subjective. Consequently, our decisions about whether to use quantitative methods or qualitative methods depend entirely on what sort of research questions we are asking, and what kinds of data will be needed to answer those questions.

Activity 1.2

Imagine you are working as part of a research team in the psychology department of The Open University. You have been asked to gather data about older people's experience of loneliness in residential care. What might you learn from conducting observations and what might you learn from conducting interviews?

Observations would allow you to see what people actually do, rather than what they say they do. So, for example, you would be able to count the number of times someone takes part in conversations, or how long they participate in other social activities. This would be quantitative data and would allow you to identify how much time people spend alone. Of course, simply being alone is not the same thing as being lonely. Joining in a conversation does not necessarily mean that someone is not feeling lonely. But this method would allow you to get a sense of the interactions taking place. Observations would also allow you to record qualitative data: rich descriptions of the kinds of interactions taking place, or of what people are doing and how they are acting when they are alone. However, interviews, which would also generate qualitative data, would allow you to ask people directly about their experiences. Your participants would be able to tell you if or when they feel lonely, and whether that has changed over time, and indeed what alleviates their sense of loneliness. They would be able to tell you *their* interpretations of things that you might have observed, rather than you having to rely on your own interpretations. Both of these methods offer you important information so you might find choosing between them quite difficult. One possible solution might be to conduct both observations and interviews and combine your data. This is not necessarily an easy solution. You would need more resources and more time, and you would need to find a way to integrate your different types of data.

Whatever choices researchers make about methods, these choices are inescapably bound up with the kind of questions they are trying to answer. *What* questions researchers are trying to answer must guide the decisions about *how* to do their research.

Summary

- There is great diversity in the kinds of research questions asked in psychology; consequently psychology requires a wide range of methods.
- Quantitative methods generate data that can be measured, counted or expressed in numerical terms and that can be compared across groups.
- Qualitative methods generate data such as interview materials and rich descriptions.
- The most appropriate research method depends on the kind of research question being investigated.

2   Reporting research: why and how

The kinds of research in which psychologists are involved can be highly consequential for people's lives. Based on what psychologists say, schools might develop new teaching methods, or change how they help troubled children; hospitals might review their practices for treating patients diagnosed with mental health problems, or supporting patients through life-changing illnesses. The justice system may introduce new rules for how witnesses to crimes may be questioned in court. Engineers may rethink the way they build machines to fit better with human tendencies to behave in particular ways, such as driving too fast in the rain. If psychologists are to make claims that inform such changes, or indeed if they are to make any claims that influence how people live, then they need to be sure those claims are reliable. Evidence matters. Evidence matters greatly. Ethically it would be deeply irresponsible, unsafe and unprofessional to make any kinds of claims as a psychologist without having the evidence to back up those claims. It would also be unscientific. Gathering and interpreting evidence is what separates the science of psychology from common sense or guesswork.

Once research has been conducted, the outcomes of the research need to be shared: they need to be made available to other researchers and to practitioners. This process of sharing research knowledge is done primarily through writing research reports. As part of your study of psychology you too will be asked to write research reports. So, this section will explain a little about the typical structure that research reports take, and will highlight some of the things that you will need to think about for your own reports. Once you are familiar with the way in which research reports are organised, you should find it easier both to read published reports and to write your own. First, though, I will explain a little about the process of publishing academic research reports.

2.1   Standing up to scrutiny

Researchers are expected to write up their results and publish them so that other researchers and practitioners can read about them and evaluate them. There are several ways of making research reports available to other people. For example, Adorno et al. (1950) published the results of their research in a book over 900 pages in length. Today, researchers frequently write blogs on the internet to talk about their research. But by far the most common way for researchers to communicate their results is through research reports written up in academic journals. The reason for this is because of a process known as 'peer review'.

All contributions to academic journals go through a procedure known as peer review. This means that before a report is accepted for publication it will be scrutinised by several people who are also experts in that field. Those experts will assess the design of the research, the methods, and the soundness of the arguments. They give their opinion, in writing, of the merits of the report and whether it should be published. Usually, they will suggest points that the researcher needs to clarify in the report, or other concerns that need to be addressed. The author of the report will then consider whether and how to incorporate these suggestions in any revisions made to the report, before it is accepted for publication. This does not mean that academic journals, or the reports they contain, are infallible, but it does mean that there is a serious process undertaken before any academic report can be published in an academic journal. However, the process of scrutiny does not stop once the article is published. Anyone reading research reports, including you as a psychology student, should always consider the strengths and limitations of the studies presented.

2.2 Writing research reports: structure and content

The aim of a research report is to provide clear information explaining what topic the research examined, exactly what the researchers were trying to find out, how they did it, what results they got, and what they think those results mean. Typically, research reports follow a well-established format. The reason for having a common format is to help make sure that the writers provide the right kind of information and to help readers work quickly and efficiently through the report, knowing where to look for particular kinds of information. When you write your own psychology research reports, you will be asked to follow a similar format.

- **Title**. Not surprisingly, a research report should begin with a title. The title is more important than perhaps you might think. The title is the place where the author has around 15 words or fewer to indicate just what the study is about. If you compose a good title, people who are interested in the kind of work you do will think about reading your report. If your title is too vague, or misleading, many people will just skip over it and look for another paper that sounds more promising. So, a good, clear title matters. It should be an informative description of the research being reported.

- **Abstract**. The next element of a research report is the Abstract. The Abstract is a short paragraph, usually around 150 to 200 words long, which summarises the entire report. In just a few sentences the Abstract should say what the research is about, what method was used to carry out the research, the results obtained, and what the results mean. This concise summary means that readers can quickly identify the main information in the report and decide whether they want to read the whole report. You might be wondering why researchers don't just read all the reports anyway. The reason is simply that there are so many of them. For instance, one estimate suggests that in psychology alone there are approximately 3000 journal articles published each month (Adair and Vohra, 2003). This means that researchers have to find an efficient way to identify those articles which are relevant to their specialist areas. Consequently, the Abstract is an important means of achieving this. Before computers were readily available, researchers would search through printed books of abstracts. Now, abstracts are collected in large online databases, which means that thousands of articles can be searched for keywords in just a matter of seconds.

The online activity *Psychology resources in the OU Library* explains how to use the Open University online library to search databases.

Hypothesis
A hypothesis is a researcher's prediction about what will happen when a quantitative study, such as an experiment, is conducted. The researcher then tests this prediction. You will read more about research questions and hypotheses in the online activity *Research questions*, and in later chapters of this book.

- **Introduction**. The Introduction sets out the background and rationale for the research. The Introduction should summarise the existing research around the topic and explain why the current study is needed. In other words, it should explain the gap in the scientific knowledge which this research report will address. A useful way to think about the structure of an Introduction is to imagine a funnel shape – wide at the top, and getting progressively narrower towards the bottom. Figure 1.5, on the next page, illustrates what I mean. Just like a funnel, the Introduction is likely to start quite 'wide' by saying what the topic is, then introducing the previous research, and then gradually narrowing the focus down to the precise issue being investigated in this particular study. The Introduction should end with a clear statement of exactly what is being investigated. The precise format that this statement takes depends on what kind of method is being used. So, for example, if the research involves experiments the Introduction should end with a precise prediction about the outcome of the experiment. This prediction is referred to as a **hypothesis**. Other methods may instead end the Introduction with a statement of the precise research question being investigated.

Whatever statement completes the Introduction, it must flow logically from the information outlined in the Introduction.

Figure 1.5   The Introduction to a research report is structured like a funnel, with a wider focus at the start, which becomes more narrow as it leads to the hypothesis or research question being investigated

- **Method**. This section describes how the research was carried out. The most important quality of the Method section is that it should provide sufficient detail to allow a different researcher to replicate the study – in other words, to repeat the study in exactly the same way. It is quite difficult giving this amount of detail clearly, so the Method section is usually sub-divided into parts, each one concentrating on a particular aspect of the method such as who the participants were, and what the procedure was. The precise format of the Method section will depend on the requirements of the particular journal in which it is published.

- **Results**. This section describes what the research found. There is a particular style for reporting your findings depending on whether you are reporting quantitative research or qualitative research, but basically this section gives a summary of your data. If data are quantitative, and therefore in the form of numbers, the results will include relevant tables and graphs and information on how these numbers were analysed. If data are qualitative, and therefore involve rich descriptions, results will summarise that data along with illustrative examples.

- **Discussion**. The Discussion is the place where you tell your reader what you think your findings mean. The Discussion should consider how your results relate back to the previous literature mentioned in the Introduction. This means explaining whether your findings are similar to those of any previous studies, and in what way; or whether your results suggest something different from those earlier studies. Importantly, this section must also outline any limitations of the research. So, not only should we evaluate carefully what we read, but you can see from this that researchers should also evaluate their own research just as carefully. The Discussion should consider what worked well in the research, and what needs to be reviewed. It should also indicate where research on this topic should go next.

- **References**. The reference list is usually the final section of a research report. All academic writing must provide references for any ideas or material cited. There are two reasons why references must be provided. In academic work it is essential to always acknowledge where ideas come from. Not to do so would be the equivalent of stealing those ideas and passing them off as if they were our own. So, if we are using an idea somebody else has already written about, or spoken about, then we must acknowledge that. When you are writing assignments for your studies you will be expected to reference the source of all of your ideas too. The second reason for providing references is that, as I explained in Section 1.1, we must provide *evidence* for our claims. Therefore, if we are drawing on evidence presented somewhere else, we must tell our readers where to find that evidence so that they can read it for themselves if they want to. This does not apply only to evidence from other researchers, by the way. If a researcher has presented evidence for something in a previous paper that they have written, they can, if it helps them to build an argument, cite that paper to support what they are saying. This is why you will often find researchers citing themselves in their writing. This isn't vanity. It is a sensible way to tell a reader where to find more evidence that the author has written about previously. It adds to the weight of their claims without the argument for each claim having to be repeated afresh every time.

- **Appendices**. Occasionally researchers will include an appendix to a research report. (The plural of appendix is appendices.) An appendix is often used to provide more details about the materials used in the research. This might include a full list of interview questions, for example, or copies of any images used as stimuli in an experiment, and so on.

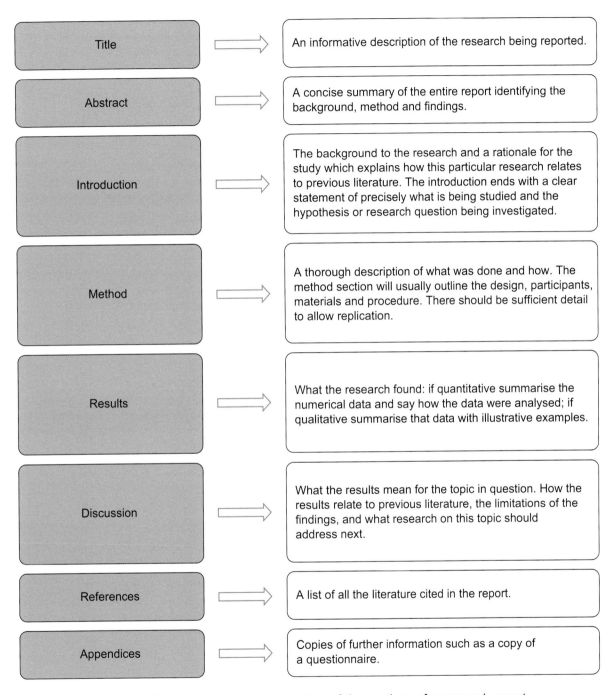

Figure 1.6   The research report template: an overview of the sections of a research report

So, these are the main sections of a research report. Figure 1.6 shows a report template which summarises all of these different sections. As you work through this book you will come across extracts from a range of research reports that have been published in academic journals. This template will direct you to which section(s) of the report you will be reading. You will see an example in the next section of this chapter where you will read three parts of a published research report: the Title, the Abstract and the Introduction. This will give you an opportunity to see what these sections look like when they are written up for publication.

Summary

- Psychological research impacts people's lives and therefore any claims made about psychology must be based on evidence.
- The most common way to present research evidence in psychology is through a research report published in a journal.
- Academic research reports are subject to an important process known as 'peer review'.
- The usual sections of a research report are the Title, Abstract, Introduction, Method, Results, Discussion, References and, occasionally, Appendices.

3   Reading primary sources: a research report on astrology and science

Scientific reports are usually written for a scientific audience and this means it can take a while to get used to how they are written. But knowing what to expect in each part of the report makes it easier to work through them. Also, the more research reports you read, the easier it becomes to make sense of them.

This section presents some extracts from Allum (2011), who looked at why some people believe astrology is a science. You might remember from Chapter 1 of *Investigating Psychology* that Adorno et al. concluded that people with authoritarian personalities were more likely to believe in superstitions and **pseudo-sciences** such as astrology. This relationship between belief in astrology and authoritarian personality was one of the things Allum wanted to test. His research report tells us what he did and what he found.

Pseudo-sciences
The appearance of scientific methods but lacking in proper application of those methods.

Figure 1.7   Report template: locating the Title, Abstract and Introduction

As Figure 1.7 indicates, I am going to concentrate on three elements: the Title, the Abstract and the Introduction, so that you can see how Allum used these sections in his report of his study.

3.1   What makes some people think astrology is scientific?

The obvious place to start our examination of this report is with the title.

3.1.1   Title

This is Allum's title for his 2011 paper:

> **What makes some people think astrology is scientific?**
>
> (Allum, 2011, p. 341)

What do you think about this as a title? Does it give you a clear sense of what his journal article is going to be about? It gives you a good idea of the basic topic, but it does not say very much about how Allum went about answering the question he asks here. Nor does it tell you anything about what that answer is. However, it did catch my attention when I was looking for journal articles for this chapter – so, in that sense, it worked for me. But, in terms of what *you* might want from a title, does it work for you?

3.1.2   Abstract

In Section 2.2, I explained the importance of abstracts in research reports. Here is the Abstract for Allum's 2011 paper:

Abstract

Citizens in both North America and Europe are apt to read horoscope columns in newspapers and magazines. While some people read these casually and purely for entertainment, some believe that astrology has scientific status and can provide real insight into events and personality. Using data from a European survey, this article explores some of the reasons why some people think that astrology is scientific and how astrology is viewed in relation to other knowledge-producing practices. Three hypotheses in particular are tested. The first is that some Europeans lack the necessary scientific literacy to distinguish science from pseudoscience. The second is that people are confused about what astrology actually is. The third is derived from Adorno's work on authoritarianism and the occult and postulates that those who adhere to authoritarian values are more likely to believe in astrological claims. Support is found for all three hypotheses.

(Allum, 2011, p. 341)

As you were reading the Abstract, did you notice how concise it was? Only 145 words. You might be surprised to realise that the full report comprises over 7000 words as well as tables, figures and an extensive list of references. In comparison then, the Abstract has given us a very clear summary of the report but in very few words.

Figure 1.8   Astrological symbols: the signs of the zodiac

Activity 1.3

Have another look at the Abstract. Can you identify:

(a) the method Allum uses for collecting data, and

(b) the three hypotheses he tests? (Remember a hypothesis is the researcher's prediction about the outcome of a study.)

Although this Abstract is very concise, it tells us that the researcher used survey data (that is, responses to a questionnaire), and that this was a survey of European participants. The three hypotheses – the precise statements of what Allum tests in his study – are: (1) that some Europeans lack the necessary scientific literacy to distinguish science from pseudo-science; (2) that people are confused about what astrology actually is; and (3) following Adorno's work on authoritarianism and the occult, those who adhere to authoritarian values are more likely to believe in astrological claims.

Box 1.1   Proof and disproof

Did you notice the last sentence of the Abstract where Allum tells us he has found 'support' for all three of these hypotheses? Note – Allum does not say he has 'proved' anything here. He tells us, cautiously and appropriately, that he has some evidence. In psychology, as in other sciences, the word 'prove' or 'proof' is rarely used. This is because it is usually only possible to 'disprove' something, not 'prove' something. For example, you might see lots of swans, and all the ones you see might be white, but this does not *prove* all swans are white. You would have to see every single swan in the world before you could make that claim. But, seeing just one black swan would 'disprove' the notion that all swans are white. By avoiding the word 'prove' and using words like 'the findings support the notion that ...', we are acknowledging the fact that while we have some evidence, new data might emerge which do not support the notion.

3.1.3 Introduction

The next extracts are taken from the Introduction to Allum's 2011 report. The extracts included below are not the complete Introduction, which was around 2700 words. Instead, I have taken some segments from it to give you a sense of how introductions work. As you read these extracts, think about how the author is setting out the background for the study, and explaining why it matters. Notice also the way in which Allum explains how his study relates to a wide range of previous literature. As you read, you may notice that with each extract the Introduction becomes gradually narrower in focus, just like the funnel effect I mentioned in Section 2.2. The first extract comes from the beginning of the Introduction.

Introduction

Anyone reading this article is likely at some point to have read their horoscope. Astrology columns are widespread in print media and on the Internet and have been a staple for a surprisingly long time. One of the earliest recorded columnists was 17th-century astrologer William Lilly, who may have predicted the Great Fire of London, albeit 14 years early (Curry, 1989). Webster-Merriam dictionary defines astrology as "divination of the supposed influences of the stars and planets on human affairs and terrestrial events by their positions and aspects." A horoscope, on the other hand, is defined as a "diagram of the relative positions of planets and signs of the zodiac at a specific time (as at one's birth) for use by astrologers in inferring individual character and personality traits and in foretelling events of a person's life." The more common understanding of horoscopes is that they are astrological forecasts, such as those that appear in newspapers. It is this definition that I use for the rest of the article. Ten years ago, just less than half of Americans read their horoscope at least occasionally in 1999 (National Science Board, 2000), and there is little reason to think that the numbers have declined since then.

It is one thing to read an astrology column for amusement or entertainment but quite another to believe that astrological predictions about events or personality will come true. A surprisingly large quantity of scientific research has been carried out to evaluate the claims of astrology. Less surprisingly, there is really no evidence to support such claims (Blackmore & Seebold,

2001; Carlson, 1985; Eysenck & Nias, 1982). It is therefore cause for concern if citizens make important life decisions based on entirely unreliable astrological predictions. For instance, people may decide for or against a potential marriage partner based on astrological sign, they may make rash financial decisions based on predicted good fortune, and so on. For this reason, in 1984, the Committee for Skeptical Inquiry (at that time the Committee for Scientific Investigation of Claims of the Paranormal) began a campaign to persuade American magazines and newspapers to attach a "health warning" to horoscope columns to indicate that they were to be read for entertainment purposes only. Only around 70 publications out of 1,000 or more in the United States that carried horoscopes at that time agreed to carry such a warning. This probably indicates that newspaper proprietors do not want to spoil their readers' enjoyment by telling them that they should really ignore all the advice given. In any case, since the 1980s, there has been a proliferation of horoscope and astrology-related websites, such as horoscope.com. This attests not only to the popularity of the topic but also to the impossibility of policing the way in which information is presented to the public.

But perhaps people do not set any store by astrological predictions and a health warning is really not necessary. After all, one does not need to believe something is true to be entertained by reading it. However, it appears that belief in astrological claims is quite widespread, at least in the United States. Losh and colleagues, in a review of 20 years of the U.S. survey data, found that many Americans believed in astrology, with polls putting the figure at around 25% (Losh, Tavani, Njoroge, Wilke, & Mcauley, 2003; National Science Board, 2002).

(Allum, 2011, pp. 341–3)

Let's stop here for the moment and review Allum's Introduction so far. Did you notice how Allum starts very broadly by identifying the topic for his paper: astrology and people who read horoscopes? He explains what he means by these terms, and that many people read horoscopes. So, right from the first paragraph we have a sense of the topic. In the second paragraph he tells us what the problem is: while some people read horoscopes for amusement, others may believe the predictions they contain and use them as a basis for important life decisions. He points out that much research has been conducted to evaluate the predictive claims of astrology but no substantial evidence has been found in support of it (notice how he cites some examples of these studies as evidence for his argument). Therefore, he says, if people are using astrology and horoscopes to make important decisions, that is a cause for concern. His third paragraph tells us that if astrology was just entertainment that would not be such a concern, but it seems that many people, in the USA at least, do believe in astrology (notice again how he cites evidence for this). This opening to the report has given us a sense of the 'big picture': many people read horoscopes and there is some evidence that some people believe them. Let's continue with Allum's Introduction:

Why should the credulity of some sections of the public toward astrology be a matter for concern for science communicators? Even if people do believe in astrology, or ghosts and alien abductions for that matter, does this have a bearing on people's understanding of and engagement with science? Again, the evidence is that it probably does. For not only do sizeable proportions of the American and European public believe in the efficacy of astrology, they also believe that it is scientific (National Science Board, 2006). The ability of citizens to distinguish between scientific and pseudoscientific claims is seen by many as an important component of scientific literacy. In a social and economic environment increasingly permeated by science, and the technological developments that flow from it, citizens require some basic competencies in order to meaningfully engage in rational judgments about a whole host of issues. For example, climate change, biofuels, stem cell cloning, synthetic biology are all topics that have acquired, or are quickly gaining, political status, which in turn require societal decisions to be made. In Miller's framework for measuring civic scientific literacy, the rejection of astrology is an empirical criterion for identifying those who are and are not scientifically literate (Miller, 2004).

(Allum, 2011, p. 343)

In this section, Allum has started to narrow the focus. Why does it matter if people believe in astrology? His argument is that if people believe in astrology this might suggest that they are not scientifically literate. In other words, if people are unable to distinguish between science and pseudo-science, this casts some doubt on their ability to make decisions based on evidence and rational argument. Allum makes the point that in society today people are increasingly required to make a host of judgements about scientific technologies, and some people consider scientific literacy to be an essential skill for making those judgements. Notice how Allum uses Miller's paper from 2004 (Miller, cited in Allum, 2011) to develop his point. Allum is not just giving us his personal opinion, he is citing other people's arguments to develop his own case. You would be expected to do this in the writing you do as part of your studies of psychology. Whenever you make any statements in your academic writing, think: 'Says who?'

This next extract comes from later on in Allum's Introduction. As you read it notice how Allum is narrowing his focus even further. Now he is talking about very specific studies – the authoritarian personality research conducted by Adorno and his colleagues.

The reference used here (Miller, cited in Allum, 2011) is an example of secondary referencing. The author of this chapter has not read Miller's original paper and indicates that here by giving the actual source of her information about Miller – Allum, 2011. For the same reason, Miller, 2004 does not appear in the reference list for this chapter.

> What is particularly interesting for the present study, though, is the connection drawn between astrology (and other forms of popular occultism) with authoritarianism, fascism, and modern capitalism. Adorno sees astrology as emphasizing conformity and deference to higher authority of some kind. Nederman and Goulding (1981) sum this up concisely as "Take things as they are, since you are fated for them anyway." Adorno posits an "astrological ideology" that he claims "resembles, in all its major characteristics, the mentality of the 'high scorers' of the Authoritarian Personality" (Adorno, 1994). The work on "Authoritarian Personality" by Adorno and colleagues has been much criticized since its appearance in 1950 (Adorno, Frenkel-Brunswik, Levinson, & Sanford, 1950; Kirscht & Dillehay, 1967) with particular criticism being directed toward the test items in the "F-Scale" (Hyman & Sheatsley, 1954). Nevertheless, it is possible to deduce a reasonably clear empirical hypothesis from "stars down to earth." Those who value conformity, obedience, and tend toward uncritical acceptance of in-group moral authority will be more likely to give credence to the claims of astrology.
>
> (Allum, 2011, p. 347)

In this extract, Allum has moved to a very specific focus: the proposed relationship between authoritarian personalities and a belief in astrology. Again notice how Allum cites the sources for his argument here. He mentions Adorno as the *source* of the suggestion that there is a link between authoritarianism and belief in astrology. Then he borrows from Nederman and Goulding (1981) to *explain* that link. (The phrase 'stars down to earth' refers to a journal article by Adorno about the content of a newspaper astrology column.)

Before I discuss this any further I want to add one final extract from Allum's Introduction. I said earlier that introductions should always end with the statement about what is being studied. You may remember from Allum's Abstract that he said he was looking at three main hypotheses. Here I am going to focus on just the final one. This is the hypothesis with which Allum ends his Introduction:

Hypothesis

Following Adorno's thesis, we should expect that people who score higher on a measure of authoritarianism will be more likely to rate astrology as being scientific.

(Allum, 2011, p. 348)

Activity 1.4

Look carefully at this hypothesis. Can you identify the link Allum makes between Adorno's work on authoritarianism and Allum's own study? What are the reasons Allum gives that lead to his hypothesis that people who are high in authoritarianism will be more likely to believe in astrology?

Allum tells the reader that previous research has connected astrology with authoritarianism. (I don't know about you but I continue to find this idea surprising!) In essence, Adorno's argument was that someone high in authoritarianism tends to defer to higher authorities and astrology could be seen to be a higher force. Therefore, someone who tends to conform uncritically to outside forces may be more likely to accept the claims of astrology. This is Allum's prediction, based logically and clearly, on previous literature.

I have presented three elements of a report here, a Title, an Abstract and an Introduction, so that you can see how these are used to outline a study, explain the background and previous literature, and state precisely what is being explored in this study. As there are no further extracts from Allum's paper in this chapter, here is a brief summary of the remainder of his report so that you know the rest of the story. Allum goes on to explain his method, which was to use data from a questionnaire he compiled with a team of colleagues for a Europe-wide survey (European Commission, 2005a, 2005b). The survey questioned participants on their knowledge of, and attitudes to, science, technology, social values and ethics. The questionnaire was administered to over 30,000 people. (This is an unusually large sample, far bigger than you would normally expect to find in most questionnaire research.) Participants were drawn from the 25 countries which made up the European Union at that time. In summary, Allum's results indicated that many people exhibited confusion between astronomy and astrology; but people who exhibited scientific literacy, that is, people who knew, for example, that experiments tested cause and effect, were less likely to believe in astrology and more able to distinguish science from pseudo-science. Allum argued that his findings suggest scientific literacy is important in assisting people to make informed, rational choices in life. Finally, in regard to the hypothesis about authoritarianism, Allum did indeed find that people with authoritarian values were more believing of astrology.

Summary

- Extracts from Allum (2011) illustrate the function of the Title, Abstract and Introduction to research reports.

- The Title and Abstract should both give a concise and informative overview of the research.

- The Introduction should explain the background to the study, gradually narrowing its focus to the specific hypothesis, or hypotheses, being tested.

- Allum's (2011) quantitative study gathered data via a questionnaire and his findings indicated that scientific literacy is important for distinguishing science from pseudo-science and therefore important for making informed choices.

4 Other ways of researching beliefs and attitudes: focusing on focus groups

In this chapter, I have described Allum's (2011) study of people's responses to questions about astrology. Allum used a subset of questions from a larger 'Eurobarometer' questionnaire to find out about people's understanding of science and why some consider astrology to be scientific. Also, in McAvoy (2012), I described the authoritarian personality studies by Adorno and his colleagues. Adorno et al. (1950) developed sets of scale questionnaires designed to assess people's attitudes and beliefs in order to say something about their personality. Both Allum (2011) and Adorno et al. (1950) used questionnaires to gather data on attitudes and beliefs which could be analysed numerically. In this section, I will present an alternative way of studying beliefs and attitudes. This study is by Kumar et al. (2011), who wanted to find out about young people's attitudes to their peers from other ethnic groups. This particular study used focus groups to explore the attitudes of white teenagers towards Middle Eastern peers. As you are reading about this study, think about the different kinds of data produced by these two methods: questionnaires and focus groups. There are some clear similarities, but some important differences too.

You read about focus groups in Section 1.2.

4.1 Talking about selves, talking about others

Kumar and her colleagues (2011) were interested in ethnic group relations in American schools with mixed ethnicity populations. They noted that previous research suggested that being white in a culture where the majority of people are white is a 'protective factor'. In effect, this means that among other things being white is taken for granted when the majority of people around you are white. In comparison, belonging to an ethnic group which is in a minority in that particular society marks members out as different. Ethnicity is made more salient as a consequence. This means that not only are attitudes to *others* influenced by being in an ethnic majority or ethnic minority, but *self-perception*, our understanding of our own identity, is also heavily influenced.

Figure 1.9
Revathy Kumar

To explore this further Kumar et al. (2011) conducted 10 focus group studies with young teenagers: two groups in five different schools in the USA. In three of the schools, white students were the majority group in the school. In the other two schools, Middle Eastern students were the majority group. The focus groups were composed of white students in order to explore the way white students talked about ethnicity when white students were in the majority in their school, and when they were in the minority in their school. Kumar et al. (2011) explained that they chose focus groups because they believed it would be easier for the students to talk about sensitive and complex issues if they were able to do so in a group of peers with whom they might share similar ideas and similar concerns, rather than in the spotlight of a one-to-one interview.

Analysis of the data indicated that the white students from schools with a *majority* of white pupils tended to express some prejudice towards Middle Eastern students, but were less likely to highlight issues about their own identity as white. 'Whiteness' was not greatly noticed by these white students when they were in the majority. Instead, their attention was on ethnically different 'others'. In comparison, white students in schools where they were in the *minority* were more likely to express prejudice towards Middle Eastern students, and also were more likely to comment on their own experiences of being white. Being in a minority made their own identity as white more noticeable to themselves, and more salient in the way they made sense of themselves and their surroundings.

Activity 1.5

Think back to the two types of method used by Allum (2011) and by Kumar et al. (2011) – questionnaires and focus groups. Try to identify some similarities and differences. To get you started, think about what participants are being asked to do. (Figures 1.10(a) and 1.10(b) might give you some additional clues.)

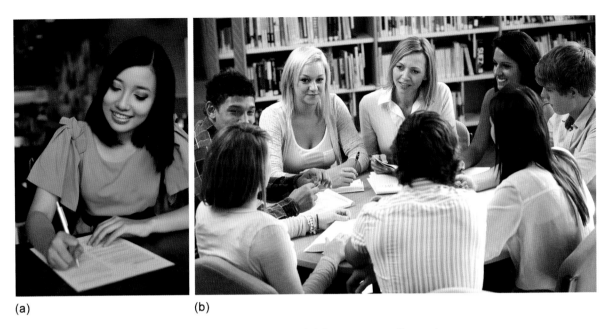

(a)   (b)

Figure 1.10   (a) student completing questionnaire; (b) focus group discussion

Here are some of the similarities and differences I identified. You may
have identified some more. One of the key similarities is that all the
participants in these studies are being asked to give **self-reports**. This
means that the data the researcher obtains about a participant is what
that participant says about themselves, subjectively, and not the kind of
data the researcher might have observed independently. All of these
studies then are potentially vulnerable to **demand effects** – in other
words, there is a risk that participants are saying things that they think
are socially acceptable, or what the researcher wants to hear, rather than
what they might think in private. But, if questionnaires are completed
anonymously by the participants this *may* help them to say what they
believe to be true rather than what they think they should say. For the
focus groups, look back to what Kumar et al. said about their reason
for choosing this method. They suggested that being in a group of
peers would enable their participants to speak more freely together. This
might alert you to another difference. In the questionnaires, individuals
complete their answers on their own. In a focus group, participants are
interacting with each other to generate their responses.

There are further similarities, though. For example, the researchers will
have needed to prepare their questions carefully in advance. Kumar
et al. (2011) included an appendix to their report which outlined all
their questions and what purpose each question was intended to serve.
Similarly, you know from McAvoy (2012) that the scales devised for the

Self-report
Any method of
collecting data that asks
participants to supply
information about
themselves, such as
their beliefs, attitudes
or feelings. Common
examples are
questionnaires and
interviews.

Demand effects
The effects on
behaviour when
participants are aware
of taking part in
research and adapt their
behaviour as a
consequence.

authoritarian personality study were revised to overcome acquiescence bias. Getting the questions right is important for both methods. However, there is a major difference in what participants could do with those questions. In the questionnaires, the questions were fixed in advance and participants had a limited range of responses available to them, pre-determined by the researcher. In contrast, while the focus groups also used carefully planned and structured questions to organise the discussion, the groups were invited to discuss their ideas freely, producing open-ended responses.

Finally, these methods produce very different data for analysis. The questionnaires used by Adorno et al. (1950) and Allum (2011) gathered data which were converted into scores to be analysed numerically. This was a quantitative method. In contrast, for the focus group, rather than condensing the data into numbers, Kumar et al. (2011) identified the key patterns in the talk, such as: what ideas the members of the focus groups generated; what mattered to them; what they considered to be important. This was a qualitative method.

Remember, all research is about selecting the kind of methods that allow you to answer the psychological questions you are interested in. There is no one correct way – but there are ways that are more, or less, suited to your particular research interests. Part of the researcher's task is to understand what can, or cannot, be achieved with any particular method.

Summary

- Focus groups are an alternative way of collecting data on people's attitudes and beliefs.
- Focus groups allow participants to interact, contributing to the discussion jointly.
- A key feature of questionnaires, interviews and focus groups is that they produce self-report data.

References

Adair, J. G. and Vohra, N. (2003) 'The explosion of knowledge, references, and citations: psychology's unique response to a crisis', *American Psychologist*, vol. 58, no. 1, pp. 15–23.

Adorno, T. W., Frenkel-Brunswik, E., Levinson, D. J. and Sanford, R. N. (1950) *The Authoritarian Personality*, New York, NY, Harper.

Allum, N. (2011) 'What makes some people think astrology is scientific?', *Science Communication*, vol. 33, pp. 341–66.

Bingham, W. and Moore, B. (1959) *How to Interview*, New York, NY, Harper.

European Commission (2005a) *Special Eurobarometer 224: Europeans, Science and Technology* [Online], Directorate General Press and Communication. Available at http://ec.europa.eu/public_opinion/archives/ebs/ebs_224_report_en.pdf (Accessed 25 April 2013).

European Commission (2005b) *Special Eurobarometer 225: Social Values, Science and Technology* [Online], Directorate General Press and Communication. Available at http://ec.europa.eu/public_opinion/archives/ebs/ebs_225_report_en.pdf (Accessed 25 April 2013).

Kumar, R., Seay, N. and Karabenick, S. (2011) 'Shades of white: identity status, stereotypes, prejudice, and xenophobia', *Educational Studies*, vol. 47, no. 4, pp. 347–78.

McAvoy, J. (2012) 'Exposing the authoritarian personality', in Brace, N. and Byford, J. (eds) *Investigating Psychology*, Oxford, Oxford University Press/Milton Keynes, The Open University.

Chapter 2
The importance of replication

Jovan Byford

Contents

Aims and objectives

After studying this chapter you should be able to:

- describe the concepts of sampling and generalisation, and how they are used in psychological research
- understand the importance of replication in psychological research
- recognise the different features of the Method section in a psychology report
- appreciate the contribution of the method and the findings of two recent studies of obedience.

1   Samples, populations and generalisations

In Banyard (2012) you read about Milgram's classic studies on obedience. You will recall that Milgram conducted his research in Connecticut, in the USA, in the 1960s. Participants were all men of similar socio-economic standing and cultural background. And yet Milgram was not interested specifically in obedience among this narrow sample of the world's population. Nor was he interested in the way in which people react to the presence of specifically scientific authority, epitomised by the researcher in a grey coat, issuing orders. In studying a particular example of obedience, Milgram was trying to shed light on a more general aspect of the human condition and human behaviour. His carefully designed and controlled set of studies was used to draw conclusions about situational factors that cause people generally to react to authority. Other researchers then investigated whether the conclusions of Milgram's studies applied to different contexts, from the behaviour of soldiers in war (Browning, cited in Banyard, 2012), to interactions between people in a virtual world (Slater et al., cited in Banyard, 2012).

You will see in the reference list at the end of this chapter that Banyard (2012) refers to Chapter 2 of *Investigating Psychology*.

That Milgram sought to draw general conclusions about human behaviour is an example of the **universalist** assumption that runs through much research in psychology. Universalism refers to the notion that phenomena observed in a **sample** of the population (participants in a study) can be generalised to the population as a whole, that is, to people beyond the specific group who took part in the research. Note, however, that when psychologists refer to 'the population' they do not necessarily mean everyone in the world or residents of a particular country. A researcher interested in the behaviour of pre-school children, for example, will conduct their study on a sample of children with the view of generalising not to everyone, but to all children within that age group. In this case 'the population' refers to pre-school children, rather than everyone. However, in research looking at general psychological phenomena (such as obedience) there is an implicit assumption that these are indeed universal and in this case 'the population', rightly or wrongly, assumes everyone.

Universalism
The assumption that phenomena observed in a study can be generalised to other contexts.

Sample
Subset of the population of interest that is studied in a piece of research.

Although generalisation is an important issue in psychology, not all psychological research seeks to generalise, or make universalist claims. A lot of qualitative research in particular is concerned with the examination of people's experiences and the emphasis there often is on what is unique, subjective, personal, or situation-specific. In contrast, generalisation is one of the goals of research involving quantitative methods, including experiments and questionnaire studies. Because psychologists cannot possibly recruit everyone in the world to take part in their study, they use samples from which they extrapolate to the population as a whole.

1.1   Sample selection

Sampling
The process of selecting participants for a study.

Selecting a sample (or **sampling**) is a complex business and there are several important considerations for researchers. First, there is the issue of *size*: the larger the size of the sample (i.e., the greater the number of participants), the more likely it is to be similar to the population. In other words, findings of studies using large samples are more likely to be generalisable to the population as a whole, compared with those using smaller samples. In Chapter 1, you read about the study by Allum (2011) which examined beliefs in astrology. This is a good example of a researcher using a large sample: Allum drew on existing data from the large Eurobarometer survey completed by over 30,000 participants across Europe. Of course, collecting data from a sample of this size requires an enormous amount of time and resources, and existing surveys are not always appropriate or relevant. So, most researchers will use smaller samples, but exercise some caution when drawing conclusions about the generalisability of their findings.

Second, there is the issue of *representativeness*. This refers to the extent to which a sample resembles the population of interest. Again, the more representative the sample, the better it is with regards to generalisability. However, here too there are practical considerations: obtaining a sample whose diversity matches that of the target population is time-consuming and expensive. Researchers will often use what is known as a *convenience sample*, that is, whichever participants are most easily accessible to them. Given that most psychological research is conducted in university departments, this has often meant recruiting participants from among undergraduate students.

Activity 2.1

When selecting the sample for his study, Milgram (1963) did not use students attending his psychology classes, even though this would have been the most 'convenient' sample. In fact, the advert used to recruit volunteers explicitly excluded 'high school and college students'. Can you think of reasons why Milgram did this?

When recruiting participants, Milgram focused on working men between the ages of 20 and 50. Of course, this was not a representative sample of either American society or the world's population. It excluded women, teenagers, those above 50, the unemployed and people with disabilities. But Milgram chose it because, in 1960s America, this was the group that would be most readily assumed to represent an 'ordinary' or average member of the public. Given that Milgram wanted to demonstrate the readiness of ordinary people to cause harm to others, it was important to select a sample that appeared to fit this description. Had he used students, it might have been argued that his research exposed a feature of the student population or characteristics of a particular generation, rather than those of an average person from the east coast of the USA.

There is another reason why sampling is important. Researchers may want to compare performance across different conditions. This is exemplified in Milgram's research, which included several variations of the original design in order to explore the influence of different aspects of the situation on obedience levels. For example, Banyard (2012) explained that Milgram tested one group of participants with the 'learner' in the adjacent room, and compared their obedience levels with those of another group, where participants were in the same room as the 'learner'. By comparing the two groups, Milgram was able to conclude that the proximity of the victim has an effect on the participants' readiness to administer shocks. When doing comparisons of this kind, it is important that the participants in the groups to be compared are as similar to each other as possible.

Imagine, for example, if in one of the variations in the obedience study the participants were middle-aged men from Connecticut, USA, while in another variation participants were recruited from among female students taking Milgram's undergraduate social psychology class. This would have made it impossible to say for certain whether any difference in obedience levels between these two groups of participants was due to the particular variation being studied (the difference in the proximity of the victim, for example) or because of the differences in age, gender, educational level or life experiences. Rather than having one group made up of middle-aged men from Connecticut, and one group made up of female college students, a better solution would be to randomly select participants for both variations from the population as a whole; this way *both* samples are more likely to be representative of the population as a whole.

This solution is not completely free of problems. Any sample, even a randomly selected one, is unlikely to represent the wider population completely. In psychological research, this is referred to as **sampling error**. Differences can occur between two samples, just because neither is an exact match to the population or to one another. Unfortunately, without actually testing the entire population, there is no way of knowing for sure whether a sample does differ or by how much it differs from the population.

Sampling error
This refers to the fact that any sample, however chosen, is unlikely to represent exactly the population from which it was drawn.

You will learn more about random samples and sampling error in the online activity *Sampling*.

Box 2.1   The WEIRD participants

According to Kimmel (1996), about 70 per cent of studies in personality and social psychology published in the USA employ university or college students as participants, with the figure rising to as high as 90 per cent in some other areas of psychology. A more recent survey of psychology journals, published in 2008, has confirmed that the trend continues (Arnett, 2008). This is a direct result of the tendency to use convenience samples and recruit participants from among students who are not only available in large numbers, but also usually quite keen to take part. This feature of psychological research is not new. As early as the 1940s, McNemar (1946, p. 333) referred to the study of human behaviour as being 'largely the science of the behaviour of sophomores' (sophomore is the term used mainly in the USA to refer to a student in the second year of university study). Also, it is not a problem limited to the USA. In the UK and elsewhere, researchers also tend to over-rely on students when selecting participants (Foot and Sanford, 2004).

The problem here is not just that the majority of participants are students, but also that the research is typically conducted on samples from wealthy, developed nations, where most of the leading universities are based. As many as 96 per cent of all participants in published psychological research come from **W**estern, **E**ducated, **I**ndustrialised, **R**ich and **D**emocratic societies. This is why the report looking into this issue suggested that the typical participant in psychological research is WEIRD (Henrich et al., 2010).

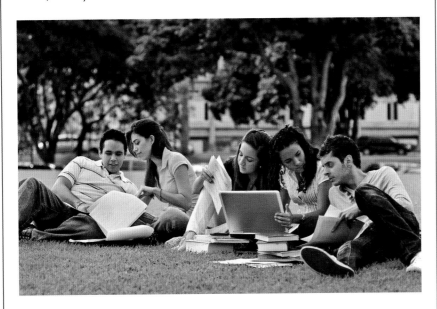

Figure 2.1 The WEIRD participants

The overuse of students and participants from developed countries has important implications for generalisation. If only 12 per cent of the world's population lives in Western, industrialised societies where the research is carried out, as suggested by Arnett (2008), then we should begin to question the extent to which it is legitimate to draw universal conclusions about human behaviour and psychological functioning from a sample that is so unrepresentative in terms of culture, wealth or lifestyle.

Throughout this module, you will encounter numerous examples pointing to the need for psychologists to recognise the diversity of the world's population because human behaviour is so profoundly influenced by culture and heritage, as well as by historical and societal conditions. You have already learned about cultural aspects of intelligence and personality, and later you will revisit these themes in relation to other topics such as attachment, social relationships, and

The relationship between culture and intelligence was discussed in the film *Limitations of intelligence testing*. The relationship between culture and personality was discussed in the film *Exploring personality in different cultures*. Both are available on the module website.

even attention. As you do so, you may want to bear in mind these words of Henrich et al. (2010):

> Recognizing the full extent of human diversity does not mean giving up on the quest to understand human nature. To the contrary, this recognition illuminates a journey into human nature that is more exciting, more complex, and ultimately more consequential than has previously been suspected.
>
> (Henrich et al., 2010, p. 29)

Summary

- Quantitative research, such as experiments, involves generalisation from a sample to the population as a whole.
- Two criteria when selecting a sample are *size* and *representativeness*.
- Researchers often use convenience samples, such as groups of psychology students, which do not adequately recognise human diversity.

2 Introducing replication

Because psychological research always involves a sample of the population, there are limits on the extent to which the results of a single study can be generalised to the population as a whole. One way of overcoming this problem is through **replication**, a concept you were introduced to by Banyard (2012).

Replication is when a study is repeated to ascertain whether the same results can be obtained using a different sample, or in different historical and social contexts. By conducting a piece of research with a different set of participants, in a different context, or at a different point in time, researchers can explore whether the findings can be generalised beyond the specific sample used in the original study. As Banyard (2012) explained, Milgram's (1963) research was repeated, or replicated, in many countries, and although there was some variation in the observed level of obedience, the basic finding was reproduced: obedience is the function of certain contextual and situational factors, such as the presence of the authority figure or the proximity of the 'learner'.

It might be worth pointing out here that the word 'replication' is used in psychology in several ways. A researcher might attempt an *exact replication*, in which case they would follow the same procedure with a view to verifying the results. A second version is *replication with extension*. This is where a researcher follows the original procedure, but adds a new dimension; for example, a new variation. You will see an example of this in Section 3. The third type is *conceptual replication*, where a researcher addresses the same question as a previous study, but does so through a slightly different approach. (See, for example, Mixon (cited in Banyard, 2012) who used role play, and Slater et al. (cited in Banyard, 2012) who used a virtual environment.)

Replication is an important concept in scientific research generally, not just in psychology. It is important because it often happens that a scientific finding, sometimes a very interesting or important one, cannot be replicated. This could be for a whole variety of reasons. It may be that the study was not conducted very well, in that there may have been a problem with the sampling or the research process that produced a one-off result. Or it might be that the researchers misinterpreted the results in some way. In rare cases, it might even be down to fraud or misconduct. Whatever the reason, the point here is that a single study,

Replication
When a result from a research study is found again in a subsequent study. Replication is important to establishing the reliability of a finding.

Replication is discussed in Chapter 2, Section 4.1, of *Investigating Psychology*.

on its own, can do no more than provide *evidence* to support a claim. Without replication, the claim cannot be confirmed or refuted. As Karl Popper, one of the twentieth century's most important philosophers of science, put it, a finding is scientifically relevant only if it 'can be regularly reproduced by anyone who carries out the appropriate experiment in the way prescribed' (Popper, 1968, p.45). This is the essence of replication.

Activity 2.2

Imagine that you are suffering from tonsillitis and your doctor suggests a course of antibiotics. She gives you a choice between penicillin, a tried and tested drug effective in the treatment of your condition, or a brand new drug which your doctor concocted in her kitchen, and which successfully cured one patient the previous week. Which option would you take?

Hopefully your doctor would never offer you this choice because only drugs that have undergone comprehensive clinical trials can be prescribed to patients (unless the patient in question is part of such a trial). Of course, the wise choice in this case would be to take the registered drug whose effectiveness has been clinically tested on a large number of patients. In fact, the whole rationale behind the process of clinical trials is that conclusions about the usefulness of a drug (or indeed a dietary supplement or cosmetic product) cannot be drawn from a single positive outcome. What is required is for the *initial* finding about a drug's effectiveness to be *replicated*, following rigorous scientific procedures.

Rigour was defined in Chapter 1 as a careful and thorough approach to methods and argument; to work rigorously means to work with systematic integrity.

In the remainder of this chapter, you will continue to learn about replication. As you will see, the importance of replication is ingrained in the way that scientific research is written up and presented: the conventions of scientific writing require authors to describe the method in sufficient detail to allow other researchers to repeat it, and to see whether they can corroborate the original finding. This feature of academic writing will be illustrated in Section 3 of this chapter using the extract from a recent attempt by Burger (2009) to replicate Milgram's (1963) findings.

Box 2.2 Why is replication important?

Replication is an important way of verifying scientific research and identifying instances where a study was not conducted very well, where the results may have been misinterpreted or, in rare instances, where authors cheated by making up their data or their findings.

Consider the following examples. John Bargh, an American psychologist, is one of the central figures in the research on social priming. This concept assumes that stimuli in the environment, even if people are not consciously aware of them, can have a significant effect on behaviour. For instance, one of Bargh's studies found that a person exposed, in the context of an experiment, to a word associated with elderly people, was more likely to walk more slowly when leaving the laboratory compared with someone who was primed with a neutral word (Bargh et al., 1996). Another study claimed that holding a warm mug when interacting with another person acts subconsciously to improve feelings towards that person (Williams and Bargh, 2008). The work on the effects of these unconsciously perceived stimuli has been hailed by many psychologists as offering major insights into human behaviour.

However, in recent years, researchers who sought to replicate the findings of some of the original priming studies found that they could not do so (e.g. Doyen et al., 2012). One explanation that has been put forward is that the methods used by Bargh and colleagues to measure the subtle effects of priming may not have been sophisticated enough, leading to spurious results. Or it could be that Bargh and colleagues repeated an experiment numerous times, but only reported the findings of those trials that supported the premise of social priming. Whatever the reason (and there is no indication that foul play was involved), the failure of replication has brought years of research into question. The Nobel Prize-winning psychologist Daniel Kahneman, who himself praised the priming studies in his writing (e.g. Kahneman, 2011), recently warned of a 'train wreck looming' in this field of research. He called for psychologists to recognise that there is a problem and to find ways of differentiating findings that stand up to scrutiny from those which do not (cited in Bartlett, 2013).

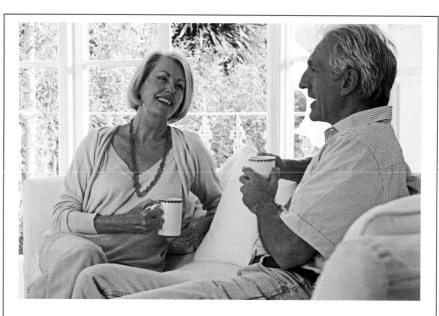

Figure 2.2   Feeling warm or warm feelings?

An even more dramatic illustration of why replication is important is the case of Diederik Stapel, a Dutch social psychologist who was exposed in 2011 for having fabricated data used in numerous studies which he published over several decades (Stroebe and Hewstone, 2013). Given that Stapel was a highly regarded researcher, the discovery of his record of malpractice shocked the world of social psychology. Of course, one fraudulent individual should not be allowed to cast a shadow over the whole discipline. Nor is this a problem limited to psychology. Nevertheless, the scandal exposed the need for closer scrutiny of claims made by researchers.

In both the Bargh and Stapel examples, psychology would have been spared a lot of embarrassment if attempts had been made to replicate specific findings before uncritically accepting their validity. This, however, points to a broader problem: in the past researchers have been reluctant to conduct replications of other people's work, mainly because such studies offer relatively little new and therefore bring less prestige. They are also less likely to be funded, or published in the high-status academic journals. This appears to be changing. Psychologists both in the USA and in Europe are reviewing the procedures for assessing research prior to publication, and funds are being made available specifically for replicating important findings.

Summary

- Replication is important for validating findings from quantitative research and for demonstrating that findings are not unique to the sample used in the original study.
- Replication is also important for identifying methodological shortcomings, and it acts as a safeguard against scientific fraud.

3   Writing the Method section

When conducting replications, psychologists need to carry out the study in a way that is as similar as possible to the original. To make this possible, psychology reports will usually include detailed accounts of how the study was carried out. In some ways, these accounts are a little like a cookery recipe: the ingredients and the procedure should be described in sufficient detail to allow anyone using it to create a culinary masterpiece similar in taste and appearance to that pictured in the cookbook. The more precise the instructions, the more likely it is that the user will be able to *replicate* the dish. Guidance such as 'add milk until you get the right texture' or 'bake until it is ready' is not as useful as 'add five ounces of full fat milk' or 'bake at 200°C for 35 minutes'. The same principle applies to psychology reports.

Figure 2.3   Replication in the kitchen

Information on how a study was carried out is typically provided in the Method section of a report, which follows the Introduction. It will generally cover three themes:

You read about the Introduction of a psychology report in Chapter 1 of *Investigating Methods*.

1   A description of the participants, including how many people took part, the gender and age of the participants, their ethnic or racial background, how they were recruited for the study, and other relevant information.

2 A description of the materials used in the study, which includes information about equipment or resources needed to carry out the study. This might include information about questionnaires or scales (if applicable), or about actual equipment (such as the 'shock generator', or the mock-up of a psychology laboratory used in Milgram's study).

3 A detailed account of the procedure which describes what occurred during the study. It is this section that should provide other researchers with sufficient detail to allow them to, first, evaluate the method and make an initial judgement about its appropriateness and, second, conduct a replication.

There is considerable variety in the way that the Method section is presented in psychology reports. For example, in some cases, the information about participants, materials and the procedure will be provided within a single section. In others, the Method section will be divided into different subsections. There are also differences in how the subsections are labelled. For example, the 'Materials' section is sometimes labelled 'Apparatus'. Precisely how a report is structured and how the sections are labelled depends largely on the conventions adopted by the publication in which it appears (e.g. a journal). Researchers need to follow these guidelines closely, in the same way that you need to follow the guidance provided on the module website when completing your assignments!

The key feature of the Method section and Procedure in particular is that they are very detailed. When writing the Method, researchers need to exercise judgement about what constitutes important information, as opposed to unnecessary or trivial detail. The key to making the right decision is *relevance*, so the writer will need to put themselves in the position of someone attempting replication and try to provide as much useful detail as possible in each of the subsections. So, just like in a recipe book, the Procedure subsection describes a *sequence of events* in a study, which means that it should be written in chronological order. It should give an account of every step, from recruiting participants, to what happened after the participants completed the study. The Method section will also include information on the steps that the researchers took to ensure that ethics guidance was adhered to.

3.1   An example of replication

In this section, we will look in more detail at an example of a Method section featured in a published report of psychological research. The report in question is by Burger (2009), published as an article in the journal *American Psychologist*. Burger chose a very effective title for the article: 'Replicating Milgram: would people still obey today?' The title informs the potential reader that this is an attempt at replication, and provides information about the basic research question. Burger was interested in finding out whether rates of obedience are likely to be as high at the dawn of the twenty-first century as they were in the early 1960s. This is an important question because it has been suggested that individuals today are more aware of the dangers of obedience and that they would therefore be less likely to follow orders.

As you might expect, for reasons of ethics, Burger was not in a position to conduct an exact replication of Milgram's study. So, he devised what he called 'the 150-Volt solution'. When reviewing Milgram's findings, Burger noticed that most people who refused to obey orders did so before the shocks reached the 150-Volt (V) level, while as many as 79 per cent of individuals who continued to administer shocks beyond that point went all the way up to 450 V. This means that a person's conduct at 150 V (whether they stop administering shocks or not) was a good predictor of their behaviour beyond that point: if they had not stopped by 150 V, they were likely to go all the way. Thus, rather than exposing participants to the stress of administering 'lethal' shocks to another human being – which was the most contentious aspect of Milgram's original study – Burger made them go only up to 150 V, and then stopped the proceedings.

Because the procedure in Burger's study was very similar, but not identical, to the original obedience research, Burger (2009, p. 9) referred to it as a 'partial replication'. Also, Burger's study sought to extend Milgram's work. As part of the original research, Milgram explored how participants would respond if they witnessed other 'teachers' refusing to follow orders. To test this, Milgram introduced a variation involving two additional 'teachers' in the room, both of whom were stooges instructed to disobey orders. The stooges would refuse to carry on at an agreed point near the end of the experiment. Milgram found that the presence of disobedient 'teachers' reduced the likelihood of participants carrying on with administering the shocks. Burger, however, wanted to see what would happen if the participants witnessed the act of disobedience *before* they started to administer any shocks, rather than late on in the experiment, when the shocks were already in the near-lethal range. So he designed variations to test this. Also, Burger used a sample consisting of both male and female participants, which allowed him to explore potential gender differences in obedience.

Finally, Burger wanted to look further at the possibility that obedience is at least partly determined by personality. You may remember that Banyard (2012) outlined studies that looked at the link between obedience and personality. These studies found a link between obedience and authoritarianism, but no link between obedience and general personality measures (Elms and Milgram; Elms, both cited in Banyard 2012). Burger chose to look at two different personality factors, namely empathy and the need to control events. He predicted that participants who have greater empathy towards others and a desire to control events will be less likely to obey, compared with those who do not exhibit these personality traits. In the study, these personality characteristics were measured using questionnaire-based scales.

What follows is an abbreviated Procedure subsection taken from the Method section in Burger's (2009) report. What has been omitted is a rather lengthy description of how participants were recruited and how the personality characteristics were assessed. In the extract, you will read the accounts of the two variations, or conditions, used in the study. First is the Base condition, which is very similar to the one featured in Milgram's original study described by Banyard (2012).

The second, Modeled refusal condition, involved an additional 'teacher', a confederate of the researcher, who refused to obey at a pre-arranged point. The extract from the article is provided in two parts. After reading the description of the Base condition, you will be invited to complete a brief activity before moving on to read the account of the Modeled refusal condition. While reading the extracts, pay particular attention to the kind of information they provide, and the level of detail.

You read about scales in Chapter 1 of *Investigating Psychology* and in the online activity *Constructing scales*.

See Chapter 2, Section 2, of *Investigating Psychology*.

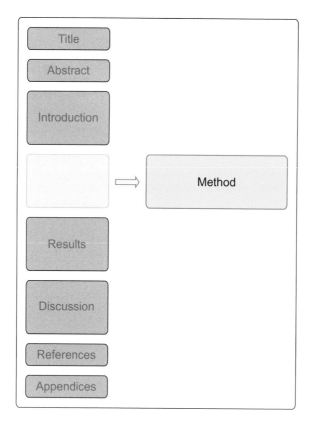

Figure 2.4   Report-writing template: locating the Method section

Procedure

Base condition. ... Upon arrival, participants assigned to the base condition were escorted by a research assistant into the lab room and introduced to the experimenter. The experimenter was a White Caucasian man in his mid-30s. Approximately one minute later, the research assistant escorted the confederate into the lab room. The confederate was a White Caucasian male in his 50s. Both the experimenter and the confederate were selected in part because of their resemblance to the experimenter and confederate used by Milgram. At this point, the experimenter gave the participant and the confederate each a $50 bill for their participation and said the money was theirs to keep even if they chose to end their participation at any time.

Using a script taken largely from the one used in Milgram's research, the experimenter explained that the research was concerned with the effects of punishment on learning. He then informed participants that one would play the role of teacher and the other the role of learner and that the roles would be decided through a random drawing. The drawing was rigged so that the participant was always the teacher and the confederate was always the learner. The participant and the confederate were then asked to read and sign consent forms. The consent form informed participants that they could end their participation at any time and still keep their money and that they might be videotaped during the study. If participants asked whether they were being videotaped, the experimenter told them they should assume they were being taped. In fact, participants were being videotaped by two hidden cameras.

The experimenter then escorted both individuals to the room next door, which contained a chair facing a table. An intercom box and a box with a set of four switches sat on the table. The experimenter asked the confederate to sit in the chair and then secured the confederate's arms to the wooden armrests with nylon straps. The experimenter explained the step was necessary "to prevent excessive movement during the experiment." The experimenter attached an electrode to the confederate's left wrist and added electrode paste, explaining that the paste would "provide a good contact to prevent blisters or burns." The experimenter also pointed out that the electrode was connected to the shock generator in the adjacent room. The participant stood a few feet away throughout this process.

The experimenter then placed a list of sample problems in front of the confederate and gave the confederate instructions patterned after those used by Milgram. The confederate was told to try to remember each of 25 word pairs read by the experimenter (e.g. *strong*–arm) and that during the test the experimenter would read the first word in each pair followed by four other words. The confederate's task was to indicate by pressing one of four buttons which of the option words was paired with the word on the original list. The experimenter also explained that incorrect answers would result in an electric shock and that the test would continue until all 25 word pairs were learned.

At this point, the confederate said, "I think I should say this. When I was in Kaiser Hospital a few years ago, they detected a slight heart condition. Nothing serious. But as long as I'm getting these shocks—how strong are they? How dangerous are they?"

The experimenter answered, "While the shocks may be painful, they're not dangerous."

The experimenter and the participant returned to the experiment room, with the experimenter closing the door to the learner's room and the lab room behind him. The participant was seated in front of the shock generator, which was built to match the one used in Milgram's research. The machine was approximately 3 feet long, 15 inches high, and 16 inches deep (91.4 cm × 38.1 cm × 40.6 cm). A label in the upper left-hand corner of the box contained the words "Shock Generator, Type ZLB, Dyson Instrument Company, Waltham, Mass. Output 15 volts – 450 Volts." There were 30 switches across the face of the machine, with accompanying volt indicators ranging from 15 to 450 in 15-volt increments. The table with the shock generator was on the other side of the wall where the confederate sat.

The experimenter gave the participant instructions on how to press the switches, demonstrating how the switch remained in the middle position after being pressed to show which switches had been used. As in Milgram's studies, the experimenter also gave the participant a sample shock if the participant agreed (only two declined). The experimenter then handed the participant a list of word pairs and reviewed the instructions with him or her. The word pairs and response options were identical to those used in Milgram's studies. The experimenter then turned the page over to reveal the response options. Each of the 25 words that began the word pairs was presented with four numbered response options. The experimenter explained that the participant should read the first word and the four options. The experimenter also said, "If he gives the wrong answer, you say, 'wrong' and then tell him the number of volts you are going to administer. Administer the punishment, read him the correct word pair once, and then go on to the next line." After reviewing the procedure one more time, the experimenter said, "Each time he gives a wrong answer, you move up one switch on the shock generator. It's important that you follow the procedure exactly."

The experimenter then pretended to turn on the intercom system (which was always on). He explained that it was a one-way system such that the confederate could hear what the participant said but could not respond through the intercom. The experimenter sat at a table approximately four feet (1.2 m) behind and a few feet to the right of the participant. The experimenter assisted participants who had difficulty with the procedures (which was often the case with the first few items) but otherwise limited comments to those described below.

The confederate responded to each test item by pressing one of the buttons on the switch box that lit up either 1, 2, 3, or 4 on the answer box in the adjacent room. The confederate gave correct and incorrect responses according to the same predetermined schedule used in Milgram's research. A computer inside the shock generator was attached to a speaker on the confederate's side of the wall. The computer was programmed so that prerecorded sounds emanated from the speaker when certain switches were pressed. The effect was that participants thought they were listening to the confederate's slightly muffled but clear voice through the wall. After participants pressed the 75-volt switch, they heard a small grunt (what Milgram described as "ugh"). Participants heard the confederate grunt after each successive shock, and each grunt was a little louder than the previous one. When the participant pressed the 150-volt switch, he or she heard the confederate yell through the wall, "Ugh. That's all. Get me out of here. I told you I had heart trouble. My heart's starting to bother me now. Get me out of here, please. My heart's starting to bother me. I refuse to go on. Let me out."

The experimenter was instructed to end the experiment when the participant either (a) refused to continue after hearing all the experimenter's prods or (b) read the next item on the test after hearing the confederate's protests following the participant's press of the 150-volt switch. If at any point during the learning task the participant expressed either verbally or nonverbally a reluctance to continue the study, the experimenter gave one of four prods, in this order: "Please continue" or "Please go on"; "The experiment requires that you continue"; "It is absolutely essential that you continue"; and "You have no other choice, you must continue." The prods were given in sequence each time the participant hesitated to continue, beginning with the first prod. Thus, if the participant responded to the first prod with more reluctance to continue, the experimenter gave the second prod, and so forth. If the participant continued to express reluctance after the fourth prod, the experimenter ended the study. No participant was allowed to press any more switches after pressing the 150-volt switch.

Again following Milgram's procedures, the experimenter gave predetermined answers to specific questions by the participant. If the participant asked whether the learner would suffer physical damage from the shocks, the experimenter said, "While the shocks may be painful, there is no permanent tissue damage." If the participant said that the learner did not want to continue, the experimenter said, "Whether the learner likes it or not, you must go on until he has learned all the word pairs correctly." If the participant asked who was responsible for any harm to the learner, the experimenter said, "I am responsible." If the participant asked about the money he or she was given for participation or wanted to give back the money, the experimenter said, "The money is yours to keep regardless." Any of these specific questions also was considered an indication that the participant did not want to continue. To make the answer a response to the participant's question or comment and to keep from sounding repetitive, the experimenter sometimes varied the wording of these statements slightly.

As soon as the experimenter announced that the study was over, he told the participant that the shock generator was not real and that the confederate was not receiving electric shocks. The confederate entered the lab room at that point to assure the participant that he was fine. After the experimenter determined that the participant understood the situation, the participant was escorted to a nearby room, where the principal investigator conducted a thorough debriefing.

(Burger, 2009, pp. 6–7)

Activity 2.3

Having read the description of the procedure involved in the Base condition, would you be able to replicate it, purely on the basis of the information provided in the extract? Is there anything that is missing from the description that you feel would have been useful?

The first thing to note about the extract you read is that the procedure is described in *chronological order*. The account takes you through the different stages of the study, from the moment the participants enter the laboratory, to the final debriefing. The second point to note is that the information is very *detailed*. Burger even provided the exact dimensions of the shock generator and the inscriptions on the labels.

Although the account of the procedure was very detailed, several potentially important details were omitted. For example, in the original study the exact position of each person (the 'learner', the 'teacher' and the 'experimenter') was regarded as crucial, which is why Milgram provided an illustration of the layout of the 'laboratory' (reproduced in Banyard, 2012, p. 69). We do not know whether the layout in Burger's study was the same. Also, while the precise measurements of the shock generator are provided, we are not told if the switches were labelled in the same way as in the original study (from 'slight shock' to 'XXX'). (However, see Figure 2.5 for images kindly supplied to the author by Jerry Burger.) Nevertheless, it is likely that in both cases Burger had followed Milgram's procedure, considering how careful he was to make his research as similar to the original as possible. For instance, he describes how he used the same script, preserved many of the original features such as the 'experimenter's' lab coat, the specific words used in the memory task, even the appearance of the confederates. As Burger (2009, p.10) observes, 'this attention to detail probably goes beyond most efforts to replicate psychology studies'.

Figure 2.5   The images show the shock generator and confederate from Milgram's study (left) and corresponding images from Burger's replication (right). The author is grateful to Jerry Burger for supplying these images for use in this text

Now read the Procedure subsection relevant to the Modeled refusal condition and compare the level of detail with the previous extract.

Modeled refusal condition. Participants assigned to the Modeled refusal condition went through the same procedures as participants in the base condition, with a few exceptions.

First, two confederates were used in the Modeled refusal condition. One of the confederates was the same man who played the learner in the base condition. The other confederate, also posing as a participant, was of the same gender as the real participant. For the women, this second confederate was a White Caucasian woman in her late 20s. For the men, the confederate was a White Caucasian man in his mid-30s. The drawing was rigged so that the participant was assigned the role of Teacher 2 and the new confederate was assigned the role of Teacher 1. Both teachers watched the learner being strapped into the chair, and both were given a sample electric shock (the confederate went first). Second, the experimenter instructed both teachers to sit next to one another in front of the shock generator, with the confederate on the left and the real participant on the right. The experimenter explained that Teacher 1 would begin the procedure. If the participant asked what Teacher 2 was supposed to do, the experimenter said he would explain that later. Third, the confederate posing as Teacher 1 read the list of word pairs and began administering the test and pressing the switches. The confederate showed no signs of hesitation until hearing the learner's "ugh!" after pressing the 75-volt switch. At that point, the confederate paused for a few seconds before continuing. After pressing the 90-volt switch and hearing another "ugh!" the confederate glanced at the experimenter and said, "I don't know about this." The experimenter responded with his initial prod, "Please continue." The confederate paused a few seconds, then said, "I don't think I can do this," and pushed his or her chair a few inches back from the table. The experimenter then asked the real participant to continue the test, picking up where the other teacher had left off. The confederate sat silently throughout the rest of the study and avoided making eye contact with the participant.

(Burger, 2009, pp. 7–8)

You probably noticed that this section is much shorter than the account of the Base condition. The main reason for this is that it is generally considered unnecessary to repeat aspects of the procedure which are the same in the two conditions. Instead, most of the description is devoted to outlining the differences between the two conditions and identifying the features of the Modeled refusal condition that distinguish it from the Base condition: specifically, the presence of another 'teacher' who was a stooge and who refused to obey orders by following a carefully prepared script. Thus, when reporting research, one of the key aims of the Procedure subsection is to set out in detail what happened in each of the conditions and how they were different. This is precisely what Burger focuses on in the above extract.

3.2   Findings

So what were the results of Burger's (2009) study? First, he successfully replicated Milgram's findings in that rates of obedience were very similar to those reported by Milgram (1963). This led Burger to conclude that 'the same situational factors that affected obedience in Milgram's participants still operate today' (Burger, 2009, p. 9). More importantly, Burger found that there was no difference in obedience levels between the Base condition and the Modeled refusal condition. Thus, seeing another person disobey orders early on in the experiment made no difference to the levels of obedience. He interpreted this as a corroboration for the importance of other situational factors, such as the presence of an authority figure, in determining whether a person will follow orders or not. Also, Burger found no gender differences in obedience: male and female participants were equally likely to follow orders from the authority figure.

When looking at the relationship between personality and obedience, Burger found that more empathetic participants generally expressed more concerns about having to follow orders, but they obeyed nevertheless. This suggests that empathy, as a personality trait, creates a feeling of discomfort about harming others, but situational factors prevail so that even the more empathetic participants end up following orders. When it comes to the effect of the desire to exercise control, Burger's findings were inconclusive, suggesting that there is not a straightforward link between obedience and the desire to be in control. So, overall, the results of Burger's (2009) study suggest that situational factors are more important than personality, which was Milgram's conclusion too.

Summary

- The Method section contains a detailed account of the research procedure, which allows other researchers to carry out replications.
- In a psychological report, the procedure must be sufficiently detailed to allow replication and should be chronologically ordered.
- Burger (2009) carried out a partial replication of Milgram's (1963) findings that reproduced and extended the original findings on obedience.

4   Beyond replication: out of the laboratory and into the archive

As we have seen in Section 3, in the context of a psychology report, the detailed description of the procedure has a very clear function. It enables the reader to judge the methodological rigour of the reported research, and it facilitates replication. What the Procedure subsection is *not*, however, is a full account of all the individual, unplanned interactions which might take place between each participant and the researcher. Take Milgram's (1963) study of obedience: most of Milgram's publications report faithfully the procedure he followed in a way not dissimilar to how Burger (2009) describes his. But what is not revealed is what actually happened when the participants came into the laboratory and were asked to administer electric shocks to another human being.

In this section, we will examine a recent study by Gibson (2013) that has sought to explore this issue. The rationale underpinning Gibson's study is that in order to understand why so many of Milgram's participants inflicted the shocks, it is necessary to scrutinise in more detail what actually went on in the laboratory. Rather than conducting new replications of the obedience studies, Gibson re-examined the vast amount of material that Milgram left behind in the personal archives held at Yale University in the USA. These archives contain detailed records of the original studies, including notes, sketches, video and audio records, and even Milgram's personal correspondence. This material not only provides a unique glimpse into the history of psychology, but also offers an opportunity for revisiting and re-interpreting data collected more than half a century ago.

The focus of Gibson's (2013) study is the audio and video recordings of the different runs of Milgram's (1963) obedience studies preserved in the Yale archives. These recordings reveal the actual interaction between the 'teacher' and the 'experimenter' that took place in Milgram's laboratory. As Gibson points out, these recordings have played a peripheral role in Milgram's own research. In the 1960s 'there were few established and generally accepted techniques for qualitative analysis within psychology', especially for exploring recordings of social interaction (Gibson, 2013, p. 294). This is why these recordings were used only for illustrative purposes, rather than as 'data' in their own right. For Gibson, however, these interactions are qualitative data worthy of closer analysis.

In his study, Gibson looked specifically at examples of disobedience, namely instances where participants refused to follow orders. He analysed the 'content and structure of the actual arguments constructed by participants in their attempt to extricate themselves from the experiments' (Gibson, 2013, p. 295). He treated what happened in the laboratory as a complex piece of social interaction, with the 'experimenter' essentially arguing why the experiment should continue, and the participant (the 'teacher') offering counter-arguments in favour of ending it. The specific focus of Gibson's interest was the use of the prod 'You have no choice, you must go on' and the participants' response to it. This was the fourth and final prod that the 'experimenter' was instructed to use: if that prod failed to elicit obedience, the task ended.

Figure 2.6   'Teacher' and 'experimenter': what went on during the interaction?

While examining the recordings, the first thing that Gibson was struck by was that this prod was remarkably ineffective: the majority of participants who heard it disobeyed. Gibson argues that this is because it was the only prod that explicitly drew attention to the participants' lack of *choice*. When he looked more closely at how participants responded to it, he found that participants engaged in an argument with the experimenter, either asserting that they actually *did* have a choice, or getting the experimenter to acknowledge that indeed that is so. Either way, in the vast majority of cases the participants were able to negotiate and argue their way out of the situation, and the experiment was terminated.

Why is this finding important? Gibson (2013) points out that the prod 'You have no other choice, you must go on' is the only one in the study which is actually phrased as an *order*. (The others were 'Please continue' or 'Please go on'; 'The experiment requires that you continue'; 'It is absolutely essential that you continue'.) And yet it is the one that participants found easiest to resist. This suggests that the phenomenon that was observed in Milgram's laboratory might not be about obeying direct orders at all, but about how the 'experimenter' manages to influence the behaviour of the 'teacher' without issuing such an order. The participants who actually administered lethal shocks did so 'without having to be compelled to do so by direct command from the experimenter' (Gibson, 2013, p. 306). Receiving a direct order in fact made them more likely to *disobey*. One possible explanation put forward by Gibson is that, because individual autonomy is considered to be very important in Western society, implying that a person does not have a choice tends to elicit resistance. In this instance, orders seem to work best when they don't sound or feel like an order.

Also, as you read in Banyard (2012), the explanation which Milgram offered for his findings is that when faced with an authority figure people suspend their capacity to make informed moral judgements and defer responsibility for their actions to those in authority. Gibson's research suggests that this might not be the case. Participants still saw themselves as preserving their individual autonomy and choice about whether to proceed. When that choice was explicitly brought into question, they disobeyed.

Cycle of enquiry
The way in which the questions that research addresses are often derived from theories or explanations, and the findings of that research then generate new questions or refinements to theory or explanation. You learned about the cycle of enquiry in the online activity *Research questions*.

Gibson's reappraisal of Milgram's findings is important because it points to the continuously evolving nature of psychological knowledge. As psychologists develop new ways of studying human behaviour, they gain new insights, and this often requires them to revisit and reassess existing theories and explanations. This process lies at the core of the **cycle of enquiry** that you learned about in the online activity *Research questions*. Also, the dynamic nature of psychological knowledge is part of the reason why psychologists tend to avoid the word 'proof' in favour of the more cautious and less definitive term 'evidence'. Implicit in the latter is the recognition that explanations are based only on the evidence currently available and that in the future other evidence is likely to emerge which will require current theories and explanations to be reconsidered.

Activity 2.4

Now that you have considered Burger's (2009) and Gibson's (2013) studies, consider the similarities and differences between them. What are the questions that the two researchers asked, and how did these influence how they went about answering them?

The first thing to note, and this is an important similarity between Gibson's and Burger's studies, is that both studies were aimed at extending the legacy of Milgram's work and exploring the factors underpinning obedience. As such, both studies demonstrate the continuing influence and relevance of Milgram's research, and the fact that after more than half a century it continues to inspire new generations of social psychologists. At the same time, it is clear that the two studies used very different methods. Burger's study remained faithful to Milgram's original approach, although the procedure was modified for reasons of ethics. Gibson, however, used a qualitative method, analysing textual material, namely transcripts of the interactions during the study. Also, you will have noticed that the two methods addressed very different questions. It is difficult to see how the subtleties of social interaction, and the arguments between the 'teacher' and the 'experimenter' – which is the focus of Gibson's study – could be studied in a laboratory or using a questionnaire. The exploration of this particular aspect of obedience clearly requires a particular type of qualitative approach, one that is suited to analysing written records and transcripts of recorded social interaction. At the same time, a qualitative method would have been less suitable for examining how personality affects obedience levels, which is one of the questions addressed by Burger (2009). These differences point, once again, to the inherent link between the research question and the method, which you read about in Chapter 1 of this book. More importantly, they illustrate how qualitative and quantitative methods can work together to illuminate different aspects of complex psychological phenomena, such as obedience.

Finally, going back to Gibson's (2013) research, there is a further implication of this study which is important in relation to the Procedure subsection of a report. Gibson clearly demonstrated that, in practice, what actually went on in Milgram's studies departed significantly from the standardised procedure and the pre-determined 'script' described in published reports of Milgram's work. The 'experimenter' did not just stand there and utter the prods like an automaton. Rather, he was engaged in a conversation and *argument* with the participants. This matters because it points to an important dilemma faced by researchers who conduct laboratory-based research that involves people interacting with one another. On the one hand, researchers need to create a controlled environment and standardise their procedure, ensuring that each participant undergoes the same experience. On the other hand, if research is to mirror the real world, what goes on in such studies cannot always be fully scripted. Gibson's research highlights this issue very clearly. More importantly, it also demonstrates that variations in the procedure or departure from the script, of the kind found in Milgram's (1963) study, need not be dismissed as a methodological shortcoming. These should be seen, instead, as a rich source of data that can be analysed, using a different, qualitative method, and a route to new insights into the nature of obedience.

Summary

- Archives of Milgram's work at Yale University provide researchers with valuable opportunities for revisiting the original obedience studies and re-evaluating the findings.

- Qualitative and quantitative methods explore different questions, but can complement each other when it comes to illuminating complex psychological phenomena.

- Gibson's (2013) work shows that the reports of Milgram's research did not capture the complexity of the human interaction that occurred during the course of his experiments.

References

Allum, N. (2011) 'What makes some people think astrology is scientific?', *Science Communication,* vol. 33, no. 3, pp. 341–66.

Arnett, J. (2008) 'The neglected 95%: why American psychology needs to become less American', *American Psychologist*, vol. 63, no. 7, pp. 602–14.

Banyard, P. (2012) 'Just following orders?', in Brace, N. and Byford, J. (eds) *Investigating Psychology*, Oxford, Oxford University Press/Milton Keynes, The Open University.

Bargh, J. A., Chen, M. and Burrows, L. (1996) 'Automaticity of social behaviour: direct effects of trait construct and stereotype activation on action', *Journal of Personality and Social Psychology*, vol. 71, no. 2, pp. 230–44.

Bartlett, T. (2013) 'The power of suggestion', *The Chronicle of Higher Education* [Online], 30 January. Available at http://chronicle.com/article/Power-of-Suggestion/136907/ (Accessed 4 May 2013).

Burger, J. M. (2009) 'Replicating Milgram: would people still obey today?', *American Psychologist*, vol. 64, no. 1, pp. 1–11.

Doyen, S., Klein, O., Pichon, C.-L. and Cleeremans, A. (2012) 'Behavioral priming: it's all in the mind, but whose mind?', *PLOS ONE*, vol. 7, no. 1 [Online]. Available at www.plosone.org/article/info%3Adoi%2F10.1371%2Fjournal.pone.0029081 (Accessed 16 October 2013).

Foot, H. and Sanford, A. (2004) 'The use and abuse of student participants', *The Psychologist*, vol. 17, pp. 256–59.

Gibson, S. (2013) 'Milgram's obedience experiments: a rhetorical analysis', *British Journal of Social Psychology*, vol. 52, no. 2, pp. 290–309.

Henrich, J., Heine, S. J. and Norenzayan, A. (2010) 'Most people are not WEIRD', *Nature*, vol. 466, 1 July, p. 29.

Kahneman, D. (2011) *Thinking, Fast and Slow*, New York, NY, Farrar, Straus and Giroux.

Kimmel, A. J. (1996) *Ethical Issues in Behavioral Research*, Cambridge, MA, Blackwell.

McNemar, Q. (1946) 'Opinion attitude methodology', *Psychological Bulletin*, vol. 43, no. 4, pp. 289–374.

Milgram, S. (1963) 'Behavioral study of obedience', *Journal of Abnormal and Social Psychology*, vol. 67, no. 4, pp. 371–78.

Popper, K. (1968) *The Logic of Scientific Discovery*, New York, NY, Harper & Row.

Stroebe, W. and Hewstone, M. (2013) 'Social psychology is primed but not suspect', *Times Higher Education*, 28 February [Online]. Available at www.timeshighereducation.co.uk/features/social-psychology-is-primed-but-not-suspect/1/2002055.article (Accessed 8 August 2013).

Williams, L. E. and Bargh, J. A. (2008) 'Experiencing physical warmth promotes interpersonal warmth', *Science*, vol. 322, no. 5901, pp. 606–7.

Chapter 3
Measuring and manipulating variables

Nicola Brace

Contents

Aims and objectives

After studying this chapter you should be able to:

- understand the difference between correlational research and experimental research
- understand the terminology associated with experiments and with experimental design
- recognise the main features of a Method section when reporting an experiment
- appreciate the merits of an alternative method of researching the impact of television on children.

1 Correlational studies and experiments

By this point in the module you have come across quite a range of methods that psychologists might decide to use in their research. Furthermore, in Chapter 1 of this book you read that the choices psychologists make about methods are linked to the kinds of questions they want to find answers to. This chapter will focus on two quantitative methods – correlational studies and experiments – both of which were discussed by Oates (2012). As you will see, these two methods answer different kinds of questions.

1.1 Establishing links

Oates (2012) explained that the term **correlation** refers to an association between two events. As one event happens, then so does another, more frequently or systematically than would be expected by chance alone. Examples that you might have come across include smoking and lung cancer, caffeine and sleeping problems, and exercise and body weight. Psychologists in their correlational research look for associations or links between a whole host of different things, which are referred to as **variables**.

Variables are 'things that vary', and in the context of psychological research regarding human animals, this can be many things including personal attributes (e.g. age, personality), behaviour (e.g. aggressive acts, contribution to social interactions) or mental processes (e.g. memory, attention). These variables will be measured via observation, questionnaires or interviews, or inferred from performance on particular tasks. In correlational research, psychologists will address the question of whether one variable changes as another variable changes.

Let's consider one question that some psychologists have explored: is there a link between the amount of psychological stress an individual experiences at work and their physical health? To investigate this, a psychologist would measure each of these two variables to see if there is any association; for example, by using a questionnaire to measure psychological stress and obtaining data on the number of days taken as sick leave as a measure of health. Common sense might suggest that there is a link between an increase in stress levels and the number of sick days, but it is important to obtain evidence to demonstrate this.

You will see in the reference list at the end of this chapter that Oates (2012) refers to Chapter 3 of *Investigating Psychology*; there, you can see Box 3.2 for his comments on correlation.

Correlation
An association between two events, meaning that they tend to occur together more often than one might expect by chance.

Variables
In psychological research these are any thing that can vary and be measured, controlled or manipulated.

Direction of effect
Describes which of two variables is the initial cause and which is the resulting effect.

An important point made by Oates (2012; see Box 3.2) is that it is not possible to draw a cause-and-effect conclusion from correlational research. Two reasons are provided. The first is that if the researcher does find an association, then it is not always possible to know the **direction of effect**.

For example, does the amount of stress experienced determine the amount of sick days taken, or vice versa? It is possible to think of explanations for both directions. On the one hand, experiencing stress might bring about poorer health, but on the other hand, being sick and having to take time off may exacerbate the level of stress experienced, especially if there is no cover for sick leave. It would be necessary to conduct further research to test each of these explanations.

The second reason is that any correlation between the two variables might actually result from a third factor. In other words, the link between stress and health might arise because both are related to something else; for example, the number of hours that people work per week or the amount of breaks taken during the working day might influence both stress levels and physical health.

Correlational research allows psychologists to identify links between different behaviours, or between behaviours and internal processes, such as memory. If links are identified, then researchers have to be cautious about the conclusions that they draw from their findings. They have to consider the direction of effect, and whether a third factor is responsible for the correlation. One important point that all psychology students are taught is that if you use a correlational method then you should not draw the conclusion that one thing *caused* the other thing.

Figure 3.1   When I eat ice cream I'm usually wearing sandals, but my footwear isn't causing me to eat ice cream!

1.2   Establishing causal links

So how does experimental research differ from correlational research? **Experiments** involve psychologists manipulating one variable to see if it has an effect on another variable, precisely so that they can draw cause-and-effect conclusions. You were introduced to an experiment conducted by Bandura et al. (1963), described by Oates (2012).

This experiment was part of the classic Bobo doll studies, which were addressing the question of whether children would imitate the aggressive behaviour they saw performed. Why did Bandura and his co-researchers decide to study this particular question? If you listened to the *Albert Bandura* audio (The Open University, 2014) on the module

Experiment
A research method that looks at the effect of an independent variable on a dependent variable. See Chapter 3, Section 2, of *Investigating Psychology* for a description of this experiment.

website, then you will have heard Bandura explain the impetus for this research:

> There was growing public concern about the effects of televised violence on children. We had almost every imaginable form of homicidal behaviour being transmitted into the homes.
>
> (*Albert Bandura*, The Open University, 2014)

Furthermore, the theories that related to child development and learning developed by Freud, Skinner and Piaget had all been proposed in the first half of the twentieth century before television was introduced into households, and therefore had not been able to take into account the impact of television. Accordingly, Bandura felt psychology needed to explore the social influence of this medium.

Bandura and colleagues set out to explore the effect of watching violence on behaviour by using the experimental method. In other words, they wanted to isolate the effects of this one particular variable, watching someone behave in an aggressive way, by controlling for other things that may also be linked to aggressive behaviour. For example, bringing children into a laboratory setting allowed them to control for factors in the environment such as the toys and interaction with others. Based on the findings from their experiment (Bandura et al., 1963), they were able to draw conclusions about whether the variable they manipulated, children watching aggressive behaviour, *caused* a change in the variable they measured, children's subsequent aggressive behaviour.

Let's examine this strength of experiments, that is, isolating a variable to test its effects, by considering a fictitious study. Imagine I wanted to find out whether the amount of sugar young children consume is linked to any aggressive behaviour they might display. I could carry out a correlational study measuring two variables: (1) the amount of aggressive behaviour shown by toddlers when playing at nursery class; and (2) the amount of sugar in their food. I might find a relationship, suggesting that a higher amount of aggressive behaviour went together with a higher amount of sugar. But I can't be sure that it is the sugar that is *causing* the increase in aggressive behaviour. If the toddlers fed a high-sugar diet are from homes where bed-time rules are more relaxed and the toddlers go to bed later, then it is possible that their behaviour in the nursery class is a result of them being more tired and irritable. To establish whether there is a *causal* link between level of sugar in diet and aggressiveness in play, I would need to design an experiment where everything except sugar intake is kept constant. I could then compare the amount of aggressive behaviour shown by two groups of toddlers, one with a higher amount of sugar in their diet and one with a lower amount, to see if there is a difference. However, everything else about the groups that might influence such behaviour would have to be the same.

Figure 3.2 More sugar, less sweet? Or is there another reason why this little girl is so unhappy?

Activity 3.1

Make a list of the things, other than sugar, that you think might influence the amount of aggressive behaviour shown by toddlers when playing. What ethical considerations spring to mind regarding this fictitious study?

You may have identified quite a long list of factors that might influence aggression. We had already mentioned that the amount of sleep might be a possible factor. You might have thought of other aspects of the children's diet, or their gender, whether first-born or not, whether an only child or not, whether they are used to playing with other toddlers, illness, and possibly lots more! You may have also wondered whether it would be ethically appropriate to ask the parents of one group of toddlers to include a level of sugar in their diet that might have a negative effect on their behaviour. Indeed, you may have decided that it isn't possible to design an experiment that: (a) can keep all those other potentially important variables constant; and (b) can meet the requirements for ethical approval.

1.3 Choosing experiments as a research method

As researchers, psychologists often face the sorts of dilemmas outlined above. On the one hand, you might want to understand the influence of variable A on variable B, but on the other hand, you recognise that there are lots of other variables that might also influence variable B. Indeed, as with much human behaviour, it can be difficult to decide which are the important factors that should be considered. When watching part 2 of the interview with Sonia Livingstone (The Open University, 2014), available on the module website, you will have heard her say that any researcher starting a particular project has to make a decision as to which particular research method they will use. In her research on internet use, she explained that she preferred the interview as a research method because as her interests are in a relatively new field of research, she isn't sure what the questions are that need to be addressed, and she wants to hear how children perceive the issues that face them. However, she also went on to say that some of her colleagues did use the experimental method, but this was when they had a particular question that they wanted to explore which would involve making a comparison. Finally, she explained that researchers have to balance the knowledge they might gain from their research against the harm that might be done to participants. This suggests that before designing an experiment one should ask:

See Chapter 2, Section 3, of *Investigating Psychology* for information on ethics.

1   Is there a good reason for the specific research question that the experiment is designed to address? This might be public concern, such as with the work by Bandura and colleagues, but mostly a rationale for the research will be based on prior research findings which will have indicated a need for further studies.

2   Would the benefits from conducting the experiment outweigh any risks to participants? As you have read, ethics are a major consideration when conducting any research.

Summary

- Two types of research are correlational studies and experiments.

- Correlational studies reveal whether there is an association or link between variables; they cannot identify cause.

- Experiments involve investigating whether one variable has an effect on another variable, and they can allow psychologists to make causal links between variables.

2   Experiments and terminology

One thing that might have struck you when reading about the Bandura et al. (1963) experiment in Oates (2012) is that there is a whole set of terms associated with experiments, some of which you also encountered in the online activity *Experiments (Part 1)*. Let's consider these terms in this section.

2.1   The variables in an experiment

2.1.1   The independent variable

The key point about an experiment is that one variable, called the **independent variable**, is *manipulated* by the experimenter; in other words, it is something that is under the control of the experimenter. In the case of the Bandura et al. (1963) study, this was 'exposure to violence', where the researchers controlled whether or not children were exposed to aggressive acts and if so how the children saw these acts performed. In order to manipulate the independent variable, experimenters create different conditions which are variations of the independent variable. For example, in the Bandura et al. (1963), study there were three **experimental conditions** and a **control condition**, and the independent variable was whether or not children were exposed to a model behaving aggressively towards a Bobo doll.

In the experimental conditions, the children were exposed to such behaviour but in different ways. In one experimental condition, Group 1 saw a live model behaving aggressively. In a second experimental condition, Group 2 saw a film of a live model behaving aggressively, and in a third experimental condition, Group 3 saw a film of a 'fantasy' model behaving aggressively. In the control condition, Group 4 was not exposed to any model behaving aggressively. As explained in the online activity *Experiments (Part 1)*, the control condition is as identical as possible to the experimental conditions, except that whatever is being studied is absent – so here exposure to a model behaving aggressively is absent. As well as comparing performance across the three experimental conditions, Bandura et al. (1963) were able to compare the performance in the experimental conditions with that in the control condition. In other words, they could look to see if there was a difference between the experimental and the control conditions. By not exposing Group 4 to a model behaving aggressively, any observation of aggressive behaviour in this group provided a 'baseline', an indication of the

See Chapter 3, Section 2, of *Investigating Psychology* for a full description of the experiment by Bandura et al. (1963). The terminology of experiments is discussed in the online activity *Experiments (Part 1)*.

Independent variable
A variable that is manipulated by the experimenter to see what effect this has on another variable.

Experimental condition
A condition in an experiment where participants are exposed to a specific variation in the independent variable.

Control condition
The 'baseline' condition, against which experimental conditions can be compared.

amount of aggressive behaviour children would normally display when they weren't exposed previously to a model behaving aggressively.

Activity 3.2

Imagine you are an experimenter and want to research whether young children imitate the actions of older siblings. Consider how you would choose to manipulate the independent variable.

Perhaps you thought about manipulating the types of actions performed by the older siblings; for example, whether they are aggressive or not, whether these actions involve a toy or not or whether they involve some form of noise. Alternatively, you might have considered the length of time the actions are performed, or the number of times they are performed, or whether they are performed by a same-sex or opposite-sex sibling. You may have identified many more possibilities as well! Often researchers will look at previous studies within the area they are researching, and manipulate the independent variable in a similar way so that they can make meaningful comparisons with these earlier findings.

When thinking about Activity 3.2, you might have decided that what you wanted to do was look specifically at the age of young children. For example, the question that might interest you most is whether 2-year-olds imitate older siblings as much as 3-year-olds do. So, the independent variable in your experiment would be the age of the children. This naturally occurring difference in age becomes the basis for creating two conditions: where in one condition the children are all aged 2; and in the other they are all aged 3. Strictly speaking, you aren't *manipulating* this variable in the same way that Bandura et al. (1963) manipulated exposure to aggressive behaviour, as the age of a participant isn't under your control (as an experimenter you cannot 'make' a child be aged 2 or 3), instead you are *selecting* your participants to fit the criteria of either being aged 2 or 3. We will return to this issue in Chapter 7; for now just note that it is not uncommon for psychologists to include a naturally occurring difference as an independent variable. Apart from age, experimenters have compared male and female participants, left- and right-handed participants, groups with different disabilities or brain damage, or indeed groups with different skills sets such as novice and expert chess players. Also note that when choosing to investigate the influence of a naturally occurring difference, it may not be possible to have a control condition; for example, when manipulating gender, age or handedness

2.1.2   The dependent variable

The dependent variable is the variable that is expected to change as a result of the manipulation of the independent variable. In other words, the **dependent variable** is thought to *depend* on the variable that is being manipulated by the experimenters. In the Bandura et al. (1963) study, the dependent variable was the amount of aggressive behaviour observed when each child was allowed to play in a room where there was a Bobo doll. Sometimes dependent variables are relatively easy to measure. They might be the speed with which someone responds to a warning signal, which can be measured using a stop watch, or a count of the number of times someone correctly spots a warning signal. However, sometimes it is much harder to measure the dependent variable. As you saw from the description of the Bandura et al. (1963) study, measuring aggressive behaviour is a more complex task. Indeed, Bandura and his co-researchers identified four different types of aggressive behaviour, and to make sure they could identify and measure the behaviour as accurately as possible they videotaped the behaviour so that they could look at it multiple times and check that the person doing the measuring was doing so accurately.

Dependent variable
A variable that is expected to change as a result of the manipulation of the independent variable.

In the experiment you will read about in Section 3, the researchers also videotaped the children's behaviour so that they could look at whether the children imitated the actions they saw performed by an adult. Videotaping the children's behaviour helps the researchers to obtain as accurate a measurement as possible – not only can the video be viewed repeatedly, more than one person can code the behaviour, allowing researchers to check how reliable the scoring is.

You read about the importance of measurement when using a quantitative method in Chapter 1, Section 1.1.2, of *Investigating Methods*.

2.1.3   Controlling other factors

The key aim when using the experimental method is to find a causal link between two variables. This link, or cause-and-effect relationship, is that the independent variable has an effect on, or causes a change in, the dependent variable. If the independent variable does have an effect on the dependent variable, then there will be a difference between the conditions in the performance or behaviour measured (the dependent variable).

From the outset, therefore, it is important when designing an experiment to try to rule out the influence of any other factor that might affect the performance or behaviour that is being measured, so that the conditions are identical except for the independent variable that is being manipulated. Bandura et al. (1963) controlled the environment as far as possible by conducting the study in a laboratory setting, and by choosing children who were matched in terms of how aggressive their behaviour was before they took part in the study. This meant that when they observed a difference between the conditions, they could rule out that this difference was down to the environment or to how aggressive the children behaved normally, and instead could conclude that it was the result of the manipulation of the independent variable.

If a difference is found between conditions, it is always important to consider whether this was the result of the manipulation of the independent variable or perhaps arose because of a factor that was not controlled for, that is, a **confounding variable**.

Confounding variable
A variable that is not controlled by the researcher but that can affect the results.

Figure 3.3   Welcome to my lab – you said I should control the environment as much as possible

2.2   The design of an experiment

In the Bandura et al. (1963) study, different groups of children were assigned to the different conditions. Not all experiments are designed like this and sometimes the same participants take part in both control and experimental conditions.

- If participants take part in all conditions, then this is referred to as a **within-participants design**, or alternatively a **repeated measures design**. These mean the same thing. Each participant is 'tested' more than once and contributes more than one bit of data.

- If participants are allocated to different conditions, then this is referred to as a **between-participants design**, or alternatively an **independent groups design**. Again these mean the same thing. Each participant is 'tested' once and contributes one bit of data.

Activity 3.3

I said above that in the Bandura et al. (1963) study different groups of children were assigned to the different conditions. Pause for a moment and identify which design Bandura et al. used.

Within-participants design

Also referred to as a repeated measures design. This is a term used to describe the design of an experiment where participants complete all conditions.

Between-participants design

Also referred to as an independent groups design. This is a term used to describe the design of an experiment where participants take part in only one condition.

Random allocation

A feature of between-participants design where participants are randomly assigned to different conditions. You read about random sampling in Chapter 2, Section 1. Random allocation is another feature of a well-designed study.

Did you spot that Bandura et al. used a between-participants design (i.e. an independent groups design)?

Which design is chosen will depend on what is being researched and each has its own strengths and limitations. The advantage of the within-participants design is that you can rule out individual differences as a potential confounding variable. Because the same participants take part in all conditions, the only thing that should change is the independent variable manipulation. However, you then have to think carefully about whether completing one condition will influence performance in other conditions; for example, will participants gain practice and so do better, or will they become overloaded and so do worse? You also need to consider whether the order in which the conditions are completed might be a factor that could influence the findings, and whether it is boring for participants to complete more than one condition.

Sometimes it is not possible for participants to take part in each condition because it is clear from the outset that completing the task in one condition will influence performance or behaviour in another condition, and so the only option is to employ a between-participants design. A crucial element of an experiment involving a between-participants design is that there is **random allocation**.

2 Experiments and terminology

For example, participants are assigned to one of the conditions according to the number generated by a computer program, or by pulling a number out of a hat, or by flipping a coin. The key point is that the researcher is not allocating participants according to any particular attributes (such as age, gender, eye colour, attractiveness, intelligence, willingness to participate, etc.). A commonly used way to assign participants to conditions is to rotate allocation through conditions. For instance, the first person to volunteer becomes participant 1, the second participant 2, the third participant 3, and so on. Participants are then invited to take part in a particular condition according to their participant number. So, if there are three conditions, then participants 1, 4, 7, 10, etc. are assigned to condition one, participants 2, 5, 8, 11, etc. to condition two, participants 3, 6, 9, 12, etc. to condition three. This will ensure that equal (or nearly equal) numbers of participants end up being allocated to each condition. This process also helps to ensure that participants are randomly allocated to conditions: the researcher does not allocate participants to conditions according to any personal attribute, but according to chance. Random allocation to conditions is important because this way any influence from individual differences, for example in participants' abilities, is more likely to be spread evenly across conditions. Consider if, instead of doing it this way, you decided to allocate all of the first 10 participants who volunteered to condition one. All these possibly 'keener' participants would be in the same condition. Having all the keen participants in one condition may well influence the results. Also, imagine if you run 10 participants one after the other and then have a break before running another 10. If the first 10 are all assigned to the same condition and the next 10 to a second condition, you might inadvertently 'test' those assigned to condition one in the morning and those to condition two in the afternoon, and so time of day would then become a potential confounding variable.

So, random allocation helps to ensure that any differences that do emerge are because of the manipulation of the independent variable, and not because of the time of day or some characteristic of the people taking part in the conditions. Note, though, if the independent variable involves a naturally occurring difference, such as age or gender, then random allocation is not possible.

Box 3.1 Matched-participants design

There is another type of design that is sometimes employed and this is called a matched-participants design. Although different participants are allocated to different conditions, as in a between-participants design, they are matched according to features thought to be crucial to the experiment. This type of design has been used when investigating the effects of brain damage. To explore whether one particular brain region is important for a particular task, such as face recognition, an experimenter might compare the performance of patients with damage to this region with that of a matched-group of patients with damage to a different area of the brain. Each participant in one group will be matched to, and so paired with, a participant in the other group according to type and extent of brain damage, and when the damage occurred, as well as in terms of performance on other related tasks; for example, memory and language tasks. They are also likely to be matched in terms of gender and age. You can probably imagine how problematic such a design can be, but this careful matching ensures that the only difference between each pair is site of brain damage.

Summary

- In an experiment, the independent variable is manipulated in order to see its effects on the dependent variable.

- As far as possible, all other factors that might influence the dependent variable are controlled so that any influence of confounding variables is avoided.

- In a within-participants design, the same participants take part in all conditions. In a between-participants design, different participants are randomly allocated to different conditions.

3   Writing research reports of experiments

The work of Bandura et al. (1963) focused on whether children might imitate aggressive acts. The children were aged between 35 and 69 months of age. In this section, you will find extracts from a research report by Hayne et al. (2003) which describes three experiments (I will focus on just one of these). The children were aged 24 and 30 months old, so younger than those participating in Bandura et al.'s experiment, and although Hayne et al. (2003) also looked at imitation, their focus was not on aggressive acts but on actions performed with toys, and how children might learn through imitation. The extracts of their report presented below provide another example of all of the sections of reports that have been covered so far in this book: the Title, the Abstract, the Introduction and the Method section

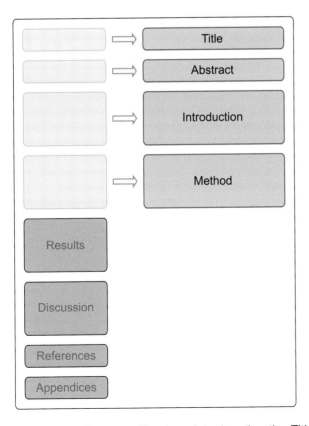

Figure 3.4   Report-writing template: locating the Title, Abstract, Introduction and Method sections

3.1   The early parts of the report

3.1.1   The Title

The title from Hayne et al.'s (2003) report:

> **Imitation from television by 24- and 30-month-olds**
>
> (Hayne et al., 2003, p. 254)

This title is short yet provides quite a lot of information and makes clear what the main focus of the study is about. However, I would have to read the Abstract to find out what it was that the young children were imitating.

3.1.2   The Abstract

The Abstract from Hayne et al.'s (2003) report:

Abstract

Infants' imitation of complex actions was examined in three experiments with 24- and 30-month-olds. In all experiments, an adult modeled a series of actions with novel stimuli and the infant's reproduction of those actions was assessed either immediately or after a 24-hour delay. Some infants watched the demonstration live, while other infants watched the same demonstration on television from a pre-recorded videotape. Both 24- and 30-month-olds imitated actions that had been modeled on television; however, their performance was consistently inferior to that of infants of the same age who watched the demonstration live.

(Hayne et al., 2003, p. 254)

The Abstract provides a summary of the experiments that were conducted and indicates the following key information:

- **What the experiments were about**. The authors explain that 'an adult modeled a series of actions with novel stimuli and the infant's reproduction or imitation of these actions was assessed'. This statement includes an explanation of the dependent variable, what the experimenters were assessing or measuring, namely the infant's reproduction of these actions (whether the infants imitated the actions).

- **The independent variables that were manipulated**. There were several independent variables. The first is whether assessment/measurement occurred immediately or after a 24-hour delay. The second independent variable is whether the children saw a live model/live demonstration or watched this on the television. The third independent variable is whether the children were aged 24 months or 30 months.

- **The key finding**. This was that all children imitated the actions they saw performed but those seeing these actions on television did not perform the actions as well as, or to the same extent as, those who saw the live demonstration.

Note that in this study the authors were not looking at whether children were imitating aggressive actions, something that would be seen as negative. Instead, they were looking at whether the children were imitating actions which reflected learning, something that would be seen as positive.

3.1.3   The Introduction

The Introduction sets out the rationale for the experiments that Hayne et al. (2003) conducted. Don't worry if you find that you have to reread the paragraphs a few times, and don't worry if despite doing so you can't follow everything covered in the Introduction. I will pick out the key points for you in the text underneath each extract. What I would like you to take away from this is how the information provided here outlines what other researchers doing similar studies had found, and indicates what particular questions have emerged from this earlier research. The Introduction starts off quite broadly and then becomes more focused on those particular aspects considered in the experiments that are reported in the paper. Essentially it explains that although even very young children can learn through imitation, how well they do so depends on a range of different variables, including what they are asked to imitate and whether they see the person performing the actions to be imitated live or on a television screen.

Introduction

Over the past two decades, imitation paradigms have emerged as valuable tools to study learning and memory in infants and young children (for reviews, see Barr & Hayne, 2000; Meltzoff, 1990). Simply put, these paradigms involve a 'monkey see, monkey do' procedure in which an adult models a behavior and the infant is given the opportunity to reproduce that behavior either immediately or after a delay. Imitation is an ideal tool for studying learning and memory in preverbal participants because it does not require language comprehension or production. Furthermore, imitation is an important means by which infants and young children acquire a wide range of new behaviors under natural (i.e. nonexperimental) conditions. Given this, studies of imitation are likely to yield an ecologically valid index of learning and memory.

A growing body of research has now confirmed that imitation emerges very early in development. Imitation of actions using objects has been documented in studies with infants as young as 6 months of age (Barr, Dowden & Hayne, 1996; Collie & Hayne, 1999). Immediate imitation of facial gestures has been documented in studies with newborns (Meltzoff & Moore, 1983, 1989) and imitation of facial gestures after a 24-hour delay has been documented in studies with infants as young as 6 weeks (Meltzoff & Moore, 1994).

(Hayne et al., 2003, p. 254)

The authors explain in the first paragraph of the Introduction that the focus of their work is on the positive contribution that imitation may make in relation to teaching things to very young children. The authors explain that imitation does not require any need to understand or use language, and so this may be one useful way by which children can acquire new behaviour. The term 'ecologically valid index' means that imitation studies are thought to reflect what happens in real life. In the second paragraph, the authors provide examples of studies that have shown how young infants imitate actions involving objects, and indeed that newborns imitate the facial gestures of others. When you watched the film *Researching young children* (The Open University, 2014) on the module website, you saw footage of three babies in their pushchairs. Did you see the imitation between the babies where baby Arthur touches the material on his trousers in a similar way to baby Lily May who is playing with the little bow on her shoe? In this film, Dorothy Faulkner explains how imitation is one way that babies learn to communicate with their mothers and how they try to establish contact with other babies. The Introduction then continues:

Despite its precocious emergence, there are also fundamental changes in the acquisition, retention and use of information acquired through imitation. A number of studies conducted with 6- to 30-month-olds have shown that older infants learn faster (Barr et al., 1996) and remember longer (Barr & Hayne, 2000; Herbert & Hayne, 2000a) than younger infants. For example, a series of experiments have shown that 12- to 30-month-olds exhibit imitation of a 3-step sequence of actions using a puppet following a single 30-sec demonstration of the target actions; 6-month-old infants, on the other hand, require twice as much exposure (i.e. 60-sec demonstration) within a single session to exhibit imitation of the same actions (Barr et al., 1996). Furthermore, despite equivalent levels of performance immediately after the demonstration, 18-month-olds exhibit retention for 14 days, while 24-month-olds exhibit retention for at least 3 months.

Older infants are also more likely to use their memories when they are tested with novel objects (Barnat, Klein & Meltzoff, 1996; Hayne, MacDonald & Barr, 1997; Herbert & Hayne, 2000b) or in novel contexts (Hanna & Meltzoff, 1993; Hayne, Boniface & Barr, 2000). In one study, for example, imitation by 6-month-old infants was disrupted by any change in the test stimulus or in the test context; imitation by 12-month-old infants was disrupted by a change in the test stimulus, but not by a change in the test context; finally, imitation by 18-month-olds was observed irrespective of changes in the test stimulus or in the test context (Hayne et al., 2000). Other studies have shown that as the complexity of the stimuli and the target actions increases, so does the age at which infants will first exhibit imitation when tested with novel objects (cf. Barnat et al., 1996; Barr et al., 1996; Herbert & Hayne, 2000b). In our view, these age-related changes in the generalization of imitation reflect age-related changes in the

> content, organization and flexibility of the underlying memory
> representation.
>
> (Hayne et al., 2003, p. 254)

In the two preceding paragraphs, the authors outline that how well
children acquire, remember and make use of the information they gain
through imitation depends on their age. For example, younger infants
have been found to need more exposure, i.e. they need to see the model
for longer, and may stop imitating the behaviour displayed by the model
sooner than older children. Other important variables are related to the
testing itself; for example, the complexity of the actions to be imitated.
So here the authors are drawing together the findings of other studies
that have identified certain variables that need to be taken into
consideration when designing an experiment to consider imitation in
young children. They don't provide that much information about these
previous studies – for example, they don't explain what is meant by 'test
context', 'change in the test stimulus' or 'complexity of the stimuli and
the target actions' – because the aim is to provide an overview and
include the necessary in-text citations and Reference section so that the
reader can go to the original sources if they are not already familiar
with these.

> Past research has shown that sometime during the second year of
> life, infants begin to imitate actions they have seen on television
> (Barr & Hayne, 1999; McCall, Parke & Kavanaugh, 1977; Meltzoff,
> 1988; Sheffield & Hudson, 1994). In a study by Meltzoff (1988),
> for example, 14-month-old infants watched a demonstration via
> closed-circuit television. Infants imitated the model's action when
> they were tested either immediately or after a 24-hour delay.
> Similarly, Barr and Hayne (1999) found that 15-month-old infants
> who watched a demonstration from a pre-recorded videotape
> imitated at least some of the target actions after a 24-hour delay
> (see Experiment 3). Attempts to document imitation from
> television by younger infants have thus far been unsuccessful (see
> Barr & Hayne, 1999, Experiments 1A and 1B).
>
> Even after infants begin to imitate actions they have seen modeled
> on television, their performance following a televised
> demonstration is inferior to their performance following a live

demonstration of the same actions (Barr & Hayne, 1999; McCall *et al.*, 1977). For example, although Barr and Hayne (1999) found evidence of deferred imitation by 15- and 18-month-old infants following exposure to a videotaped demonstration of the target actions, the level of imitation exhibited by these infants was consistently lower than that of infants who were exposed to the same demonstration presented live. Furthermore, an early study by McCall *et al.* (1977) suggested that this lag in performance may persist until the age of 36 months. Some aspects of the McCall *et al.* procedure, however, may have made the task extremely difficult, raising questions about the age at which infants' performance in the video version of an imitation task matches their performance on the live version.

(Hayne et al., 2003, pp. 254–5)

In this part of the Introduction, the authors touch on the research that has looked at imitating actions shown on television. They explain that previous findings suggest that this does not occur in very young infants (those younger than 15 months) and starts at some point during the second year of life. They also describe how young children's imitations of certain actions are more frequent when they have seen these being performed live rather than on videotape.

The purpose of the present study was to examine age-related changes in imitation from television by 24- and 30-month-olds. In all of the following experiments, an adult performed a series of specific actions with novel stimuli and infants' reproduction of those actions was assessed either immediately or following a 24-hour delay. Some infants watched the demonstration live and some infants watched the same demonstration on television from a pre-recorded videotape. Age-matched control groups were not exposed to the target actions; their performance provided a measure of the spontaneous production of target behaviors against which the performance of infants in the live and video conditions could be compared.

(Hayne et al., 2003, p. 255)

In this last paragraph, the authors outline the design of their study which, they explain, they used in all of the experiments they describe in this report (three in total). In the experimental conditions, the children saw an adult perform certain actions with novel stimuli, and in the control condition, the children did not see an adult perform those particular actions. Furthermore, the children in the control condition were matched in terms of age to those in the experimental condition.

The authors were interested in:

- comparing two age groups (24- and 30-month-olds)
- seeing whether the children reproduce actions immediately after seeing them or after a delay of 24 hours
- comparing children who saw the adult perform the actions live and children who saw a recorded version on the television screen.

3.2   The Method

Let's now look at the Method section of the first of the three experiments that Hayne et al. (2003) report. As you read in previous chapters of this book, the Method should provide sufficient information to enable someone else to replicate the study. In the extract featured next, the Method is subdivided into three parts: 'Participants', 'Apparatus' and 'Procedure'. When reporting experiments, sometimes there is a further subsection at the start entitled 'Design', which includes information on independent and dependent variables and what other variables were controlled to minimise or eliminate the effects of confounding variables. Here, much of this information is included towards the start of the 'Procedure' subsection. The authors will have followed the conventions set out by the particular journal that the report was submitted to, namely *Developmental Science*.

Participants

Sixty infants were recruited from public birth records and by word of mouth. The majority of infants were Pakeha (New Zealanders of European descent) and came from a wide range of socioeconomic backgrounds. Thirty infants (15 male, 15 female) were 24-month-olds and 30 (15 male, 15 female) were 30-month-olds. All infants were tested within 2 weeks of their 24- or 30-month-old birthday.

(Hayne et al., 2003, p. 255)

In this first subsection, full information is provided on the participants, including how they were recruited, their background, and their gender and age. Normally you would find here information about the participants that is relevant to the study carried out. For example, it might be necessary to provide information on language proficiency if the task involves text, or on visual acuity if the task is a perceptual one. Information about age and gender are routinely provided.

Apparatus

The stimuli for the present experiment were identical to those used in our prior studies of imitation by 18- to 30- month-olds (Herbert & Hayne, 2000a, 2000b). There were two types of stimuli (rattle and animal). To limit the possibility that the results were unique to a particular stimulus set, there were two versions of each stimulus type (for photographs of these stimuli, see Herbert & Hayne, 2000b). The stimuli were constructed in such a way that the exact same target actions could be performed with each version (see Table 1).

Table 1   The three target actions for each set of stimuli. There were two types of stimuli (rattles, animals) and two versions of each type. The stimuli were constructed in such a way that the exact same target actions could be performed with each version

Stimulus type	Version	Step 1	Step 2	Step 3
Rattles	Green rattle	Push ball through diaphragm into cup	Put stick on jar, attaching with Velcro	Shake stick to make noise
	Red rattle	Push ball through diaphragm into red ball	Put plug into hole in red ball	Shake stick to make noise
Animals	Rabbit	Pull lever in circular motion to raise ears	Place eyes on face, attaching with velcro	Put the carrot in the rabbit's 'mouth'
	Monkey	Pull lever in circular motion to raise ears	Place eyes on face, attaching with velcro	Put the banana in the monkey's 'mouth'

(Hayne et al., 2003, p. 255)

The term 'apparatus' refers to the equipment used to carry out the experiment, and also to information about the stimuli (so what is usually described under the subheading 'materials'). Here we learn that the 'stimuli' are two types of toys suited to the participants' age and likely to attract their attention.

You might be uncertain about what is meant by: 'To limit the possibility that the results were unique to a particular stimulus set'. Here the authors are acknowledging that stimulus type might be an important variable; possibly children might imitate actions performed with a rattle but not when performed with another toy because there is something specific about a rattle. So the experimenters chose two types of stimuli, rattles and animal toys, allowing them to check that children imitate the actions performed with both types to a similar extent.

What is also highlighted here is that two versions of each type of stimuli were constructed in such a way that exactly the same actions could be performed with each. In other words, the actions the children saw were kept constant (controlled) across the two versions of each type of stimulus.

Activity 3.4

Stop reading for a moment and think about Table 1 in the preceding extract – what purpose does it serve?

You may remember that, unlike essays, reports can include useful tables and figures. Here Table 1 is really helpful in providing information about what the stimuli were and what actions were performed. I can see at a glance that a green and a red rattle were used, and also a toy rabbit and toy monkey. The table provides a clear and concise description of each of the actions performed with each rattle and each toy animal. I can see the similarity in the sequence of actions performed at steps 1, 2 and 3 with each stimulus type. If I wanted to build on this research, I would also look at the previous research reports by some of the authors cited in this section to read the information they provide there. For example, Figure 3.5 shows images of the stimuli used (the rattles and animal toys). These images had been included in one of those previous reports.

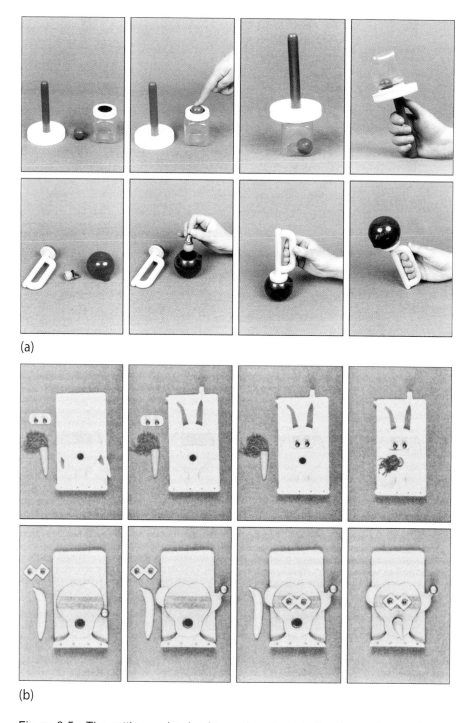

(a)

(b)

Figure 3.5   The rattles and animal toys described in the Apparatus section
(Source: Herbert and Hayne, 2000)

Procedure

Infants were tested in their own homes at a time of day that their caregiver identified as an alert/play period. During the initial visit, the purpose of the study was explained to the caregiver and informed consent was obtained.

At each age, independent groups of 10 infants (5 male, 5 female) were assigned to one of three experimental conditions (live, video or control). Stimulus type (rattle or animal) and order of presentation were counterbalanced across age and condition.

For infants in the *live condition*, the female experimenter was positioned directly opposite the infant and was seated on the floor. At the beginning of the session, the experimenter interacted with the infant for 5 minutes or until a smile was elicited. The experimenter then modeled a 3-step sequence using one version of each stimulus type (see Table 1). The actions were modeled three times in succession out of reach of the infant. The experimenter did not verbally describe the actions or label the stimuli. The entire demonstration session lasted approximately 60 seconds. The order of presentation of the stimulus sets was counterbalanced across age and condition.

Infants in the *video condition* watched the same actions performed on a pre-recorded videotape that was presented on the family television. Although the experimenter in the video was different from the experimenter who was present in the infant's home, all other aspects of the video demonstration were matched to the live demonstration, including the speed at which the actions were performed. If the infant looked away from the demonstration at any time, the experimenter called his or her name and pointed to the display on the floor or on the television screen. In no instance did a child in either condition fail to reorient immediately.

The test procedure occurred 24 hours after the demonstration and was identical for infants in both conditions. The same experimenter who had visited the infant during the demonstration session also conducted the test. Each infant was tested with both sets of stimuli that had been used during the demonstration the day before. During the test, the infant was given the first set of stimuli and his or her behavior was videotaped for 60 seconds.

> The infant was then given the second set of stimuli and his or her behaviour was videotaped for an additional 60 seconds.
>
> To assess the spontaneous production of target actions in the absence of adult demonstration, infants in the *control condition* were exposed to the stimuli for the first time during the test. For these infants, the test was scheduled within 2 weeks of their 24- or 30-month-old birthday. The test procedure was identical to that experienced by infants in the live and video conditions.
>
> (Hayne et al., 2003, p. 256)

The first paragraph of the Procedure tells us that the young children were tested at home. This is an important point because whether children are tested in a strange or familiar environment is likely to influence their behaviour. (Although it may be a benefit to test children in a familiar environment, the trade-off is that the testing environment is not kept constant across participants.) In line with guidance on ethics, informed consent was obtained.

Counterbalancing
An aspect of experimental design that includes all possible orders in which participants complete tasks or conditions, or in which experimenters present stimuli – this is to control for order effects.

The second paragraph provides clear information on the design of this specific experiment. Twenty children were allocated to each condition, 10 from each age group. It is also made clear here that there were three conditions in this first experiment: the live condition (children saw a live model perform the actions); the video condition (children saw the actions performed on a television); and the control condition (children did not see the actions).

This second paragraph also provides information on how other important variables were controlled. Equal numbers of children in each condition and in each age group saw each version of each stimulus type (remember there were two versions of the rattle and two versions of the animal toy). Also, half of the children within each condition and age group saw the actions performed first with one of the two rattles and then with one of the two animal toys, whereas the other half saw the actions performed first with one of the two animal toys and then with one of the two rattles. This is known as **counterbalancing** and is a common way of controlling for what are known as **order effects**.

Order effects
A term used to describe the influence that performing one task may have on performing another task, and therefore a consideration for any experiment with a within-participants design.

If the children had seen the actions performed first with a rattle and then with the animal toy, and if the children then later only imitated the actions with the rattle, you wouldn't know whether this was because they were choosing to perform the actions with just the rattle, or whether this was because they were imitating just the *first* sequence of actions they had seen being performed.

The third and fourth paragraphs describe what happened in the live and video conditions. In the fifth paragraph we learn how the experimenters tested the children. They videotaped the children when they were given each version of the stimulus type that they had seen being used previously. In this first experiment, imitation after a 24-hour delay was considered. The final paragraph describes how the control condition was conducted.

3.3   The findings

Hayne et al. (2003) initially wanted to conclude from this first experiment that the children were less likely to imitate what they saw on television than what they saw live; however, they noted that there is an alternative explanation for their findings. In the live condition, it was the same female adult who was seen performing the actions and who then tested the infants. In the video/television condition, the female adult who was seen performing the actions was different from the female adult who tested the infants. So, the authors could not rule out that it was the change in the experimenter, rather than seeing the actions performed on television, that was responsible for the children showing less imitation in that condition compared to the live condition. As well as carrying out a follow-up of this first experiment, which ruled out the change in the experimenter as a confounding variable, Hayne et al. also report a third experiment in the paper. Based on their findings from all three experiments, they concluded that although the young children imitated the actions they saw performed on television, this imitation was consistently inferior when compared with the imitation of the actions seen performed live.

Summary

- A report by Hayne et al. (2003) looked at learning through imitation; how very young children imitated the actions performed by a model.

- In the Introduction, Hayne et al. provided a review of the previous literature and at the end of this section they outlined the key variables under investigation.

- In the Method section, Hayne et al. provided information about the participants, the design and the stimuli used in their experiment, in sufficient detail that another researcher would be able to attempt to replicate their experiment.

- The results showed that children as young as 24 months would imitate the actions of a model, even one seen on television; however, most imitation was observed when these were performed by a live model.

4 Another way of studying the effects of watching television

In this chapter I have introduced you to a study by Hayne et al. (2003) that used the experimental method to look at the effects of viewing television on children's behaviour. Hayne et al. found that children as young as two years of age imitated actions seen on television, but not as much as when they saw someone performing the actions in front of them live. To what extent do these findings tell us about the learning from television that occurs in real life? The term **ecological validity** refers to the degree to which what happens in a study reflects everyday normal behaviour.

This is an issue that Hayne et al. (2003) raise when discussing their own findings. They point out that often children watch the same things on multiple occasions, just as they might look at the same book over and over again, whereas in their study they saw only a short presentation of the actions during a single session. The authors suggest that their findings might therefore actually underestimate the amount of learning from television that occurs in everyday life.

Consequently, when running an experiment in a laboratory setting, although this setting affords better control over the variables which then allows you to make causal links, when you are interpreting the findings it is important to consider how different the laboratory setting is compared with real life. Also, experiments involve controlling some factors to focus on the influence of one or two variables. This means that Hayne et al. (2003) were not seeking to explore all the possible factors that might determine whether and to what extent children imitate what they see on television.

Ecological validity
The extent to which a study reflects naturally occurring or everyday situations.

Activity 3.5

The experiments you have read about so far in this chapter have told you that children imitate behaviour that they see on television. What we know from this research is that children can imitate both desirable and undesirable behaviours. What this research doesn't tell us is what behaviours children are actually watching on television. Which research method would you use to find this out?

It is unlikely that you would choose an experiment because this research question is not asking you to find out why children are behaving the way they do: it is not looking for cause and effect. You might choose to interview parents because they could tell you about the kinds of programmes their children watch. They could also tell you how much television their children watch. However, it is unlikely that they could estimate accurately how many instances of particular kinds of behaviour their children were exposed to. Perhaps you considered carrying out observations of children to see first-hand what they are viewing on television. Did you consider that rather than observing the children you could just watch television programmes aimed at young children yourself to examine their content? This would allow you to identify the different kinds of behaviour that children were exposed to in their programmes and to count the number of times these occurred.

Figure 3.6   What is shown on television can be subjected to analysis

Looking at the content of what is shown on television is something that has indeed been done, and to show you how I will describe one particular study. Larson (2003) chose to look exclusively at the television adverts aimed at young children. Larson explains that the key reason for doing so was that previous research had found that children would usually attend more to the adverts than to the actual programmes (Alexander and Morrison, cited in Larson, 2003), and that they generally spent a large amount of time watching television, with one report suggesting that children aged between two and seven years watched 25 hours per week (Rideout et al., cited in Larson, 2003), and so would be exposed to a very large number of adverts.

So, how did Larson carry out the study? Television programmes shown during the week from 2 p.m.–5 p.m. and on Saturdays from 7 a.m.–12 noon were recorded for a total of 7 months, spanning all seasons of the year. These programmes had been rated as being suitable either for all children, including those as young as 2, or as suitable for children aged 7 to 14 years of age. In total, the recordings comprised 892 adverts and 595 of these involved a real or an animated child character. Larson was particularly interested in the child character that many adverts introduced, as this may serve as a model that children imitate. A method known as **content analysis** was then applied to the adverts, which involved looking at the content and coding it according to particular criteria.

Larson coded whether the child character was real or animated, along with the gender and race of the character. Another feature of interest was whether an aggressive act was displayed; for example, whether this involved 'physical aggression' (hitting another being), 'object aggression' (hitting an object), 'verbal aggression' (such as insults) or 'fortuitous aggression' (such as explosions).

The method used by Larson, content analysis, was therefore useful in terms of providing an estimate of how many of the 892 adverts had a character the children might imitate, and of these how many depicted some type of aggression. 595 adverts showed a real or animated child character and 219 of these (37 per cent) involved at least one aggressive act. Coding of the adverts also provided information about the kind of aggressive acts that children might see in the adverts when watching television programmes suited to their age. Many were coded as fortuitous aggression (42 per cent), followed by object aggression (29 per cent), then physical aggression (16 per cent) and finally verbal aggression (14 per cent).

Content analysis is a very useful technique for analysing the content of communications that people encounter in everyday life, such as books, poetry, music, websites, newspapers, archives and paintings. Choices have to be made about exactly what to count, and as with any other method, full information on this and the sample will be included in the Method section to enable replication, and limitations of the coding scheme will be acknowledged. One thing to note: you do not have any participants!

Content analysis
Involves analysing the content of written material or audio-visual material, and coding this in terms of pre-selected features. You will read about content analysis in Chapter 6, Section 2, of *Investigating Psychology*.

Summary

- Ecological validity is important when considering the findings of an experiment.
- Content analysis is a useful technique for exploring the content of different forms of communications that are encountered in daily life.

References

Bandura, A., Ross, D. and Ross, S. A. (1963) 'Imitation of film-mediated aggressive models', *Journal of Abnormal and Social Psychology*, vol. 66, no. 1, pp. 3–11.

Hayne, H., Herbert, J. and Simcock, G. (2003) 'Imitation from television by 24- and 30-month-olds', *Developmental Science*, vol. 6, no. 3, pp. 254–61.

Herbert, J. and Hayne, H. (2000) 'Memory retrieval by 18–30-month-olds: age-related changes in representational flexibility', *Developmental Psychology*, vol. 36, no. 4, pp. 473–84.

Larson, M. S. (2003) 'Gender, race and aggression in television commercials that feature children', *Sex Roles*, vol. 48, nos. 1/2, pp. 67–75.

Oates, J. (2012) 'Learning from watching', in Brace, N. and Byford, J. (eds) *Investigating Psychology*, Oxford, Oxford University Press/Milton Keynes, The Open University.

The Open University (2014) 'Albert Bandura' [Audio], *DE100 Investigating psychology 1*. Available at https://learn2.open.ac.uk/mod/oucontent/view.php?id=462766&section=2.1 (Accessed 14 May 2014).

The Open University (2014) 'Interview with Sonia Livingstone: Part 2' [Video], *DE100 Investigating psychology 1*. Available at https://learn2.open.ac.uk/mod/oucontent/view.php?id=499536&section=2.2 (Accessed 14 May 2014).

The Open University (2014) 'Researching young children' [Video], *DE100 Investigating psychology 1*. Available at https://learn2.open.ac.uk/mod/oucontent/view.php?id=462766&section=7 (Accessed 14 May 2014).

Commentary 1

You have just completed your reading of Part 1 of *Investigating Psychology* and Part 1 of *Investigating Methods*, and so by now you have become acquainted with a range of methods that psychologists use in their research, as well as with some of the broader issues that have to be considered when conducting and reporting research. Let's remind ourselves of what these were.

As you read in Chapter 1 of this book, the methods psychologists choose and the type of data they collect must suit the question they want to address. This might involve asking people questions, either a particular group of people or a sample of the general population, and psychologists can do so either by constructing questionnaires or by conducting interviews. Each of these methods has its own strengths and limitations and you will have come across these in Section 4 of each of the chapters you have read. For example, while questionnaires have the advantage that they can be distributed to a large number of people, the information provided in them is often limited. In contrast, conducting interviews will involve smaller numbers of people but interviews will tend to provide more in-depth information. In Section 4 of Chapter 1, you also encountered focus group research where small groups of participants are interviewed together. Both questionnaires and interviews (whether singly or in groups) are sometimes referred to as 'self-report' research methods, as they are both ways of getting first-hand information from participants about their opinions or feelings.

In other research, psychologists might seek to measure behaviour or performance instead of asking participants to respond to questions. They can do so either by carrying out observations of behaviour or by asking people to participate in experiments. With both observations and experiments, the researchers record participants' behaviour and/or responses. Again, each of these two methods has its own strengths and limitations. As you read in Chapter 3, observing behaviour allows researchers to look for correlations between variables, in other words, to look at whether changes in one variable appear to be matched in some way by changes in another. Experiments go further by allowing researchers to control variables in order to make causal links between them, that is, to say whether a change in one variable *causes* a change in another. However, it might not be possible to manipulate the variable of interest for ethical reasons; if you want to understand how stress affects performance at work it would not be ethical to make some people feel stressed in order to measure the effect! While observations might not allow causal links to be inferred, they do allow researchers to make a record of behaviour as it unfolds in a particular situation and to study factors that it would be unethical to manipulate in an experiment. This record of behaviour can be analysed in its own right, or it can be used to suggest new research questions. Indeed, all research can become a source of inspiration, and possibly even data, for later studies. As you read in Section 4 of Chapter 2, the recorded interactions between participants and experimenter in the Milgram study became the source of data for a more recent study.

All of the methods you have seen so far can be used in different ways, generating even more variety in what researchers might do. For example, questionnaires might involve a set of questions or items to elicit people's opinions or attitudes towards something, along with questions about gender, age, income and so on. Alternatively, items in a questionnaire may be constructed to make up a particular scale or index, such as the F-scale, which was designed to measure potential for fascism. As you read in Chapter 1, interviews vary in the extent to which the interviewers adapt their questions according to the participants' responses. Interviews may be structured so that all participants are asked the same questions, in the same order, or only semi-structured or unstructured. And, as you read in Chapter 3, experiments also vary in their design, and may be conducted either in a laboratory setting or in a more familiar setting such as the home.

Moreover, these are not the only methods that psychologists use to collect their data. You have also read about psychometric tests, such as the IQ test introduced in Chapter 1 of *Investigating Intelligence*; meta-analysis, which was described in *Investigating Psychology*, Chapter 3, Section 4.4; and archival research, which was described here in *Investigating Methods* in Chapter 2. In Parts 2 and 3 of the module, you will come across other ways of collecting data including content analysis, ethnography, case studies, and neuroimaging.

You have read that such a wide range of research methods is necessary in part because psychology is a diverse discipline. So far, you have had a taste of three different sub-disciplines: the psychology of individual differences, exemplified in personality and intelligence research; experimental social psychology, exemplified in studies of the effects of an authority figure on obedience; and developmental psychology, illustrated through studies of children's learning. There are many more! Certain research methods may better suit certain sub-disciplines of psychology; for example, developmental psychologists often carry out observations, and this is because young children are unlikely to possess the communication skills necessary for completion of questionnaires or participation in interviews. Questionnaires and psychometric tests feature relatively more frequently in studies of individual differences than in other areas of psychological research, and you saw examples of this in Chapter 1 of *Investigating Intelligence* and Chapter 1 of *Investigating Psychology*.

Importantly, the choices a researcher makes about methods are always linked to the research question: there may be little point running an experiment if your aim is to find out how people feel about particular issues. Moreover, the research question itself will be rooted in earlier research. This can take many forms. It might be that the researchers intend to make a contribution to a particular set of findings about the same issue. For example, the study by Hayne et al. (2003) described in Chapter 3 was one of many looking at infants' imitation of complex action. One of the contributions from Hayne et al. was to explore some of the particular influences on that imitation. Or, think back to the study by Allum (2011) that you read about in Chapter 1. This study sought to test a prediction based on the notion of authoritarianism developed by Adorno et al. and in so doing added to our knowledge there. Alternatively, researchers might aim to replicate an earlier finding in order to add weight to, or verify, the claims made. You read of the importance of this in Chapter 2 and you saw an example of it in Burger's (2009) study, which addressed similar issues to Milgram's (1963) study.

So, the studies introduced in Section 3 of each of the chapters in Part 1 all built on earlier research. All three carefully set out the rationale for their research, and explained how it related to earlier research. This is done in the Introduction section of the research reports. You saw two examples of the Introduction to a research report in Chapters 1 and 3. You also saw examples of the Method section in Chapters 2 and 3. One key point made several times across Part 1 was that the purpose of the Method section is to provide sufficient detail for someone else to replicate the study. In other words, when writing up research you should always bear in mind that someone else might want to repeat what you have done. Hence, the Method section needs to provide detailed information about the design of the study, participants, ethical considerations and how the study was carried out.

Now that you have had the opportunity to read extracts from three different research reports, perhaps you have noticed that these have quite a distinct style. Reports should be written in a manner that suits the intended audience. As the research reports considered in *Investigating Methods* are all intended for an audience of psychologists, they tend to contain technical terms that psychologists use (and which you will become familiar with as you study this module). Like other kinds of reports, research reports are subsectioned, and each section and subsection is titled. With research reports, however, the headings and the broad structure are largely fixed so that they follow a recognisable layout. Having an agreed format like this enables researchers to find information in reports quickly. Also, you may have noticed the style of writing in the extracts. Research reports aim to be concise, clear and precise. This is another important feature of writing in psychology.

So far the chapters have only presented the first three sections of a report: the Abstract, Introduction and Method. In Part 2 of *Investigating Methods* you will find out about the Results section. This is because the next part of this book will focus on the different types of data that psychologists collect and what they do with these data.

Before moving on, check that you understand what these terms mean:

Chapter 1:

- Standardisation
- Objectivity
- Subjectivity
- Hypothesis

Chapter 2:

- Sample
- Population
- Generalisability
- Sampling error
- Replication

Chapter 3:

- Correlation
- Experiment
- Direction of effect

- Experimental condition
- Control condition
- Independent variable
- Order effects
- Dependent variable
- Confounding variable
- Within-participants design
- Between-participants design
- Random allocation

Part 2

Chapter 4
Describing quantitative data

Nicola Brace

Contents

Aims and objectives

After studying this chapter you should be able to:

- describe different levels of quantitative data: nominal, ordinal and interval

- understand the use of descriptive statistics to summarise data

- understand how a mean and a standard deviation are calculated

- describe how to report the results of an experiment in a research report

- appreciate the merits of using an alternative way of investigating the application of conditioning techniques.

1   Data collected in research

At this point in the module you have read about quite a few studies using different methods, and about the data collected in these studies. In each instance you were presented with a description of the data. For example, Banyard (2012, p. 72) described the findings of Milgram's obedience study, writing that 'only five of the forty participants refused to continue beyond this point (300 volts)'. Also, Toates (2012) included several figures presenting the findings of studies, including a figure which described the time it took for a cat to learn to escape from a puzzle box (see Figure 4.3, p. 160) and a figure showing what happened when rats were introduced to a maze a number of times, in terms of both time to run the maze and the number of errors made (see Figure 4.5, p. 163). These are just a couple of examples where you have read descriptions of findings that were expressed in words or in graphs, and you will come across many more throughout the rest of your studies.

An important aspect of learning how to conduct psychological research is learning how to describe the data collected in a particular study, either to fellow psychologists when writing journal articles or when summarising the findings of a study for a press release to the general public. How best to do so depends on the type of data collected. The first thing to consider is whether the study involved quantitative data as in the examples above, or qualitative data. It is possible to measure, count and describe using numbers data that are quantitative, but it is not possible to describe qualitative data using numbers. This particular chapter will focus only on quantitative data, and qualitative data will be considered in Chapter 6. The second thing to consider is the type of quantitative data that was collected, and this is what I shall focus on next.

Analysing qualitative data is the focus of Chapter 6.

1.1   Types of quantitative data

In psychological research it is common to talk about how different types of quantitative data result from different ways of measuring variables – the 'levels of measurement' – and I will introduce you to these now.

1.1.1   Nominal level

Nominal level

Measurement involves naming an attribute of the participants or their responses.

Measurement at the **nominal level** involves categorising and coding participants' responses. For example, the data recorded might be whether participants responded to something or agreed with something, and so what is recorded is either 'yes, they did' or 'no, they did not'. Or perhaps the way participants behaved towards an event is categorised into whether they attempted to intervene and help out or whether they ignored what was happening, and so what is recorded is 'intervened' or 'ignored'. Alternatively, the variable of interest may relate to an attribute or characteristic of the participants and what is recorded is whether they are female or male, left- or right-handed, extrovert or introvert, and so on.

When recording and analysing data like these, researchers use numbers as codes or labels. (If you look up the definition of 'nominal' then you will find that it relates to or consists of a name.) For example, if a researcher was interested in whether participants were extroverts or introverts, the researcher could code 'extrovert' as '1' and 'introvert' as '2'. However, the researcher could just as easily have coded 'extrovert' as '2' and 'introvert' as '1'. Assigning a number to extroverts and introverts allows the researcher to differentiate between these two groups of participants. Importantly, the size of the number is irrelevant and has no direct relationship with what is being measured. For example, if women are coded as '2' and men as '1', the numbers do not imply that women are twice as much as men!

You might be wondering why there is a need to code categories, such as introvert and extrovert, using numbers. Why not use the names of the categories as the codes? The answer is that the computer software that psychologists use to analyse data requires that the data be entered as numbers, not words. You might also be curious about what the researcher does with this type of data after it has been coded. The answer is that they will count how many '1s' and '2s' there are in order, for instance, to determine how many extroverts and introverts were in the sample.

1.1.2   Ordinal level

Measurement at the **ordinal level** provides information about order and the responses from, or observations about, the participants can be put in order according to rank or according to a rating scale. For example, participants might be shown photographs of ten faces and be asked to put them in rank order of attractiveness. Figure 4.1 shows another example of ranking.

Ordinal level
Measurement on a scale that allows data to be put in an order, but differences between the points on the scale are not the same.

Figure 4.1   Dogs ranked according to size

Alternatively, participants might be asked to provide a rating on a scale, such as in surveys or with the F-scale (Adorno et al., 1950) illustrated in Figure 4.2, where they provide an indication of the extent to which they agree with a particular opinion.

F-scale items						
Item No.	Strongly oppose	Moderately oppose	Slightly oppose	Slightly support	Moderately support	Strongly support
1 Obedience and respect for authority are the most important virtues children should learn.						
	☐	☐	☐	☐	☐	☐
2 Although leisure is a fine thing, it is good hard work that makes life interesting and worthwhile.						
	☐	☐	☐	☐	☐	☐
3 Books and movies ought not to deal so much with the sordid and seamy side of life; they ought to concentrate on themes that are entertaining or uplifting.						
	☐	☐	☐	☐	☐	☐
4 People can be divided into two distinct classes: the weak and the strong.						
	☐	☐	☐	☐	☐	☐
5 It is only natural and right that women be restricted in certain ways in which men have more freedom.						
	☐	☐	☐	☐	☐	☐

Figure 4.2   An example of how items from the F-scale could be presented (Source: adapted from Adorno et al., 1950)

Note that ordinal data *only* provide information about order; they *do not* tell us about the size of the difference between the items on the scale. The difference between the face ranked as most attractive and second most attractive is not necessarily the same as that between second most attractive and third most attractive. Similarly, the difference between 'strongly oppose' and 'moderately oppose' is not necessarily the same as that between 'moderately oppose' and 'slightly oppose'.

1.1.3   Interval level

Interval level

Measurement on a scale where the differences, the intervals, between the points on the scale are the same.

Measurement at the **interval level** provides information about *order* on a scale and also about the *size* of the difference between the items on the scale. For example, a study might involve measuring the performance of participants during a particular task in terms of how long they take. Imagine participant 1 took 30 minutes, participant 2 took 25 minutes and participant 3 took 20 minutes. These data tell us participant 1 took the longest and participant 3 was fastest, but we also know that the difference between participants 1 and 2 is the same as between participants 2 and 3, and that is 5 minutes. This is also the case if the study involved measuring the number of mistakes the participants made. The difference between someone making ten mistakes and someone making eight mistakes is the same as someone making eight mistakes and someone making six mistakes.

If the scale being used is also one where zero means that there is none of whatever variable is being measured, then this is a ratio scale. (Not every variable can have a zero value: it would not make sense to say there is 'zero temperature', for example.) This distinction between ratio and interval is not something you need to worry about on this module; instead you should focus on understanding the differences between nominal, ordinal and interval levels.

Activity 4.1

Below are very brief descriptions of three studies. Decide whether the variables involve measurement at nominal, ordinal or interval level.

1   Psychologists asked parents at a school event whether they used rewards (e.g. praise), punishments (e.g. time out on a naughty step) or both as conditioning techniques with their children.
2   Psychologists asked shoppers to rate on a five-point scale the effectiveness of different rewards for re-using plastic bags.
3   Psychologists measured how many trials using positive reinforcement dogs needed to learn the command 'sit'.

In the first study, the researchers are recording whether parents use rewards, punishments or both, so their responses are allocated to one of these three categories. This is an example of nominal data. In the second study, the researchers are using a scale which has five points (e.g. 'very effective', 'effective', 'moderately effective', 'slightly effective', 'not effective'), which is an ordinal scale. In the third study, the researchers are measuring the number of trials it took to train the dogs to sit, and so are using an interval scale. Don't worry if you didn't follow this as I will take you through each of these next.

1.2   An example of nominal data

Let's imagine the first study described in Activity 4.1 and pretend that a group of researchers conducted a very short interview with 100 parents attending a school event, where they first briefly outlined conditioning techniques and then asked each parent to describe the techniques they used at home. Here are the responses for the first ten parents.

Responses from parents	
Parent 1	Reward only
Parent 2	Punishment only
Parent 3	Reward only
Parent 4	Reward only
Parent 5	Reward only
Parent 6	Punishment only
Parent 7	Reward only
Parent 8	Reward only
Parent 9	Punishment only
Parent 10	Reward and punishment

Figure 4.3   Example of data sheet showing responses from the first ten parents

What does the data sheet in Figure 4.3 tell us? We can see that the first parent must have reported that they only use conditioning techniques to reinforce good behaviour (e.g. by using rewards such as gold stars, sweets, extra pocket money) as this response was categorised as 'reward only'. The second parent must have reported that they only used conditioning techniques to stop bad behaviour (e.g. confinement to a room, or restricted television viewing) as this response was categorised as falling into the category 'punishment only'. The next seven responses were categorised as either 'reward only' or 'punishment only'. The tenth parent must have reported that they rewarded good behaviour and punished bad behaviour, as their response was categorised as 'reward and punishment'.

Remember that with nominal data, researchers count the number of responses that fall into each category. Let's do that with the responses from these first ten parents. You can see in Figure 4.3 that there are a total of six responses that were coded as 'reward only', one response that was coded as 'reward and punishment', and three responses that were coded as 'punishment only'. These counts are displayed in Table 4.1 below.

Table 4.1   Data from ten parents

	Reward only	Reward and punishment	Punishment only
Totals for first 10 participants	6	1	3

Working out how many of these first ten responses fell into each category was relatively easy. To do this accurately for 100 responses most researchers would use computer software which requires the data to be entered as numbers rather than words. For example, here I would use the following coding scheme, where a code of '1' is allocated to the 'reward only' category, '2' to 'reward and punishment' and '3' to 'punishment only'. These numbers, 1, 2 and 3, would simply be the numerical label for each category.

Now imagine that the researchers have categorised and coded all 100 responses and analysed this using computer software. The table below shows the total number of responses falling into each category – note these add up to 100.

Table 4.2   Data from 100 parents

	Reward only	Reward and punishment	Punishment only
Totals for 100 participants	50	45	5

Activity 4.2

Now that all 100 responses have been categorised, coded and counted, which of the following claims about the data is incorrect?

1   The study showed that over half of the parents approached used the conditioning techniques of rewarding good behaviour and punishing bad behaviour.

2   Fifty per cent of parents said that they rewarded good behaviour and did not punish bad behaviour.

3   Only 5 out of 100 parents reported punishing bad behaviour but not rewarding good behaviour.

The first claim is in fact incorrect as 45 out of 100 is *less than* half of the parents sampled, so less than half of the parents approached used the conditioning techniques of rewarding good behaviour and punishing bad behaviour. Using terms such as 'over half' or 'nearly half' or 'approximately three-quarters' can be a very effective way of describing findings to the general public. The second claim is correct as half of the parents (50 out of 100) said they only used rewards, and another way of expressing this is 50 per cent. The third claim is also correct as only five of the responses fell into the category 'punishment only'.

In Activity 4.2, two different ways are used to describe the findings of our hypothetical study:

*   Proportions (e.g. ½ or 0.5) and percentages (e.g. 50 per cent) – however, using either does not provide us with any information about the total number of responses or behaviours that were categorised and counted.

*   X out of Y (e.g. 5 out of 100) is often the preferred option in psychology texts and articles as this is more informative with 'X' being the number falling into a particular category and 'Y' being the total number of responses or behaviours that were categorised and counted.

As well as describing the findings using words, or showing these in a table such as in Table 4.2, the data can be represented graphically. In Figures 4.4a and b are two ways of displaying the made-up data from our hypothetical study. The first is a pie chart (Figure 4.4a), which is often used to show proportions, and here it is easy to see that the responses falling into the 'reward only' category make up half of the total number of responses obtained in this hypothetical study. However, a bar chart (Figure 4.4b) is often preferred when reporting the results from psychological studies, because it is more informative as it is easier to 'read' the number of responses falling into each category from the numbers included on the left-hand side.

Pie charts and bar charts are described in the online activity *Constructing and interpreting bar charts.*

(a)

Figure 4.4a   Pie chart showing the use of different conditioning techniques in a sample of 100 parents

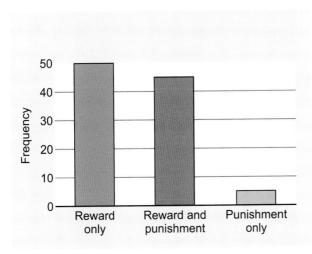

(b)

Figure 4.4b   Bar chart showing the use of different conditioning techniques in a sample of 100 parents

1.3   An example of ordinal data

Let's imagine the second study described in Activity 4.1 and pretend that a group of psychologists created a short questionnaire to ask people about their views on recycling schemes, including the effectiveness of using tokens to reward the re-use of plastic bags. For example, a section of the questionnaire might have looked like Figure 4.5:

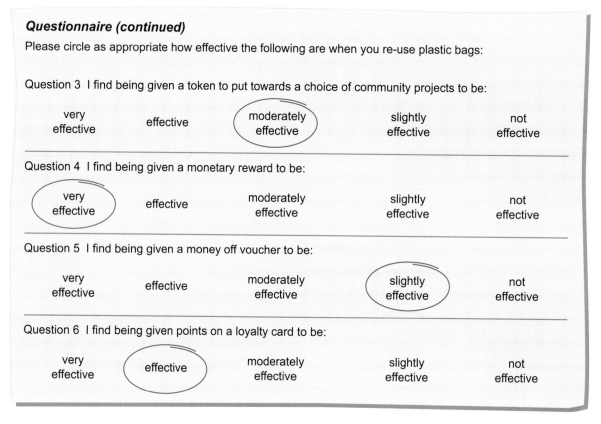

Questionnaire (continued)

Please circle as appropriate how effective the following are when you re-use plastic bags:

Question 3 I find being given a token to put towards a choice of community projects to be:

| very effective | effective | moderately effective | slightly effective | not effective |

Question 4 I find being given a monetary reward to be:

| very effective | effective | moderately effective | slightly effective | not effective |

Question 5 I find being given a money off voucher to be:

| very effective | effective | moderately effective | slightly effective | not effective |

Question 6 I find being given points on a loyalty card to be:

| very effective | effective | moderately effective | slightly effective | not effective |

Figure 4.5   Extract from questionnaire showing the responses of one participant circled

What would you do with the responses to the questions above? Perhaps you remember from Part 2 of the online activity *Constructing scales* that you assign a score to each response. In this instance, I would use the following score scheme:

'not effective' = 0 points

'slightly effective' = 1 point

'moderately effective' = 2 points

'effective' = 3 points

'very effective' = 4 points

I would then score each participant's response to each of the four questions. By adding together the scores from all of the participants to each question, I would be able to see which question achieved the highest score, and so which scheme respondents felt was most effective, and which question achieved the lowest score, and so which scheme was considered least effective.

1.4 An example of interval data

Let's imagine the third study described in Activity 4.1 where psychologists measured how quickly young dogs learned to obey the command 'sit' using positive reinforcement techniques. The psychologists decided to compare partial reinforcement with continuous reinforcement. This is an experiment. The independent variable (that manipulated by the experimenter) is whether a partial or continuous reinforcement is used, and the dependent variable (that measured by the experimenter) is the number of trials it takes for the dog to sit at the command 'sit'.

Put yourself in the shoes of the experimenter. You have recruited ten participants (dogs) at a dog training class, gaining consent from their owners, and you check that none sit when the word 'sit' is said. All are border collies, aged between 6 and 8 months. You take the first dog into a separate room. You say 'sit' and simultaneously push down on the dog's lower back to encourage the dog into a sitting position. You then reward the dog with a treat and let go of the dog. This is trial number one. You then repeat the same procedure, say 'sit', push down on the dog's rear and reward the dog with a treat and this is trial number two. You continue to do the same thing over and over until on trial ten you find that you do not have to push down on the rear. You then move away from the dog and say 'sit' to check that the dog has indeed learned the command 'sit'. Because you rewarded the dog on each trial, you record that the dog was on a continuous reinforcement schedule.

In real research a far larger number of dogs would be needed – we have kept this to ten in this example to make the calculations easier.

Figure 4.6   One young collie who has been trained to sit

Now you take the dog back to the training class and collect the second dog. You repeat the same procedure except this time you use a partial reinforcement schedule and reward the dog every other trial. At trial 15 you establish that the dog sits when you say 'sit'. You record that it took 15 trials for the dog to learn the command 'sit' and also that the dog was on a partial reinforcement schedule.

You continue in this way, alternating between the two types of reinforcement schedules until you have data for all ten dogs. The next page shows what your record sheet looks like.

	Number of trials to learn 'SIT' command	Type of conditioning schedule
Dog 1	10 trials	Continuous reinforcement
Dog 2	15 trials	Partial reinforcement
Dog 3	4 trials	Continuous reinforcement
Dog 4	22 trials	Partial reinforcement
Dog 5	11 trials	Continuous reinforcement
Dog 6	30 trials	Partial reinforcement
Dog 7	12 trials	Continuous reinforcement
Dog 8	16 trials	Partial reinforcement
Dog 9	10 trials	Continuous reinforcement
Dog 10	18 trials	Partial reinforcement

Figure 4.7   The record sheet showing the number of trials it took each dog to learn the command and whether they received continuous or partial reinforcement

Note how the record sheet includes actual numbers for each participant. Here you are collecting interval data and that means taking a measurement on a scale with equal intervals. You have already established before starting the experiment that none of the dogs would sit when told 'sit', so the scale must start at '1' (in other words the lowest score possible is '1'). The scale continues upwards in whole numbers (2, 3, 4, etc.) and the end point is unknown. For these ten dogs it stops at 30 because the highest score in this particular data set is 30, but there may be dogs who would take 40 or 50 trials.

You decide to reorganise the sheet to allow you to compare better how the dogs performed in the two conditions. Table 4.3 shows what it could look like.

Table 4.3   The number of trials to learn the command 'sit'

Continuous reinforcement condition	Partial reinforcement condition
10	15
4	22
11	30
12	16
10	18

Activity 4.3

Imagine you are on the phone to a colleague who is interested in your study. How would you describe the data displayed in Table 4.3? Can you think of an alternative to reading out all ten scores?

Perhaps you indicated that the dogs on the continuous reinforcement schedule learned to sit in fewer trials than those on the partial reinforcement schedule but could not find an easy way of saying by how much. Perhaps you also indicated that, within each condition, some dogs took more trials than other dogs but found it difficult to describe succinctly the extent of the differences.

When trying to describe interval data collected in an experiment involving two conditions, there are two key features to comment on:

1   How participants performed in one condition compared with the other. In an experimental report, it is usual to provide information about the *average* performance in each condition.

2   How performance varied within each of the conditions. In an experimental report, information on the *spread* of scores is provided alongside average performance.

Exactly how psychologists work out average and spread of scores is the focus of the next section.

Summary

- Psychologists collect different types of quantitative data.
- Measurement in quantitative research can result in nominal, ordinal or interval data.
- Quantitative data can be summarised using tables or graphs.

2   Calculating the mean and the standard deviation

Box 4.1   Note on calculations

In this section, I will show you how to carry out some calculations. To perform these calculations yourself, all you need to be able to do is use the following buttons on a calculator: add (+), subtract (−), divide (÷ or /), multiply (×), square (^{2}) and square root ($\sqrt{\ }$). You also need to be familiar with adding together and multiplying positive and negative numbers. These were covered in the online activity *Working with numbers*.

Let's return to the hypothetical data from a study using conditioning to teach young collies to sit. If I wanted to describe these data in a research report, then I would want to provide two pieces of information. The first concerns the average performance in each condition to allow comparison across conditions. I would do this by calculating something called the 'mean'. The second concerns the spread of scores in each condition and I would do this by calculating something called the 'standard deviation'. Each of these is described below.

2.1   The mean

One way of comparing performance across several conditions would be to calculate a total score for each, i.e. to add together the individual scores as shown in Table 4.4a.

From the totals shown in Table 4.4a, we can see that the dogs in the partial reinforcement condition took considerably more trials to learn the command 'sit', that is 101 trials, when compared with those in the continuous reinforcement condition, which only took a total of 47 trials. Note, though, that these totals do not provide us with information about how each individual dog performed, or whether all the dogs in either condition responded to the conditioning in a similar way or differed in how long it took them to learn to respond appropriately to the command 'sit'.

Table 4.4a   The data for each dog in each condition and the total for each condition

	Continuous reinforcement condition	Partial reinforcement condition
	10	15
	4	22
	11	30
	12	16
	10	18
Total	47	101

Another important point to consider is that looking at the two total scores only makes sense if there are the same number of participants (in this example dogs) in each condition. If we had more dogs in the partial reinforcement condition than in the continuous reinforcement condition then it would not be possible to directly compare the totals. Ideally, you want a way of comparing performance that is not reliant on having equal numbers in each condition. One way of doing this is to divide the total by the number of participants/dogs in each condition.

Adding the individual scores together and dividing the total by the number of scores results in a descriptive statistic called the **mean**.

Table 4.4b   The mean for each condition

	Continuous reinforcement condition	Partial reinforcement condition
	10	15
	4	22
	11	30
	12	16
	10	18
Total	47	101
Mean	47/5= 9.4	101/5=20.2

Mean
An average that is calculated by adding together all the items and then dividing the total by the number of items.

The mean is one way of describing an average score – there are other ways of calculating average scores which you will learn about in the online activity *The mean, the mode and the median.*

In Table 4.4b, you can see that in the continuous reinforcement condition the mean is 9.4, and in the partial reinforcement condition the mean is 20.2. These two figures provide a simple and direct way of comparing performance in the two conditions. In research reports these means are frequently presented in a table, and an example of how to do so is shown in an extract from a published report in Section 3.2. Whether you choose to present the means in a table or a sentence, it is important to indicate what the means tell you. In this case, I would write that the means suggest that dogs learn the command 'sit' in fewer trials when continuous reinforcement is used compared with when partial reinforcement is used. You might have noticed the particular wording I used: 'that the means *suggest* ...' – at this point I cannot draw inferences or make conclusions about the data; to do so requires me to employ a different branch of statistics called **inferential statistics** and you will read about this in Chapter 8.

Inferential statistics
Statistical tests that permit conclusions to be drawn from quantitative data generated by research.

Box 4.2   Drawing conclusions from numbers

Why do I need inferential statistics to draw conclusions? The fact that the scores differ across conditions is to be expected. If I performed the same task twice, for example if I ran a kilometre, then it is extremely unlikely that my performance on those two occasions would be identical. If two people performed the same task, it is also extremely unlikely that their performance would be identical. So, when a researcher wants to see if there is a meaningful difference between the performance of participants in two or more conditions, then they need a way of factoring out this normal variation in the scores. Inferential statistics tests do this, and when these tests reveal a difference, this is referred to as a 'statistically significant difference', or by saying that 'the difference between conditions was statistically significant'.

2.2   The standard deviation

As well as having a descriptive statistic that describes the average performance in each condition (the mean), there is a different descriptive statistic that describes the differences in the scores within each condition. Are they all quite close to the mean or are some quite a bit smaller and some quite a bit larger than the mean? In other words, how spread out or dispersed are the data in each condition? The simplest way of indicating spread is the **range**, and this is calculated by taking the smallest or lowest value in the data set away from the largest or highest.

Range
A measure of dispersion representing the difference between the smallest and the largest score in a data set.

However, this only provides information about the difference between the smallest and the largest scores and doesn't tell us about the other scores in between. An alternative way of providing information about the dispersion or variability of all of the scores is to calculate something called the **standard deviation**. This involves a number of steps:

- **Step 1**. Deduct the mean score from each individual score – this tells us how far each individual score deviated from the mean. Table 4.5a shows the data from the collie dogs, where the mean score (shown in bold) is subtracted from each individual score. Remember that in the continuous reinforcement condition the mean was 9.4, and in the partial reinforcement condition it was 20.2.

Standard deviation A descriptive statistic that represents the average amount by which individual values in the data differ (or deviate) from the mean.

Table 4.5a   Calculating the difference between the mean and the individual scores for each condition

Continuous reinforcement condition	Partial reinforcement condition
(10–**9.4**) = 0.6	(15–**20.2**) = –5.2
(4–**9.4**) = –5.4	(22–**20.2**) = 1.8
(11–**9.4**) = 1.6	(30–**20.2**) = 9.8
(12–**9.4**) = 2.6	(16–**20.2**) = –4.2
(10–**9.4**) = 0.6	(18–**20.2**) = –2.2

- **Step 2**. Carrying out Step 1 has resulted in ten new scores, so how do we summarise these? We could add these together and divide by the number of scores. This would tell us the mean amount (the average amount) each score deviated from the overall mean. But if you look at the new scores in Table 4.5a, then you will see some have a minus sign and some a positive sign, and adding these together is problematic as they will cancel each other out (at least to some extent). For example:

$(+2) + (-2) = 0$ and $(+5) + (-3) = 2$

To avoid this we have to first square the new numbers, that is, multiply each number by itself. For example:

$(+2) \times (+2)$ is $(+4)$, and $(-2) \times (-2)$ is also $(+4)$

Have a look at Table 4.5b where we have squared each of the new scores. Can you see how squaring the numbers has got rid of any minus numbers?

Table 4.5b   Squaring the difference between the mean and each score to calculate squared deviation scores

Continuous reinforcement condition	Partial reinforcement condition
$0.6^2 = 0.36$	$(-5.2)^2 = 27.04$
$(-5.4)^2 = 29.16$	$1.8^2 = 3.24$
$1.6^2 = 2.56$	$9.8^2 = 96.04$
$2.6^2 = 6.76$	$(-4.2)^2 = 17.64$
$0.6^2 = 0.36$	$(-2.2)^2 = 4.84$

Note: the superscript ^{2} indicates that you are squaring the number, i.e. multiplying it by itself once.

- **Step 3**. We can now calculate the average of these squared deviation scores. You might think that this involves adding them together and dividing by the number of scores – in actual fact you divide by 'the number of scores minus 1' – see Table 4.5c. This results in a descriptive statistic called the **variance**.

Variance
A measure of dispersion which involves subtracting the mean from each score and squaring the result, and then arriving at an average of these values. By taking the square root of the variance, the standard deviation can be calculated.

Table 4.5c   Averaging the squared deviation scores to calculate the variance

	Continuous reinforcement condition	Partial reinforcement condition
	0.36	27.04
	29.16	3.24
	2.56	96.04
	6.76	17.64
	0.36	4.84
Variance	**39.2/(5–1) = 9.8**	**148.8/(5–1) = 37.2**

Box 4.3 Dividing by n–1

You might be wondering why the minus 1; why divide by 4 and not 5? If you want to calculate the average amount of deviation in a condition then you would reasonably expect to divide by the number of scores (n) in that condition. The reason for dividing by n–1 is quite complex but doing so results in a better estimate of the sort of variation among the scores that you might see when training the population of collie dogs; although the study involved only a sample or subset of these collie dogs, you might remember from Chapter 2 that generalisation is one of the goals of quantitative research.

- **Step 4**. To see at a glance how the individual scores tended to vary, one more step is necessary, and that is to take the square root of the variance. Remember that we squared the deviation scores so we ended up with numbers much larger than the actual deviation scores, so to return back to an appropriate size we need to find the square root, and in doing so we've calculated the standard deviation (see Table 4.5d).

Table 4.5d   The variance and the standard deviation for each condition

	Continuous reinforcement condition	Partial reinforcement condition
Variance	9.8	37.2
Standard deviation (s.d.)	$\sqrt{9.8} = 3.13$	$\sqrt{37.2} = 6.1$

So, calculating the standard deviation, involves:

1 finding the deviation scores (each individual score minus the mean)
2 squaring the deviation scores (multiplying each deviation score by itself)
3 calculating the average of these squared deviation scores (this is the variance)
4 finding the square root of the variance.

This might sound quite a complex task, even when dealing with just a small hypothetical data set comprising only five scores in each condition (if such a study were actually carried out a much larger sample would be used!). Don't panic though. There are software packages that will do these calculations for you and you will not be expected to calculate the standard deviation on this module. The reason why we are showing you what these calculations involve is to help you understand what the standard deviation is and how it represents the dispersion or variability of the data. You need this understanding so that you can interpret the figures when you encounter them in the Results sections of research reports.

In this section, I have shown you how to calculate the mean and also the standard deviation. These are referred to as **descriptive statistics**.

Descriptive statistics are used to provide information about a set of data. The mean is a descriptive statistic that describes the average score. The standard deviation is a descriptive statistic that describes how spread out the scores are.

Descriptive statistics
These are used to describe features of a data set; for example, the mean and the standard deviation.

Activity 4.4

You will encounter the mean again in the online activity *The mean, the mode and the median*, but before moving on why not practise calculating the mean here?

Imagine the following hypothetical study, involving ways of helping overweight individuals lose weight.

- Condition one involves a therapeutic technique involving hypnosis.
- Condition two involves a therapeutic technique involving a conditioning technique.
- Condition three is a control condition where the participants talk with a therapist but the therapist does not use any particular technique.

Thirty individuals were matched in terms of their obesity, and randomly allocated to one condition (normally many more participants would be recruited but I don't want you to have to add up too many data points!). Each cell in Table 4.6 shows the score for one participant, and the scores represent the number of pounds in weight lost after two months of seeing the therapist.

Calculate the means for the hypothetical data from the three conditions and reflect on what these means indicate.

Figure 4.8   How accurate do you think the scores would be if participants weighed themselves?

Table 4.6   Hypothetical data from a study on the effects of therapeutic techniques

Condition one (Hypnosis)	Condition two (Conditioning)	Condition three (Talk only)
12	10	4
2	5	2
19	8	9
16	10	3
18	9	10
4	13	7
14	15	6
12	14	18
15	12	4
10	10	3

The means are: Condition one 12.2; Condition two 10.6; and Condition three 6.6. Remember, I can't make conclusions about whether there are 'statistically significant differences' between the conditions until I have performed inferential statistical tests, but the means suggest that more weight was lost when a therapeutic technique was used compared with the 'talk only' control condition, and the most weight was lost when hypnosis was used.

Summary

- Quantitative data can be summarised numerically using descriptive statistics.

- The mean is an average and can be calculated to allow comparison across conditions.

- The standard deviation can be calculated to provide an indication of how far the scores in a condition deviate from the mean for that condition.

3   Reporting the results of an experiment on advertising

In this section you will see an example of how descriptive statistics are used in research reports. First, some background. You may remember that Toates (2012) considered the relevance of Skinner's work on behaviourism to today's world, and described the application of conditioning to changing recycling behaviour. You might also remember hearing in the audio on Watson, *J.B. Watson* (The Open University, 2014), that Watson went on to work in advertising where he applied conditioning theory. He developed the idea of brand loyalty, that people were not just buying items but also the emotional responses that were linked to, or associated with, those items.

A related question that has been addressed in psychological research is: how do people acquire preferences for certain brands over others? In other words, how do we learn to like or dislike certain products? One explanation is that the product becomes associated with something that we already perceive as positive or negative. Liking something because it has been associated with something positive is often referred to as **evaluative conditioning**.

Evaluative conditioning has similarities to classical conditioning. In classical conditioning, also referred to as Pavlovian conditioning, a conditional stimulus (e.g. a sound) acquires the capacity to trigger a response (e.g. salivation) because of its earlier pairing with the unconditional stimulus (e.g. food).

In studies looking at evaluative conditioning, a neutral stimulus, such as a new product, is paired with a positive stimulus, such as a successful actor or athlete, and the response to the neutral stimulus will be measured. Evaluative conditioning can have a powerful effect, and one we are often unaware of. Our like and dislike of people's names is a good example. Most of us will have some names we like and some names we dislike, and quite often the latter will be the names of people from our past who we also disliked. Because we disliked the person, and that disliking became associated with their name, we also ended up disliking the name.

As evaluative conditioning can result in us liking something or not, and this can happen without us being aware of it, it has become a technique that is regularly used in advertising. The research report selected for

Evaluative conditioning
Liking or disliking something because it has been associated with something positive or negative.

You read about classical conditioning in Chapter 4, Section 2.2, of *Investigating Psychology*.

inclusion here is by Chen et al. (2012) who looked at evaluative conditioning and at attitudes towards sporting events (which in the advertising world are a particular type of product). The main aim of the research was to explore whether pairing a celebrity with a sporting event makes people feel more positive about the event. Perhaps as you would expect (but it is always good to show this empirically!), the researchers found that this was indeed the case.

3.1   Experiments on the use of celebrities to promote a brand

Chen et al. (2012) carried out four experiments in total. Two of the experiments (Experiments 1 and 3) involved two conditions: in one condition a celebrity athlete was paired with a sporting event (the experimental condition) and in the other no such pairing occurred (the control condition). So the independent variable was whether or not a celebrity was paired with a sporting event. Half of the participants were assigned to the experimental condition and the other half to the control condition. Eighty Taiwanese undergraduates from different universities participated in Experiment 1 and 80 spectators of a basketball game participated in Experiment 3.

Table 4.7   The design of Experiments 1 and 3

	Experimental condition	Control condition
Experiment 1	Celebrity paired with baseball event (Group 1)	Celebrity not paired with baseball event (Group 2)
Experiment 3	Celebrity paired with basketball event (Group 1)	Celebrity not paired with basketball event (Group 2)

The procedure involved showing participants a series of images in a slide show. Two images were important: one was of the celebrity endorser, and the other was of the sporting event (in Experiment 1 this was a baseball event and in Experiment 3 this was a basketball event). The other images in the slide show were of five fictitious products and ten images of abstract paintings and scenery. In the experimental condition, participants saw the two key images paired (i.e. one after the other) in the slide show, so that participants saw the image of the event and then the next slide showed the celebrity, and this pairing was shown five times during the presentation of the slides amid the other images. In the control condition, participants saw the same images but in a random order and so the key images of the celebrity and the sporting event were not paired (i.e. they were not shown one after the other).

The dependent variable involved asking the participants to provide responses on a set of seven-point scales, which together were designed to measure their attitude towards the sporting event.

Figure 4.9   Do you like baseball or basketball, and could your response be the result of conditioning?

In the other two experiments, Chen et al. (2012) also manipulated whether the celebrity was a sportsperson (and as this was a sporting event this celebrity had 'high congruence' and so was a good match) or alternatively the celebrity was a pop singer (someone who had 'low congruence' with a sporting event and so was a poor match). Experiments 2 and 4 involved four groups of participants. Participants were first allocated either to the celebrity endorser with 'high congruence' or to the one with 'low congruence'; then each of these two groups were split further so, as in Experiments 1 and 3, half saw the slide of the celebrity paired with the slide of the sporting event (i.e. one was shown immediately after the other) and the other half saw the same images but in a different order so that the two key slides were not paired.

Table 4.8   The design of Experiments 2 and 4

	Experimental condition	**Control condition**
Experiment 2	Celebrity paired with baseball event, high congruence (Group 1)	Celebrity not paired with baseball event, high congruence (Group 2)
	Celebrity paired with baseball event, low congruence (Group 3)	Celebrity not paired with baseball event, low congruence (Group 4)

Experiment 4	Celebrity paired with basketball event, high congruence (Group 1)	Celebrity not paired with basketball event, high congruence (Group 2)
	Celebrity paired with basketball event, low congruence (Group 3)	Celebrity not paired with basketball event, low congruence (Group 4)

3.2   Introducing the Results section from Experiment 1

In Part 1 of this book, we provided examples of the first few sections of a research report (the Abstract, Introduction and Method sections). In the case of Chen et al. (2012), as you would expect, their Abstract summarised their study, its context, method and findings. The Introduction provided the rationale for investigating evaluative conditioning and for studying it in the way they did. Their Method section explained the design of the experiment, the participants, the procedure and the materials. The section that follows is where the authors report a summary of their data and the analyses performed, and this is usually called 'Results'.

In an experimental report, the Results section has three key functions:

1   To describe the data collected using descriptive statistics, often presented in tables or in graph form. You have been introduced to two descriptive statistics, the mean and the standard deviation, in Section 2.

2   To report the results of other analyses using inferential statistics which are performed on the data to allow conclusions to be drawn. You will be introduced to these in Part 3 of this book.

3 To state whether the results of the statistical analysis supported the hypothesis or hypotheses being tested.

Before we look at the Results section of the first of Chen et al.'s (2012) experiments, let's consider the data they collected. In their research report, the authors wrote that a seven-point semantic differential scale was used, which is a seven-point scale with opposite adjectives at each end. The authors reported that the adjectives were: 'good/bad, high quality/low quality, like very much/dislike very much, superior/inferior, attractive/unattractive, pleasant/unpleasant, interesting/boring' (Chen et al., 2012, p. 213).

Let's imagine what the data for one participant might have looked like. In their report, Chen et al. (2012) wrote that participants were asked to answer the questions presented after the slide show had finished. Unfortunately, they do not include the exact instructions that accompanied the questions, but it is likely to have been something like 'Indicate your feelings towards the baseball/basketball event by ticking 1–7 as appropriate, where 1 represents the most negative response and 7 the most positive'. Table 4.9 lists responses that I have made up to show you how a participant might have answered the questions.

Table 4.9 Hypothetical responses from one imaginary participant

	7	6	5	4	3	2	1	
Good				✓				Bad
High quality			✓					Low quality
Like very much				✓				Dislike very much
Superior			✓					Inferior
Attractive			✓					Unattractive
Pleasant				✓				Unpleasant
Interesting			✓					Boring

What do you think Chen et al. did then? In the paper they wrote: 'All items were averaged to represent overall attitude towards the event' (2012, p. 213). So this suggests that they took an average of the scores assigned to each response. Let's do that now using some made-up data from one participant.

- **Step 1**. Score each item (Table 4.10a). You may remember from your reading about the F-scale in the online activity *Constructing scales* that we have to check whether scale items all run in the same direction, that is, whether they all have positive and negative responses at the same end of the scale. If they do not, we must reverse the scoring for those items running in the opposite direction. In this case, all the items on this questionnaire are listed in such a way that the positive end of the scale is always to the left (scoring 7 points) and the negative end of the scale is always to the right (scoring 1 point). This means, luckily, that I don't have to reverse any of the items because in this example all the items run in the same direction.

Table 4.10a   Hypothetical scores for each item/question

Good/Bad	4
High quality/Low quality	5
Like very much/Dislike very much	3
Superior/Inferior	4
Attractive/Unattractive	4
Pleasant/Unpleasant	3
Interesting/Boring	5

- **Step 2**. Add up the scores to achieve a total (Table 4.10b).

Table 4.10b   The sum of the hypothetical scores for each item/question

Good/Bad	4
High quality/Low quality	5
Like very much/Dislike very much	3
Superior/Inferior	4
Attractive/Unattractive	4
Pleasant/Unpleasant	3
Interesting/Boring	5
Total	**28**

- **Step 3**. Divide the total by the number of items to achieve the average (Table 4.10c).

Table 4.10c   An average of the scores

Good/Bad	4
High quality/Low quality	5
Like very much/Dislike very much	3
Superior/Inferior	4
Attractive/Unattractive	4
Pleasant/Unpleasant	3
Interesting/Boring	5
Total	**28**
Mean	**28/7 = 4**

So, the mean score for this hypothetical data is '4', and this score of '4' represents overall attitude towards the event.

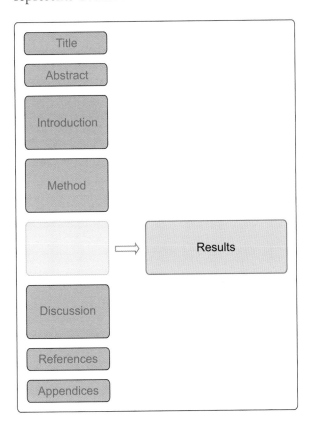

Figure 4.10   The report-writing template: locating the Results section

Returning to the report by Chen et al. (2012), here is an extract of the Results section for Experiment 1.

Results [Experiment 1]

Table 1 reports means and standard deviations by conditions for 80 subjects. The mean of attitude towards the event was 3.98 for the treatment group, compared to 3.12 for the control group. This difference was statistically significant (t=3.74, p< .001). Results of this experiment revealed that individuals exposed to the systematic pairing of the event with the celebrity did develop a more favourable attitude towards the event than individuals in the control condition (no systematic baseball event/celebrity pairing). This supported H1.

TABLE 1   Means and Standard Deviations for experiment by condition

CONDITION	N	MEAN	STANDARD DEVIATION	T	P-VALUE
TREATMENT	40	3.98	1.34	3.74*	0
CONTROL	40	3.12	0.53		

*P<.05

(Chen et al., 2012, pp. 213–14)

The first two sentences in the extract are reasonably straightforward, although note that the authors use the term 'treatment group' to refer to the experimental condition. These two sentences relate to the first function of the Results section mentioned earlier, namely to describe the data collected. Mean attitude scores are compared in the second sentence – note that the mean for the control group is lower, suggesting a less favourable attitude. You have to consider what is being measured and how the scoring was carried out to decide what a higher or lower score actually means; here a higher score signifies a more favourable attitude to the event.

The third sentence refers to the difference in the attitude scores for the two conditions as being 'statistically significant' – you will learn about statistical significance later in this module in relation to inferential statistics. Chen et al. (2012) used a particular inferential statistic suited to comparing two conditions which enabled them to draw conclusions about their data. The conclusion they reached for Experiment 1 is presented in the fourth sentence: 'Results of this experiment revealed that individuals exposed to the systematic pairing of the event with the celebrity did develop a more favourable attitude towards the event than individuals in the control condition (no systematic baseball event/celebrity pairing).' So, the researchers' descriptive statistics indicated a higher score in the condition where the celebrity was paired with the event, and the other statistical analysis they performed allowed them to conclude that pairing the celebrity with the event did have a statistically significant effect on the attitude expressed.

The final sentence refers to H1; H stands for hypothesis and at the end of their Introduction Chen et al. (2012) set out the two hypotheses they were testing, the first (H1) being:

H1: Individuals exposed to the systematic pairing of a sporting event with a celebrity will develop a more favourable attitude towards the sporting event than individuals in the control condition (no systematic sporting event/celebrity pairing).

(Chen et al., 2012, p. 212)

The results that Chen et al. (2012) observed support this first hypothesis. No reference is made to the second hypothesis because this is not tested in Experiment 1.

If you now look at Table 1 in the extract above, again you'll see that Chen et al. refer to the experimental condition as 'treatment' and the control condition as 'control'. They include a column called 'N' which is standard notation for 'number' and tells you that there were 40 participants in each condition. Next to that is a column called 'MEAN' and here they report a mean of 3.98 for the experimental condition and a mean of 3.12 for the control condition. The fourth column called 'STANDARD DEVIATION' shows how much the scores deviate from the mean, 1.34 for the experimental condition and 0.53 for the control condition. If the standard deviation is a large number then this suggests that overall there is a lot of variation in the scores within the condition. If it is small then this suggests that the scores are quite close to the mean. In Table 1 the standard deviation for the experimental condition is slightly larger than that for the control condition, so this suggests that the scores in the experimental condition are a little more spread out (or deviate to a greater extent from the mean) than the scores in the control condition.

So what about the other experiments that Chen et al. (2012) conducted? Experiment 3 was very similar to Experiment 1, except that the sporting event involved basketball and the participants were not undergraduates but spectators at a basketball event. The results of Experiment 3 were very similar to Experiment 1, and again supported hypothesis 1. The researchers had therefore replicated the findings of their first experiment. (You read about the importance of replication in Chapter 2.) What about the findings of Experiments 2 and 4? Chen et al. found that the influence of pairing a celebrity with a sporting event on the attitude expressed towards the sporting event was more marked when the celebrity was a sportsperson rather than a pop singer. Indeed, when it was a pop singer the researchers could not conclude that the attitudes in the experimental condition were different from those in the control condition. In other words, the celebrity had to be a sportsperson for the attitude expressed to be more favourable towards the sporting event.

Summary

- In the Results section of an experimental report, the data collected are described and the findings of statistical analyses are reported.

- The paper by Chen et al. (2012) involved evaluative conditioning experiments that tested whether pairing a celebrity with a sporting event makes people express a more favourable attitude towards that event. A more favourable attitude emerged only when the celebrity was highly congruent with the event.

4 Exploring the use of conditioning techniques

The experimental method has been used in a range of studies seeking to find out more about how we come to like or dislike products. Questions addressed include why did the sales of Courvoisier cognac increase by 20 per cent when artists Busta Rhymes and Puff Daddy released a song and music video with the title 'Pass the Courvoisier Part Two'? Can evaluative conditioning promote children's liking of vegetables? Can unpleasant images paired with snack foods enhance healthy food choices?

It is to be expected that much of the research looking at the application of conditioning to advertising has used the experimental method. This is because the way experiments are designed means that researchers can study whether one thing has an effect on another. So, this method allows researchers to identify whether the particular pairing (evaluative conditioning) introduced influences how a particular product is viewed, and what factors influence whether this effect arises. There are of course research questions related to the application of conditioning theory where alternative methods would be more appropriate.

Activity 4.5

Imagine that you wanted to find out how well psychology graduates understand the concepts involved in operant conditioning. Reflect for a moment on the merits of interviewing graduates individually or in a focus group.

Interviewing graduates individually would allow you to assess the accuracy of their understanding of the concepts. You would also be able to ask about their views on how well they felt they had understood the concepts, whether they felt confident about their understanding of these concepts, and whether they ever put them to use in their daily lives. It is possible, though, that graduates would feel uncomfortable at being asked to define or explain these concepts in an interview situation. They might feel that they were being pressed to give an answer and that they couldn't take the amount of time they would like to think about the concepts before giving their answers.

Chapter 1 of both
Investigating Psychology
and *Investigating Methods*
discuss some of the
advantages of the
questionnaire method.

It would be difficult to assess the accuracy of the graduates' individual understanding of the concepts when using a focus group; however, you would be able to get a sense of which concepts were raised and discussed by the group, and whether collectively they could arrive at accurate explanations. You would probably also obtain rich data concerning their views on this particular topic; for example, by hearing them discuss its importance or usefulness.

Alternatively, a questionnaire might be a good method for assessing how well psychology graduates understood operant conditioning concepts. It would avoid putting them on the spot, and the completion of the questionnaire could be done in a quiet environment and at their own pace. The graduates' understanding of the terms could be assessed through multiple-choice questions, and open-ended questions could ask about their views on this approach to learning and about whether they used any conditioning techniques themselves.

One possible downside of using a questionnaire is that you as the researcher would have no way of knowing whether the participants attempted the multiple-choice questions by drawing solely on their understanding or whether they had a peek at the information provided in their study materials, or indeed whether they sought help from others. Nevertheless, the advantages of questionnaires are that they can be administered to a large group and are resource efficient, and this means they are a popular research method.

Warren-Smith and McGreevy (2008) used a questionnaire to find out whether accredited horse trainers, referred to in the report as equestrian coaches, understood the concepts of operant conditioning.

Before I describe their study, it might be helpful to refresh your memory of some basic operant conditioning terms:

- Positive reinforcement involves adding or introducing a stimulus once the desired response is shown.
- Negative reinforcement involves subtracting or taking away a stimulus once the desired response is shown.
- Both positive and negative reinforcement should lead to an increase in the frequency of the desired response.
- Primary reinforcers are those associated with the animals' biological needs (e.g. food, water, warmth).

- Secondary reinforcers are those that were previously neutral stimuli but were paired with primary reinforcers as in classical conditioning (e.g. praise).
- Punishment involves adding or introducing a stimulus once a particular response is shown, which then leads to a decrease in the frequency of that response.

In their research report, Warren-Smith and McGreevy (2008) explain that inappropriate behaviour in horses is one of the main causes of horses being destroyed. Clearly, a horse that does not behave as required is a safety risk for anyone riding the horse. Both positive reinforcement and negative reinforcement are used to train animals, and although punishment is not always effective, unfortunately it too is also used. The authors point out that negative reinforcement is particularly important because riders use tactile contact to control the horse, and correct behaviours are reinforced by removing the pressure from the reins (via the bit) or from the rider's legs.

Figure 4.11   This looks like a well-trained horse

Warren-Smith and McGreevy designed a two-page questionnaire and they provided full details of this questionnaire in the Method section of their research report. The final four of 20 questions asked about horse training interventions and focused on coaches' understanding of reinforcement and punishment and how they would use these in training. Based on the description provided in the report (2008, pp. 154–5), these questions would have looked similar to the questions in Figure 4.12. Note how the coaches are not asked to define these concepts, or answer multiple-choice questions, but instead are asked to provide examples of how they use the concepts in their training. This approach avoided the appearance of a test of knowledge and also encouraged responses that revealed what the coaches actually do when they think they are drawing on conditioning techniques in their horse training.

The questionnaire was sent to all 830 equestrian coaches in Australia who were accredited at the time, but only 206 were completed and returned (it is often the case with questionnaires that many are not completed, and completion rates are usually reported in the research report). From the responses, Warren-Smith and McGreevy were able to work out how well the coaches understood certain conditioning concepts. Warren-Smith and McGreevy scored the second open-ended part to questions 17–19 as 'correct' if they were in line with Skinner's (1953) definitions, or as 'partially correct' if these partly, but not completely, agreed with the definitions, or as 'incorrect'.

Questionnaire

Please indicate the usefulness of the following by circling the appropriate response and providing an example:

Question 17 Positive reinforcement: very useful   useful   unsure   unhelpful   very unhelpful

Provide an example of how you would use this in horse training

Question 18 Negative reinforcement: very useful   useful   unsure   unhelpful   very unhelpful

Provide an example of how you would use this in horse training

Question 19 Punishment: very useful   useful   unsure   unhelpful   very unhelpful

Provide an example of how you would use this in horse training

Question 20 Your horse has just performed a movement well in a training session; this can include a dressage movement, a good jump, good transition, acceptance of the bridle, etc. Rank the following in order (1 most important to 6 least important) in terms of their effectiveness as a reward for this performance:

scratching on the withers ☐
patting on the neck ☐
rubbing on the neck ☐
giving a handful of preferred food ☐
turning out for free run ☐
releasing the aid ☐

Figure 4.12 An example of how the last four questions might have looked in the questionnaire

The researchers wrote that the most striking result was the relatively low number of respondents who could accurately provide an example of positive reinforcement (only 2.8 per cent were scored as 'correct') and negative reinforcement (only 11.9 per cent were scored as 'correct').

Although 80 per cent of respondents said that they found positive reinforcement very useful, the examples provided showed that 50.6 per cent confused this with negative reinforcement. Similarly, negative reinforcement was confused by 51.5 per cent of respondents with punishment.

When Warren-Smith and McGreevy looked at the responses to question 20, they found that 78.2 per cent of respondents ranked the release of pressure as the most effective reward. As this involves stopping something unpleasant, this is in fact negative reinforcement, and so it is negative rather than positive reinforcement that is most favoured. Scratching the withers is a primary reinforcer as it is inherently rewarding for a horse, and it is also considered to be an effective reward (e.g. McBride et al., cited in Warren-Smith and McGreevy, 2008). However, only 7.4 per cent of the respondents considered this to be the most effective reward. A pat on the neck is a secondary reinforcer when appropriately paired with a primary reinforcer (e.g. McGreevy, 2004, cited in Warren-Smith and McGreevy, 2008), but those rating the pat as the most effective reward were also most likely to have provided an incorrect explanation of positive reinforcement.

The questionnaire method proved to be an effective tool for finding out how learning theory was being applied in real life. From just a few questions, Warren-Smith and McGreevy (2008) found evidence suggesting that operant conditioning concepts were poorly understood by equestrian coaches in Australia. Importantly, they were also able to gain a sense of the techniques that were being favoured in the training of horses. Their findings can be used to inform any changes to the training of accredited equestrian coaches.

Summary

- Research on conditioning has involved the experimental method; however, interviews and questionnaires are helpful when exploring how well conditioning is understood and applied in real life.

- Warren-Smith and McGreevy (2008) used a questionnaire to explore accredited horse coaches' understanding of operant conditioning concepts.

References

Adorno, T. W., Frenkel-Brunswik, E., Levinson, D. J. and Sanford, R. N. (1950) *The Authoritarian Personality*, New York, NY, Harper.

Banyard, P. (2012) 'Just following orders', in Brace, N. and Byford, J. (eds) *Investigating Psychology*, Oxford, Oxford University Press/Milton Keynes, The Open University.

Chen, C.-Y., Lin Y.-H. and Hsiao, C.-L. (2012) 'Celebrity endorsement for sporting events using classical conditioning', *International Journal of Sports Marketing & Sponsorship*, April, pp. 209–19.

Skinner, B. (1953) *Science and Human Behavior*, New York, NY, The Macmillan Company.

The Open University (2014) 'J. B. Watson' [Audio], *DE100 Investigating psychology 1*. Available at https://learn2.open.ac.uk/mod/oucontent/view.php?id=441824&section=3 (Accessed 14 May 2014).

Toates, F. (2012) 'Changing behaviour', in Brace, N. and Byford, J. (eds) *Investigating Psychology*, Oxford, Oxford University Press/Milton Keynes, The Open University.

Warren-Smith, A. K. and McGreevy, P. D. (2008) 'Equestrian coaches' understanding and application of learning theory in horse training', *Anthrozoös*, vol. 21, no. 2, pp. 153–62.

Chapter 5
Making associations

Nathalia Gjersoe

Contents

Aims and objectives

After studying this chapter you should be able to:

- appreciate the use of scattergraphs to display correlations
- explain what is meant by a positive and negative correlation and the correlation coefficient
- appreciate the use of contingency tables to display associations
- understand how to undertake and report coding of behaviour
- describe two different tests of attachment.

1   Describing data in correlational studies

In Chapter 3, we distinguished between the experimental and correlational approaches to research. In an experiment the researcher manipulates the independent variable to consider its effect on the dependent variable, while in a correlation the researcher measures two naturally occurring variables and looks for associations between them. You saw how experiments are designed to look for differences between conditions, and how data from experiments can be summarised using descriptive statistics such as the mean and standard deviation, which can be presented in research reports using tables and graphs. In this chapter, I will describe how data from correlational studies are displayed and described. In addition, I will illustrate how complex behaviour can be coded to allow researchers to identify associations.

The difference between correlational studies and experiments was explained in Chapter 3, Section 1, of *Investigating Methods*.

Calculating, reporting and interpreting descriptive statistics such as the mean and standard deviation were described in Chapter 4 of *Investigating Methods*.

Activity 5.1

Suppose that you want to find out whether there is any relationship between doing the online activities in a study module and the grade achieved in that module.

1   How might you answer this question using an experimental design?

2   How might you answer this question by carrying out a correlational study?

3   Why might a correlational study be preferable in this case?

For the first question, you could design an experiment to test whether completing online activities led to higher grades by finding two groups of students who were matched in terms of their general ability and asking Group 1 to do all the activities (the activities condition) and Group 2 not to do any of the activities (the no-activities condition). Then you would compare the grades achieved by each group. Remember that experiments involve manipulating the independent variable – in this case, whether or not students did the activities.

In answer to the second question, you could examine the same question by designing a correlational study where you explore whether there is a relationship between the number of online activities that students happen to do (variable 1) and their subsequent module grade (variable 2). Because you are measuring two things that are naturally occurring (i.e. occurring without your intervention), and you are not manipulating an independent variable, this is a correlational study and not an experiment.

The final question asks you to consider why a correlational study might be preferable. Did you spot the ethical considerations which would make an experiment problematic? An experiment would require you to instruct some students not to complete the online activities and therefore risk them doing badly on the module for the sake of your research. With a correlational study, you would be able to record whether or not students complete the online activities and their final grade. You would not be interfering with their study choices or risking having a negative influence on their final grade. If you found that students who did more of the online activities got higher grades, then you would know that the number of online activities completed is associated with the grade achieved. Note, though, you could not say that doing the online activities *causes* students to get higher grades. It might be that students who do more of the online activities also do more of the chapter activities or that they have more time overall to study.

You read about establishing causal links in Chapter 3, Section 1.2, of *Investigating Methods.*

1.1   Levels of measurement in correlational studies

The data collected in studies involving experiments or correlations can be nominal, ordinal or interval.

You read about these different levels of measurements in Chapter 4, Section 1, of *Investigating Methods.*

Activity 5.2

Below are very brief descriptions of three correlational studies. Identify the two variables being measured in each example, and say whether the variables are being measured at the nominal, ordinal or interval level.

1 Psychologists measured whether boys committing a high or low number of anti-social acts are more likely to be excluded from school.

2 Psychologists compared the number of cuddles that mothers gave children and rated those children's level of aggression in nursery.

3 Psychologists examined whether happy or unhappy people ate more chocolate.

In the first study, psychologists are comparing two variables. One variable is whether the boys commit a high or low number of anti-social acts, and the other variable is whether or not they are excluded from school. Therefore this is an example of a correlational study that would be measuring two variables at the nominal level. In the second study, one variable is the number of cuddles, which yields interval data, and the other variable is the rating of aggression (on a scale from not aggressive to very aggressive), which yields ordinal data. Finally, in the third study, psychologists explore the relationship between the variable 'happiness' (happy or unhappy), which is nominal, and the amount of chocolate eaten, which is an interval variable.

If you find that one variable is associated with another then the next step is to look at the nature of this association. Correlations are directional. Correlations can be positive – as one variable goes up, so too does the other. For example, 'The older I get the more I forget' implies a positive correlation. As one variable (age) goes up, so too does the other (forgetting). Correlations can also be negative – as one variable goes up the other goes down. For example, 'The older kids get, the less obedient they become' implies a negative correlation. As one variable goes up (age) the other goes down (obedience). A negative correlation can signal just as strong a relationship between two variables as a positive correlation.

Activity 5.3

Which of the following hypothetical findings describes a positive correlation and which describes a negative correlation?

1 People who do more exercise rate their body satisfaction more highly.

2 Children who get more cuddles cry less.

3 Students who procrastinate less get higher marks.

The first hypothetical correlation is positive because as one variable increases (exercise) so does the other (body satisfaction ratings). The second example is a negative correlation because as one variable increases (number of cuddles), the other decreases (amount of crying). The final example also describes a negative correlation because as one variable decreases (procrastination) the other variable increases (marks). Have you noticed that when we use the terms 'positive' or 'negative' to describe a correlation, we do not mean a 'good' or 'bad' correlation?

1.2   Plotting interval data from correlational studies

An easy way of seeing whether variables appear to correlate, and whether the correlation is positive or negative, is to display the data in a graph.

To do this we use a graph called a scattergraph. Scattergraphs are also sometimes called scatterplots or scattergrams but all these words mean the same thing. This type of graph is used in correlational studies when both variables are measured at the *interval* level. A scattergraph is simply a graph where a participant's score on one variable is plotted against their score on another variable. Let's take a look at the scattergraph in Figure 5.1a.

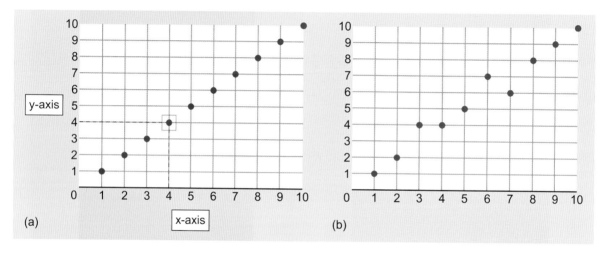

(a)   x-axis   (b)

Figure 5.1a   Scattergraph showing a perfect positive correlation Figure 5.1b   Scattergraph showing a near-perfect positive correlation

Chapter 4 of *Investigating Methods* and the online activity *Constructing and interpreting bar charts* introduced bar charts which can be used when reporting experiments, and these display any differences between conditions.

The scattergraph shares some properties with the bar chart that you learned about in the online activity *Constructing and interpreting bar charts*. Like the bar chart it has two axes – these are the strings of numbers that run along the bottom and side of the data. The horizontal line of numbers along the bottom of the graph is referred to as the 'x-axis' and the vertical string of numbers on the left is referred to as the 'y-axis'. These represent interval amounts (here from 0 to 10) of the two variables that are being compared. Each dot on the graph represents the data from one participant. For instance, in Figure 5.1a the dot with a red square around it represents a participant who scored 4 on both the variable on the x-axis and the one on the y-axis. You can tell this by following an imaginary straight line down from the dot to the x-axis and reading what number on the x-axis it intersects with. In the same way, you can follow the line from the dot to the number on the y-axis. A scattergraph tells you how each participant scored on both variables.

The scattergraph illustrated in Figure 5.1a shows a perfect positive correlation. That is, participants who score high on one variable also score high on the other variable to exactly the same degree. It is very unlikely that you would ever see a perfect correlation in psychological research – at most you might see a near-perfect correlation, as in Figure 5.1b. For instance, this sort of pattern in a scattergraph might represent a study examining the relationship between children's age and vocabulary size – older children are likely to have larger vocabularies. When the data points on a scattergraph slant upwards like this, it suggests that there is a positive correlation between the variables. Compare this with the scattergraph in Figure 5.2a.

You can practise interpreting scattergraphs in the online activity *Interpreting correlation.*

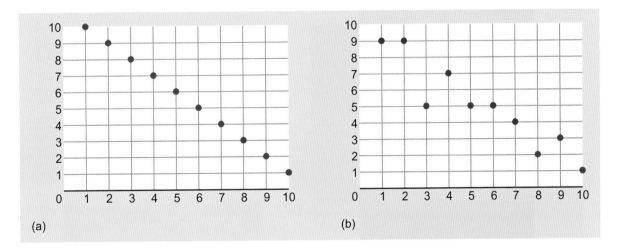

(a)

(b)

Figure 5.2a   Scattergraph showing a perfect negative correlation
Figure 5.2b   Scattergraph showing a near-perfect negative correlation

The scattergraph in Figure 5.2a shows a perfect negative correlation and Figure 5.2b shows a near-perfect negative correlation (which you are more likely to see). That is, participants who score high on one variable tend to score low on the other. For instance, this sort of pattern in a scattergraph might represent a study examining the relationship between the amount of alcohol consumed and accuracy in a test – participants who have consumed more alcohol are likely to perform less accurately. When the dots in a scattergraph slope down from left to right like this, it suggests that there is a negative correlation in the data.

All the data points in Figures 5.1 and 5.2 lie along a single straight line or nearly straight line. Figure 5.3 shows a scattergraph where the variables appear to be correlated but less closely.

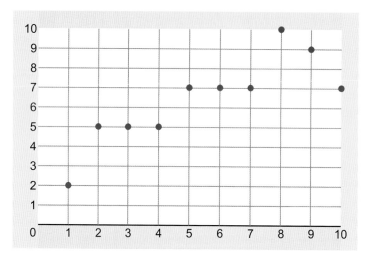

Figure 5.3   Scattergraph showing imperfect positive correlation

As you can see in Figure 5.3, the dots still cluster in an upwards direction but they are not so closely aligned as in Figures 5.1a or 5.1b. The strength of a correlation is represented by how closely the dots are clustered together along a positive or negative line. Although the dots are quite widely clustered in Figure 5.3, it is still clear that they are arranged in an upwards direction, suggesting a positive correlation. Compare this with the scattergraph in Figure 5.4 which represents two variables that have no correlation. Here the data points seem to be scattered randomly all over the graph and there is no spread of data points in any consistent direction.

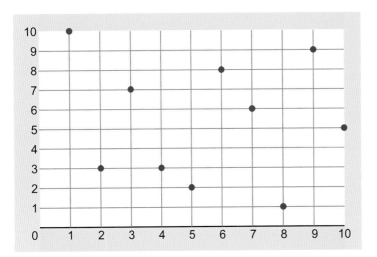

Figure 5.4   Scattergraph showing no correlation

Activity 5.4

Plot the fictional data shown in Table 5.1 on the graph axes provided in Figure 5.5a below, then answer the following questions. These data represent invented examples of the sort of data that Bowlby (cited in Custance, 2012) might have collected in his forty-four thieves study.

The data points for Boys 1, 2 and 3 have been entered for you.

You will see in the reference list at the end of this chapter that Custance (2012) refers to Chapter 5 of *Investigating Psychology.* Bowlby's study is described in Section 5.2.

Table 5.1   Fictitious data mimicking Bowlby's correlational study

Participant number	Amount of time (in days) separated from mother before age 5 (maternal deprivation)	Number of anti-social acts committed by age 15 (anti-social acts)
Boy 1	5	3
Boy 2	1	2
Boy 3	0	0
Boy 4	10	7
Boy 5	24	10
Boy 6	3	1
Boy 7	8	4
Boy 8	14	5
Boy 9	22	8
Boy 10	10	9

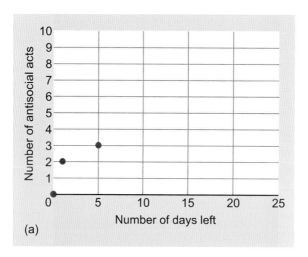

(a)

Figure 5.5a   Scattergraph showing correlation between maternal deprivation and anti-social acts

1   What variable is measured on the x-axis?

2   What variable is measured on the y-axis?

3   What does each dot on the graph represent?

4   Is there a correlation between maternal deprivation and anti-social acts? How can you tell?

5   What direction is the correlation – positive or negative?

6   What does the correlation tell us about the cause of children's anti-social behaviour?

How did you get on? A completed version of the graph can be found at the end of this chapter (Figure 5.5b), but here are the answers to the questions.

1   Maternal deprivation, measured by the amount of time the child is separated from the mother before age 5.

2   The number of anti-social acts committed by the age of 15.

3   The amount of maternal deprivation experienced by the boys and the number of anti-social acts they have committed.

4   The correlation between maternal deprivation and anti-social acts can be seen from the fact that the dots cluster along a rough line (you can check this on Figure 5.5b).

5   The fact that the dots cluster in an upwards direction suggests that there is a positive correlation between maternal deprivation and anti-social acts.

6   This correlation tells us nothing about the *causes* of anti-social behaviour in children. Note also, though, as you learned in Chapter 4, without inferential statistics we do not know if this result could be generalised beyond the sample from which the data were taken.

1.3   Using the correlation coefficient

So far this section has focused on simply assessing correlations by looking at how the data points on the scattergraph cluster. If they cluster together in an upwards direction it implies a positive correlation, if they cluster in a downwards direction it implies a negative correlation, and if they do not cluster in any consistent direction it suggests there is no correlation. However, researchers are interested not just in whether a relationship exists between two variables but also in the strength of that relationship. The stronger the relationship, the more useful it is in enabling a researcher to predict what will happen to one variable if the other one changes.

To determine the strength of a correlation, researchers calculate a number called the **correlation coefficient**, which is referred to as 'r' in research reports. The correlation coefficient is always a number between -1 and $+1$. A negative number indicates a negative correlation and a positive number indicates a positive correlation. For instance, the data in Figure 5.1a illustrate a perfect positive correlation so this would be written as $r = +1$. Conversely, the data in Figure 5.2a illustrate a perfect negative correlation so this would be written as $r = -1$. The closer the correlation coefficient is to $+1$ or -1 the stronger the correlation is. What about the data in Figure 5.4 which show no correlation? Here the data are not correlated in either direction so the correlation coefficient would be exactly halfway between $+1$ and -1, that is, $r = 0$. Have a look at Figure 5.6 below, which shows all of the scattergraphs with their respective correlation coefficients.

You learned about the relationship between sampling and generalisation in Chapter 2, Section 1, of *Investigating Methods*.

The need for inferential statistics was introduced in Chapter 4, Box 4.2, of *Investigating Methods*.

Correlation coefficient
This is a measure of the strength and direction of the relationship between two variables.

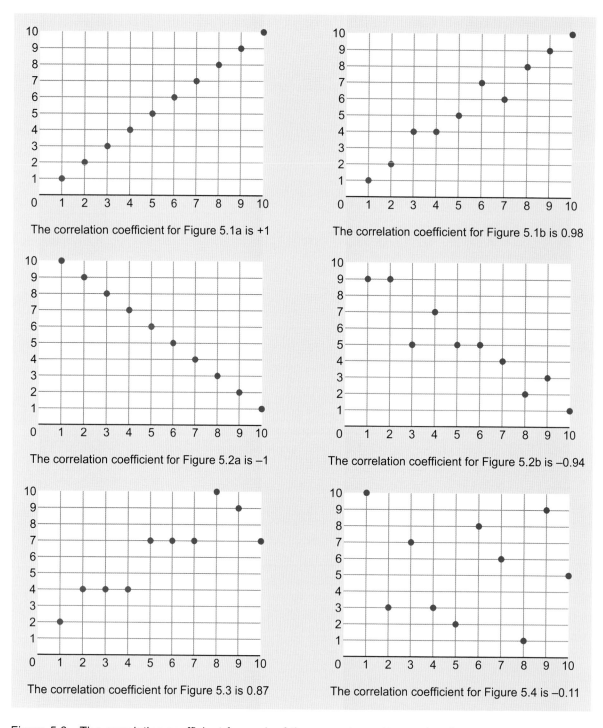

Figure 5.6   The correlation coefficient for each of the example scattergraphs above

The correlation coefficient is a descriptive statistic, like the mean and standard deviation that you learned about in Chapter 4. The correlation coefficient is tricky to calculate by hand but there are several calculators online that make it very straightforward. Here you do not need to know how to calculate the correlation coefficient, but you do need to know how to interpret it when you see it. The correlation coefficient is a way of summarising the participants' responses to give one figure that communicates the overall strength of the relationship between the two variables. Like other descriptive statistics, the correlation coefficient does not let you infer that the relationship between the variables is statistically significant. Even when you find a strong correlation coefficient between two variables, you cannot know for sure that it has not occurred by chance until you have conducted further inferential statistics, which you will learn about in Part 3.

Activity 5.5

Put the following correlation coefficients in order of strength of relationship from weakest to strongest:

0.1

−0.6

−1

0

0.9

Answer

Remember that both 1 and −1 are equally strong correlation coefficients and imply perfect correlation, while 0 implies no correlation at all and is therefore the weakest correlation coefficient value. The closer that the correlation coefficient is to 1 or −1, the stronger it is.

The answer is: 0, 0.1, −0.6, 0.9, −1.

Summary

- Correlational studies explore the association between two variables.

- A positive correlation implies that as the score on one variable increases so too does the score on the other; a negative correlation implies that as the score on one variable increases the score on the other variable decreases.

- Interval data from correlational studies are displayed using a scattergraph.

- The strength of a relationship is calculated by the correlation coefficient, which is symbolised by the letter 'r'. The correlation coefficient is a number from -1 to $+1$, and the closer the correlation coefficient is to -1 or $+1$, the stronger is the relationship between the variables.

2 Presenting nominal data from correlation studies

In the previous section, you learned how interval data from correlational studies can be displayed in scattergraphs. It is also possible to explore the association between two variables when these are measured at the nominal level. In Chapter 4, you learned that you get nominal data by categorising characteristics and behaviour. Remember that nominal data results from placing participants in distinct categories – a person cannot be both high and low in aggression or have both a high and low IQ. In this section, you will explore how relationships in nominal data like this can be reported using contingency tables. A contingency table is a way of summarising the relationships between variables, as you will see next.

Box 5.1   Transforming interval or ordinal data for contingency tables

Where one of your variables is measured at the nominal level and the other variable is measured at the ordinal or interval level, it is possible to transform the one measured at the ordinal or interval level to generate nominal data. This allows you to display both variables in a contingency table. For instance, measuring age by year is an example of interval data, but age could be recoded into categories such as 'under 18', '18 to 45' and 'over 45' or simply into 'young' and 'old'.

2.1   A two-by-two contingency table

Contingency tables allow researchers to report nominal data and identify possible patterns which might indicate that one variable is associated with another variable. In Activity 5.4, you plotted a scattergraph using fictitious data based on Bowlby's forty-four thieves study (cited in Custance, 2012). The data in this activity were interval (amount of time in days and number of anti-social acts), but the two variables could have been recorded in a way that gave nominal data, i.e. one variable could have been 'Whether or not the child was separated for at least a week from their mother before the age of 5', and the other variable could have been 'Whether the child committed an anti-social act or not by age 15'.

Activity 5.6

There are now several databases in Britain that collect data on thousands of children, such as the Millennium Cohort Study (at the Centre for Longitudinal Studies.) which has collected information about children born in 2000, from the year they were born and every subsequent year. These databases make an excellent resource for exploring correlations between different variables. To examine the association between separation from the mother and later anti-social behaviour, imagine you had access to such a database containing this information, and imagine you have selected a sample of 500 children at random. The fictitious data from the first seven children in this sample are displayed below, in Table 5.2.

Table 5.2   Fictitious anti-social behaviour data – boys and girls

Participant number	Separated for at least a week from mother before age of 5?	Committed an anti-social act by age 15?
001	Yes	No
002	Yes	Yes
003	No	No
004	Yes	Yes
005	No	No
006	No	No
007	No	Yes

As you can see from this data set, we have four categories that the young people can fall into:

1 Children who were separated and who did commit an anti-social act ('Yes' in columns 2 and 3).

2 Children who were separated and who did not commit an anti-social act ('Yes' in column 2, 'No' in column 3).

3 Children who were not separated and who did commit an anti-social act ('No' in column 2, 'Yes' in column 3).

4 Children who were not separated and who did not commit an anti-social act ('No' in both columns 2 and 3).

Let's create a table that can incorporate each of these four categories.

Table 5.3a   Contingency table activity

	Separated for at least a week from mother before age of 5?	
	Yes	No
Committed an anti-social act by age 15? Yes		
No		

The name 'contingency table' comes from the fact that the numbers in each cell are contingent (dependent) upon the category in the column *and* the category in the row.

Now that we have created this table, filling in the cells is just a matter of adding up how many young people fall into each category. In Table 5.3b the data from all 500 young people is displayed. (Remember this is fictitious data.)

Table 5.3b   Contingency table with data added

	Separated for at least a week from mother before age of 5?	
	Yes	No
Committed an anti-social act by age 15? Yes	47	29
No	119	305

When Bowlby examined the data he collected for his study, he noted that, unlike non-offenders, most of the young offenders had been separated from their mother for at least one week before the age of 5. Looking at the data in Table 5.3b, do you think there was a similar association between being separated from the mother and committing an anti-social act in our fictitious data?

Answer

Bowlby's conclusion has two elements to it:

1 Most of the young offenders had been separated from their mother.

2 Most of the non-offenders had not been separated from their mother.

The fictitious data in Table 5.3b show that:

- of those who had committed an anti-social act, 47 had been separated and 29 had not – meaning most had been separated. This is very similar to Bowlby's conclusion regarding offenders
- of those who had not committed an anti-social act, 119 had been separated and 305 had not – meaning most had not been separated. This is also very similar to Bowlby's conclusion regarding offenders.

2.2   Larger contingency tables

The contingency table you created in Activity 5.6 is a very simple 2x2 design – that is, there are two rows of data and two columns of data. There is no real limit to how big a contingency table can be; it depends on the number of categories you want to compare. Let's say you wanted to explore the association between separation from the mother at an early age and different types of anti-social behaviour. Imagine you were able to obtain more detail from the fictitious database used in Activity 5.6, which allowed you to work out the type of anti-social behaviour the young person had taken part in. You might end up with a contingency table that looks like the one below and would be described as a 4x2 design (4 rows and 2 columns).

Table 5.4a   Larger contingency table

Type of anti-social behaviour	Separated for at least a week from mother before age of 5?	
	Yes	No
None	119	305
Vandalism	9	8
Shoplifting	13	5
Physical assault	25	16
Total	**166**	**334**

Once again, each number is contingent on the categories listed in the row (type of anti-social act) and the column (separated or not). One thing to note is that because far more young people were not separated than were, the two columns have quite different totals (166 compared with 334). This makes it inadvisable to directly compare the numbers in each row – we would expect those in the 'No' column to be larger just because there are more people in this category. Instead, you need to look for patterns in each column and compare these by row. For instance, looking at the table above, is the largest number for each column in the same row? Here, the largest number for both columns is in the same row, namely 'None'. Is the smallest number for both columns in the same row? Here, the smallest number for those separated is in the row for 'Vandalism', whereas that for the children who were not separated is in the row for 'Shoplifting'. Furthermore, looking across both rows 'Vandalism' and 'Shoplifting', of the children who were separated a higher number committed shoplifting than vandalism, but the opposite is true for those who were not separated.

It can be quite difficult spotting patterns like these, though, so have a look at this alternative way of representing the same data in Table 5.4b.

Table 5.4b Data in a contingency table presented as percentages

	Separated for at least a week from mother before age of 5?	
Type of anti-social behaviour	Yes	No
None	72%	91%
Vandalism	5%	2%
Shoplifting	8%	2%
Physical assault	15%	5%
Total	**100%**	**100%**

Here I have converted the simple counts in Table 5.4a into percentages.

Now it is possible to compare the values in the cells directly. This time, we can see that of the children who had not been separated only 9 per cent were involved in anti-social behaviour, whereas 28 per cent of children who had been separated had committed anti-social acts. In both cases, the most common anti-social behaviour was physical assault but, again, a higher percentage of children who had been separated committed physical assault at 15 per cent compared with 5 per cent for children who had not been separated.

The online activity Working with numbers explains how to calculate percentages.

2.3 Exclusive and exhaustive

The categories in contingency tables must be 'exclusive'. That means that the categories cannot overlap – each participant can only be in one cell of the table and not two. If someone were to have one blue eye and one brown eye, for instance, then the researcher would have to select just one eye-colour to categorise the person or exclude that person from the data set. In the example above, children might have been involved in both fights and vandalism, but this information would be lost as they could only be included in one of the categories. This is a drawback of measuring at the nominal level to explore complex human behaviour.

Researchers try to get around this limitation by ensuring that contingency tables are also 'exhaustive'. That is, that the categories included cover all possibilities and everyone tested. One simple way of ensuring this is by including a 'Miscellaneous' or 'Other' category. For instance, if children in the example above committed anti-social acts other than vandalism, shoplifting or physical assault, then an 'Other' category would have been included to represent those individuals. Alternatively, if some of the children had been involved in both vandalism and physical assault, then an additional category 'Vandalism and physical assault' would have been created to include just these individuals. In Section 3, you will learn about the importance of choosing appropriate categories to describe your behaviour of interest and ensuring that you have enough categories to capture that behaviour.

Summary

- A contingency table is a way of displaying the relationship between two nominal variables.

- Contingency tables can be any size provided that each data point is contingent (i.e. dependent) upon the categories in both the row and the column.

- Contingency tables are 'exclusive' and 'exhaustive'.

3 Coding behaviour

In the previous sections of this chapter you saw how relationships between variables can be explored using correlations (Section 1) and contingency tables (Section 2). But how do researchers record behavioural data in the first place? How do they break the rich and complex stream of human behaviour, thought and variability down into units that they can measure?

In this section, you will learn about how researchers select categories and use these to code participants' behaviour, and how this process is reported. Oates (2012) describes how Bandura and colleagues coded the aggressive behaviour of children in their study of social learning.

Structured coding schemes are pre-specified categories that determine what behaviours the observer attends to during a study. They enable researchers to code behaviour in a systematic and reliable way that will be consistent across different participants and researchers. This is because everybody who has been taught how to use the coding scheme should code behaviour in the same way. It is important to include any coding schemes and a description of coding decisions in research reports so that readers can assess how coding was carried out and be able to replicate the coding scheme.

You will see in the reference list at the end of this chapter that Oates (2012) refers to Chapter 3 of *Investigating Psychology*.

Structured coding scheme
This is a set of pre-specified categories that is used to code behaviour.

3.1 Examining the attachment bond between dogs and their owners

Custance (2012) outlined Ainsworth's Strange Situation Procedure (ASSP). Ainsworth invited mothers and their babies into the lab and then observed their interaction over a series of episodes designed to be moderately stressful for babies and therefore activate their attachment behaviours. Each baby experienced the same set of episodes in the same order while observers coded their responses through a one-way mirror.

Box 5.2   ASSP episodes from Custance (2012)

- **Episode 1**. The mother and infant enter an unfamiliar room that contains two chairs and a selection of toys. The infant is allowed to explore the room while the mother sits and reads.

- **Episode 2**. A stranger enters the room, chats briefly with the mother and then attempts to interact with the child.

- **Episode 3**. The mother leaves the room and the stranger attempts to comfort or play with the child. This episode is cut short if the child becomes very upset.

- **Episode 4**. Reunion occurs. The mother re-enters the room, pauses for a few seconds by the door to allow the child to initiate approach, and then interacts with the child as normal. The stranger leaves the room.

- **Episode 5**. The mother leaves the child alone in the room. This episode is cut short if the child becomes very upset.

- **Episode 6**. The stranger re-enters the room, pauses by the door and then attempts to comfort and play with the child.

- **Episode 7**. Reunion with the mother occurs and the stranger leaves.

The research report selected for inclusion here is by Prato-Previde et al., published in 2003 in the journal *Behaviour*. The research presented in this article was described by Custance (2012). Instead of examining attachment relationships between babies and their mothers, the authors repeated the ASSP to examine whether the relationship between dogs and their owners could be classified as an attachment.

Figure 5.7   Can the relationship between owners and their dogs be characterised as an emotional attachment? Do dogs feel the same way?

Prato-Previde et al. (2003) adapted the ASSP episodes but focused their coding on behaviours that they felt indicated an attachment bond. Specifically, these were security-, proximity- and comfort-seeking behaviours such as:

- whether the dog's play and exploration lessened in the presence of just the stranger and when alone, but recovered after reunion with the owner

- whether the dogs stopped exploring and returned to the owner's side when the stranger entered the room

- whether dogs engaged in play with the stranger while the owner was in the room but stopped once the owner left.

These kinds of behaviours are described by Ainsworth and Bell (1970) as evidence that babies treat their mother as a secure base, and Prato-Previde et al. (2003) suggested that evidence of similar behaviours in dogs would indicate that they too had formed an attachment bond to their owners.

Figure 5.8   Set of images from Prato-Previde et al. (2003, p. 233) showing dog behaviour in each of the episodes of the adapted ASSP

3.2 How to report a structured coding scheme

The extract from Prato-Previde et al., which is presented in Section 3.2, comes from the Method section of their report.

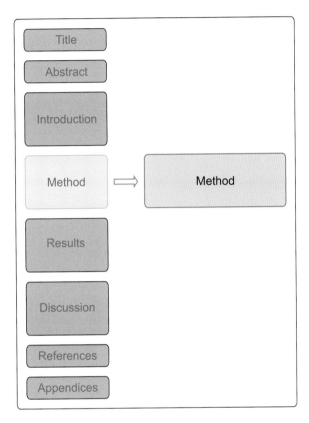

Figure 5.9 Report-writing template: locating the Method section

In Part 1 of this book you learned about the importance of reporting the details of your study design so that readers can assess whether your results and interpretation are trustworthy. The Method section must include a clear and detailed explanation of what you did to enable a reader to make decisions about whether the study you conducted was appropriate to answer your research question and whether you have interpreted your results in an appropriate way; and, if necessary, enables a reader to replicate your research to see if they obtain the same result.

You read about replication in Chapter 2 of *Investigating Methods*.

As we saw in the section above, the behaviour that a researcher chooses to include in their structured coding scheme is vitally important information. Researchers normally include their entire coding scheme in any research report. If the coding scheme is very long and detailed, it might be included in an Appendix at the back of the paper for readers to refer to. Normally, however, it is included in the Method section of the paper.

Table 5.5   Extract showing coding scheme from Prato-Previde et al. (2003)

Behavioural category	Definition
Mutually exclusive categories	
Exploration	Activity directed toward physical aspects of the environment, including sniffing, close visual inspection, distal visual inspection, and gentle oral examination such as licking
Passive behaviour	Sitting, standing or lying down without any obvious orientation toward the physical or social environment
Locomotion	Walking, pacing or running around without exploring the environment or playing
Individual play	Any vigorous or galloping gaited behaviour directed toward a toy when clearly not interacting with the owner or stranger; including chewing, biting, shaking from side to side, scratching or batting with the paw, chasing rolling balls and tossing using the mouth
Social play	Any vigorous or galloping gaited behaviour performed when interacting with the owner or stranger; including running, jumping, active physical contact and chasing toys
Following	Following the person around the room or to the door
Approach	Approaching while clearly visually oriented to the person, either spontaneously or when called

Withdraw	Avoiding interaction with the owner or the stranger by either moving away, very clearly turning away or looking away
Oriented to door	Staring fixedly at the door, either when close to it or from a distance
Oriented to person	Staring fixedly at the owner or stranger, regardless of whether the behaviour was reciprocated
Oriented to chair	Staring fixedly at the owner's or stranger's empty chair
Scratch the door	All active behaviours resulting in physical contact with the door, including scratching the door with the paws, jumping on the door, pulling on the door handle with the forelegs or mouth
Other behaviours	Any activity not included in the behavioural catalogue, such as self-grooming, self-scratching or drinking
Non mutually exclusive categories	
Physical contact with person	Being in physical contact with owner or stranger
Physical contact with chair	Being in physical contact with owner's or stranger's chair
Contact with objects	Being in physical contact with the owner's or stranger's shoes or clothing
Vocalising	Any kind of vocalisation, *i.e.* barking, growling, howling, whining: vocalisations were recorded as bouts
Greeting behaviour	All greeting behaviours toward the entering owner or stranger, such as approaching, tail-wagging, jumping, physical contact

(Source: Prato-Previde et al., 2003, pp. 234–5)

Table 5.5 is an extract from Prato-Previde et al.'s (2003) research report in which they detail what 'behavioural categories' they focused on and how they defined them. Reporting your definition for categories is very important as readers might interpret a phrase like 'Individual play' in any number of ways. Carefully describing how you define the variable

Operational definition
Describes exactly what your variables are and how they are measured in your study.

you want to measure, and the categories which comprise that variable, is known as an **operational definition**.

Operational definitions are very important when deciding what behaviour to code as they help you to focus on the most relevant behaviours but also enable other people reading your work to decide what to make of your findings. By carefully stating what they mean, Prato-Previde et al. make it clear to the reader what behaviours they coded.

The extract in Table 5.5 is taken from the Method section of Prato-Previde et al.'s report. Read through the extract to get a sense of how many different behaviours Prato-Previde et al. coded and how they operationally defined each of those behavioural categories.

Let's take a look at some of the features of this coding scheme in more detail. There are certain structural details of the table to notice. The left column lists the behavioural category and the right column gives the operational definition. There are also sub-titles as part of this table – 'Mutually exclusive categories' and 'Non mutually exclusive categories'. Mutually exclusive categories refer to categories of behaviour that occur by themselves. For instance, a dog cannot be both sitting passively and engaging in social play at the same time. Non-mutually exclusive categories refer to categories of behaviour that can occur at the same time – for instance the dog could be engaging in vocalising behaviour such as whining or barking at the same time as greeting behaviour such as tail-wagging.

Now let's take a closer look at the types of behaviour listed under 'Mutually exclusive categories'. The authors list 12 different types of behaviour that the dog could be engaged in and they also have an 'Other behaviours' category which they can use if the dog isn't behaving in any of the ways listed above. Can you think of any possible responses the dog might have that aren't included in this list and that might be put in the 'Other behaviours' category? The authors provide a few examples such as self-grooming, self-scratching or drinking.

A very important aspect of this coding scheme is that it provides clear definitions of what is meant by each of the coding categories with examples of the sorts of behaviours that might be included in that category. For instance, the authors make a distinction between 'Exploration' and 'Locomotion'. Under their coding scheme, exploration includes any activity directed towards physical aspects of the environment while locomotion refers to any other movement around the room that does not include exploration of the environment or playing. Without these clear and concise definitions, different coders may interpret the categories in different ways and other researchers reading about the study may struggle to understand or replicate the study.

3.3 How to code behaviour

Having decided what behaviour to code, how do researchers go about carrying out this coding? There are many different ways this could be done. I will illustrate two ways. First, I will borrow the coding scheme from Prato-Previde et al. (2003) to show a simple level of 'yes/no' coding of behaviour. In Section 3.4, I will explain how Prato-Previde et al. actually carried out the coding in their study, which was a little more complex.

So let's begin with the simpler version. When conducting structured observations, observers often make use of a 'grid' of behavioural categories. Imagine what the grid might look like for some elements of Prato-Previde et al.'s coding scheme outlined in Table 5.5. Below in Table 5.6a is a grid showing three of their 'mutually exclusive categories'. The columns include the first five episodes outlined in their research report (they looked at eight in total). In Episode 1, the dog enters the room with their owner and is free to explore. Episode 2 involves a stranger entering the room, who interacts briefly with the owner and then with the dog to initiate play. In Episode 3, the dog is left on its own in the room with the stranger who continues to attempt to play with and reassure the dog. In Episode 4, the owner returns, pauses to allow the dog to initiate interaction, and then greets the dog as they would normally. The stranger then quietly leaves the room. In Episode 5, the dog is left alone but observed by the owner and researchers via a monitor.

Activity 5.7

This is a simple coding task to familiarise you with using a coding grid. Each row is dedicated to coding one behaviour (remember we are only looking at the first three categories of behaviour from Prato-Previde et al., 2003) and each column is labelled with an episode. Based on the description for one dog on the next page, fill in the coding grid in Table 5.6a with a 'Yes' if the dog did engage in any of these behaviours during the relevant episode and a 'No' if they did not.

As a reminder, here are the definitions for these categories:

- Exploration: activity directed toward physical aspects of the environment, including sniffing, close visual inspection, distal visual inspection, and gentle oral examination such as licking.
- Individual play: any vigorous or galloping gaited behaviour directed toward a toy when clearly not interacting with the owner or stranger; including chewing, biting, shaking from side to side, scratching or batting with the paw, chasing rolling balls and tossing using the mouth.
- Following: following the person around the room or to the door.

Table 5.6a   Example coding grid for Dog 1

	Episode 1: owner and dog	Episode 2: owner and stranger and dog	Episode 3: stranger and dog	Episode 4: owner returns and stranger leaves	Episode 5: owner leaves
Exploration					
Individual play					
Following					

Use the following description to enter the data in Table 5.6a. In Episode 1, when the dog entered the room with just the owner, it explored the toys and the environment, and began chewing a ball. In Episode 2, when the stranger entered, the dog went immediately back to the owner and sat beside her. When the owner got up to leave the first time (Episode 3), the dog followed her to the door and then sat by it until she returned. When the owner returned, the dog followed the owner to the chair, picked up the ball again and recommenced chewing. When the owner left again, the dog continued chewing while watching the door.

Table 5.6b   Example coding grid for Dog 1 with data added

	Episode 1: owner and dog	Episode 2: owner and stranger and dog	Episode 3: stranger and dog	Episode 4: owner returns and stranger leaves	Episode 5: owner leaves
Exploration	Yes	No	No	No	No
Individual play	Yes	No	No	Yes	Yes
Following	No	No	Yes	Yes	No

How did you get on? Do your answers match mine in Table 5.6b? Possibly you found some coding decisions straightforward, but others more complicated. Let's look at the category for 'Following'. The dog does not display any such behaviour in the first two episodes, but clearly does so in the third and fourth one. However, it may not always be that clear cut. Let's look at the category for 'Individual play'. In episode 4, the dog followed the owner to the chair and was chewing the ball. But does this count as individual play given that the dog followed the owner? I decided it did because there was no interaction between the dog and the owner. These decisions can take some time. Can you imagine doing this with all 17 categories that Prato-Previde et al. (2003) selected?

This method of coding, where you decided 'Yes' or 'No' for each category, is one of the more simple coding systems. This is because it does not take account of *how often* a particular behaviour occurred during a particular episode, or with what *degree of intensity*. Prato-Previde et al. (2003) did in fact code for frequency, and when looking at the greeting behaviour of the dogs, they also scored the intensity of the greeting, as you will read below. With these more complicated coding systems, it is usually necessary to work from video recordings of behaviour, which is precisely what Prato-Previde et al. did, and we will look at this next.

3.4   Prato-Previde et al.'s (2003) coding

You saw how Prato-Previde et al. (2003) reported the categories and how these were operationalised in Table 5.5. In the extract below, they explain how they went about recording the behaviour. They provided this explanation in the final subsection of the Method section, 'Data collection and analysis', parts of which are reproduced below.

Data collection and analysis

The behaviour of each dog during the experimental episodes (ep.1–8) was recorded on videotapes and each session was analysed by two trained observers recording a total of 17 behavioural categories. These categories were selected after a preliminary analysis of the videotapes and on the basis of previous work based on the strange situation procedure (*i.e.* Ainsworth & Bell, 1970; Ainsworth, *et al.*, 1978; Topal *et al.*, 1998).

(Prato-Previde et al., 2003, p. 235)

In the first line the authors explain how the study was recorded (on videotapes) and that it was analysed by two trained observers. Each observer would have watched the footage and used the same coding scheme (outlined in Table 5.5) to categorise the behaviour of each of the dogs. The 'experimental episodes' (Episodes 1–8) refer to the different episodes that the dog participated in (e.g. arriving with the owner, being left alone with the stranger, etc.). The reference to '17 behavioural categories' indicates the list of behaviours included in the coding scheme in Table 5.5.

It is usual in this type of research to have more than one observer. This is to allow the researchers to check whether their categories are explained clearly enough for other researchers to be able to code the behaviours in the same way. By having two observers, Prato-Previde et al. will have looked at how closely the coding of their two observers matched and will have calculated a correlation coefficient.

You read about the correlation coefficient in Section 1 of this chapter.

A high correlation coefficient ('r') between observers would suggest that they completed the coding in a similar way. A low correlation coefficient would suggest that there were many differences of opinion between the observers over the coding of the same behaviours and, therefore, that the categories needed to be defined more clearly and the coding redone.

In the next extract below, Prato-Previde et al. (2003) explain their method of coding in relation to one particular category. I have chosen this paragraph because it gives you a flavour of how it is possible to capture much more information than the simple 'yes/no' approach in Activity 5.7. The category they write about here is greeting behaviour.

> The greeting behaviour of the dogs towards the owner (ep. 4 and 7) and the stranger (ep. 2 and 6) was recorded both quantitatively (duration of greeting in seconds before the resumption of another behaviour) and qualitatively (in terms of an intensity score) considering the first minute of each reunion episode. The greeting intensity score was as follows: if no greeting behaviour occurred, the score was 0 (no greeting); if the dog initiated approach, but then showed a mild greeting with limited physical contact and tail wagging, the score was 1 (mild greeting); if physical contact was full and the greeting behaviour was intense (i.e. jumping up on the owner, vocalising and strongly wagging the tail) the score was 2 (intense greeting).
>
> (Prato-Previde et al., 2003, pp. 235–6)

Observers coded the length of time that the dog greeted the person, producing a quantitative score for each dog in each of the episodes. The authors also refer to an additional 'qualitative' score referring to the intensity with which the dog greeted the person. It is very important to note that the authors here are not using the word 'qualitative' in the way that it is normally used. They are using this term here to indicate their subjective interpretation of the 'quality' of the greeting in contrast to the duration of the greeting. The authors outline how they coded the intensity of the dogs' greeting responses so that this could be replicated by another researcher. They give examples of what sort of behaviour would lead the observer to code the interaction with a 0 (no greeting), a 1 (mild greeting: limited physical contact and tail-wagging) or a 2 (intense greeting: jumping up on owner, vocalising, and strongly wagging tail).

3.5   What Prato-Previde et al. (2003) found

Overall, Prato-Previde et al. (2003) found that adult dogs' behaviour in the Strange Situation Procedure closely resembled that of human babies. Their evidence supports the conclusion that the relationship between dogs and their owners is an affectional bond but they could not conclude it was also an attachment bond. An affectional bond refers to the fact that the dog might prefer their owner to a stranger but an attachment bond implies a much deeper emotional relationship where the dog treats the owner as a secure base from which to explore the world. The problem Prato-Previde et al. had in interpreting their results was that those behaviours indicating that the dog was treating the owner as a secure base were affected by the order in which episodes occurred. This meant that it was difficult for the researchers to tell if differences in behaviour between the episodes occurred because the dog was treating the owner as a secure base or simply because they had grown tired and bored over the course of the episodes. However, a subsequent study by Palmer and Custance (2008) showed that even when the order of episodes was mixed up ('counterbalanced'), dogs showed the same behaviours. This led them to conclude that the relationship between dogs and their owners was indeed an attachment bond, like that between babies and their mothers.

Summary

- Coding behaviour normally involves the use of clearly defined, pre-determined categories.

- Prato-Previde et al. (2003) provide an example of such coding in their study of the relationship between dogs and their owners.

- Behaviour is often video-recorded and multiple observers will carry out the coding.

- It is important to report the categories and coding method so that the study can be replicated.

4 Another attachment measure: examining children's stories

In this chapter I have referred to how Ainsworth (cited in Custance, 2012) developed a set of behavioural categories that helped her (and many researchers since) determine babies' attachment styles. I have also explained how Prato-Previde and colleagues (2003) simplified and adapted this set of behavioural categories to explore whether the relationship between a dog and their owner could also be classified as an attachment. Both of these studies used a very similar research design – the babies and dogs all took part in a set of episodes, and their behaviour was observed through a one-way mirror and classified using a set of pre-determined categories. In this section, I will present an alternative way of assessing children's attachment styles. The Story-Stem Assessment Profile (SSAP) is a method used by clinicians and researchers to explore attachment relationships in children aged 4–8 years. Rather than observing and coding behaviour through a one-way mirror, the story-stem technique involves the researcher interacting with the child and observing how they play. As you read about this method, think about the similarities and differences between this and the classic Ainsworth's Strange Situation Procedure (ASSP).

4.1 The Story-Stem Assessment Profile

The SSAP is a set of 13 beginnings of stories, referred to as 'story stems'. Children are presented with dolls and other props, the beginning of a story is acted out with the dolls, and then the child is asked to finish the story using a combination of language and role-play with the dolls to describe what happens next. As well as the story-stem assessment, clinicians will also interview parents or carers to explore their relationship with the child. This section describes one story stem developed by the Anna Freud Centre and the Great Ormond Street Hospital and how it would be used in a clinical setting.

You can hear about the work of Anna Freud in the audio *Anna Freud and child observation*, available on the module website.

Figure 5.10   The sorts of dolls and props that might be used in the SSAP

The assessment generally takes about an hour during which the experimenter plays with the child, introducing them to a number of different story beginnings ('stems') which they ask the child to complete using a combination of verbal storytelling and role-play with the toys available. The child's responses and interactions with the researcher are videotaped. The interaction is then analysed by experts who have received substantial training in using a rating system that identifies specific criteria in children's responses. Each story presents a family scenario with an inherent dilemma. Described below is one such story stem reported by Mayes et al. (2007). The dilemma in this story stem, which is acted out by the researcher, is that two children have been told that they can ride on their bikes provided they are careful, but they ride too fast and one falls.

Example Story Stem

In the next story, Child 1 is at home. There's a knock at the door, and it's Child 1's friend (Child 2).

Child 2 says: "let's go and play on our bikes!"

Child 1 says: "I'll go and ask my Mum"

So, s/he went and asked her/his Mum.

> Child 1: "Mum, can we go and play outside on our bikes?"
>
> Mum says: "Yes, but be careful!"
>
> We have to pretend the bikes.
>
> They went really fast on their bikes and they went "wheeeeee" (dramatize wild bike riding), but "oh" – what happened (show Child 1 fallen on ground with friend standing)
>
> Show me and tell me what happens now?
>
> (Mayes et al., 2007, p. 168)

At this point, the props are given to the child to act out the remainder of the story. Sometimes the children's responses can be distressing and therefore I will not repeat them here. Instead, I will focus on explaining the procedure.

The story stem and the children's responses are video-recorded. Then, researchers who have been trained in coding the story responses watch the videos and code the children's responses according to a set of pre-determined criteria. The videos are watched by at least two researchers and the main points to emerge are compared for consistent interpretation, and any disagreements are discussed. If disagreements cannot be resolved, then other researchers may be asked to code the same videos to settle the difference. Coders observe how the children use the toy characters to tell the story. They might look for whether the toy 'child' characters are used to perform frustration or aggression, for example, or whether the toy 'parent' characters are made to appear childlike.

After the video has been coded, it is assessed alongside an interview with the parent or carer to assess the relationship from both the child's and the adult's points of view. Based on hundreds of interviews with children who have been maltreated and those that have not, the Anna Freud Centre has developed a scale of children's responses to this battery of stories. The concepts identified in a child's video are mapped on to this scale to examine how this child compares with other children in their age group.

The ASSP and SSAP are similar in a number of ways. Both use children's behaviour to identify their relationships and attachments. Both involve the child coming into a laboratory and being exposed either to a set of pre-determined episodes or pre-determined story-stem scenarios. In both the ASSP and the SSAP, the child's responses are coded using a set of pre-determined categories. For both the ASSP and SSAP, researchers must receive extensive training in how to conduct the study and code the results.

The SSAP, unlike the ASSP, uses a combination of research strategies. Researchers record the child's response to pre-determined story stems and try to interpret the response as a way of assessing the child's relationships with their parents or carers. The SSAP also interviews the parents or carers. This allows them to assess the relationship from the adult's point of view as well. The ASSP focuses only on the infant's behaviour during the episodes. This does not mean that one is inherently better than the other. Both the SSAP and ASSP are valuable tools that serve specific purposes, and researchers must draw on those research tools and strategies that best suit their clearly defined needs.

Activity 5.8

Think back again to the description of the ASSP by Custance (2012) and compare it with the description of the SSAP above. Try to identify some other differences between the two techniques. Think about what the techniques identify, what participants are being asked to do, and what is involved for the researcher.

Although the ASSP and SSAP both try to find out about children's attachment bonds, there are a number of differences between the two techniques. Perhaps most evidently, the ASSP focuses on the attachment relationships between babies and their mothers while the SSAP is designed to explore the relationships of older children, usually aged around 4–8 years. This difference in population leads to other differences in the design. For instance, the SSAP can focus on children's verbal and non-verbal responses to stories because by 4 years of age children normally have sufficient language abilities to be able to understand these scenarios and respond. This would not be an appropriate way of assessing babies, however, so the ASSP focuses on how babies *behaviourally* respond to a series of moderately stressful events. Babies below 12 months of age normally form one strong attachment to a primary caregiver, and the ASSP focuses on that relationship. Older children, however, often have several close attachments that might include other members of their family, siblings and friends. While the ASSP focuses on just the relationship between the baby and the main attachment figure, the range of stories used in the SSAP means that researchers can also explore children's relationships with other important people in their lives

Summary

- The SSAP is a way of collecting data about children's relationships through children's responses to a set of story-stem scenarios.
- A key feature of the ASSP and SSAP is that they code children's responses according to a pre-determined set of behavioural categories.
- Both the ASSP and SSAP compare individual children's responses to norms in order to assess children's attachment style and needs.

Answer to Activity 5.4

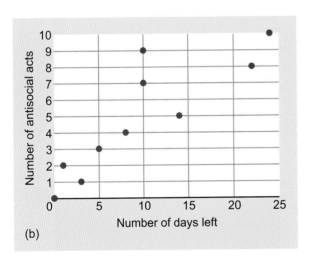

(b)

Figure 5.5b   Completed scattergraph showing correlation between maternal deprivation and anti-social acts

References

Ainsworth, M. D. and Bell, S. M. (1970) 'Attachment, exploration, and separation: illustrated by the behaviour of 1-year-olds in a strange situation', *Child Development,* vol. 41, no. 1, pp. 49–77.

Centre for Longitudinal Studies (no date) *Millennium Cohort Study* [Online]. Available at www.cls.ioe.ac.uk/page.aspx?&sitesectionid=851&sitesectiontitle=Welcome+to+the+Millennium+Cohort+Study (Accessed 5 November 2013).

Custance, D. (2012) 'Determined to love?', in Brace, N. and Byford, J. (eds) *Investigating Psychology,* Oxford, Oxford University Press/Milton Keynes, The Open University.

Mayes, L., Fonagy, P. and Target, M. (2007) *Developmental Science and Psychoanalysis: Integration and Innovation,* London, Karnac.

Oates, J. (2012) 'Learning from watching', in Brace, N. and Byford, J. (eds) *Investigating Psychology,* Oxford, Oxford University Press/Milton Keynes, The Open University.

Palmer, R. and Custance, D. M. (2008) 'A counterbalanced version of Ainsworth's Strange Situation Procedure reveals secure-base effects in dog-human relationships', *Applied Animal Behaviour Science,* vol. 109, no. 2, pp. 306–19.

Prato-Previde, E., Custance, D. M., Spiezio, C. and Sabatini, F. (2003) 'Is the dog–human relationship an attachment bond? An observational study using Ainsworth's Strange Situation', *Behaviour,* vol. 140, no. 2, pp. 225–54.

Chapter 6
Addressing qualitative data through thematic analysis

Lucinda Kerawalla

Contents

Aims and objectives

After studying this chapter you should be able to:

- recognise different types of qualitative data

- describe when you might use thematic analysis and outline how thematic analysis is carried out

- appreciate how the findings from a thematic analysis of interview data can be reported

- outline how data mining can be used alongside qualitative data to study online friendships.

1 Introduction to qualitative data and thematic analysis

This chapter focuses on qualitative research methods, the types of data they produce and a commonly used type of qualitative data analysis called thematic analysis.

1.1 Types of qualitative data

In Chapter 1, you read about some of the differences between qualitative and quantitative research methods and the different types of data they produce. To recap, quantitative data are numerical and can be represented in charts, tables and graphs. Quantitative data can be described in terms of descriptive statistics such as the mean and standard deviation, and are subjected to inferential statistical tests so that inferences can be drawn in relation to the hypotheses being tested. Qualitative data deals with *meanings* and *experience*. This distinction is illustrated in the following example of two different reports of the same tennis match (inspired by Dey, 1993).

> Example 1:
>
> Smith won the match, 6-4, 6-3, 7-6. He served 2 double faults and 15 aces. The average speed of his serve was 95 mph.
>
> Example 2:
>
> There was a real buzz in the stands at Wimbledon today as the French player walked on to the court and began the warm-up session. There was some concern that his hamstring injury might impede his performance but this was unfounded as he ran and stretched for every ball sent hurtling across the net by his opponent. The crowd were enthralled as he …

As you can see, the report in Example 1 consists of a set of quantitative results such as the overall score, and the report in Example 2 is a qualitative description of the game. Of course, it is possible for a qualitative researcher to capture many different types of data that represent the same game of tennis; they could, for example, attend the match in person and make extensive notes, or make a video-recording or take photographs. Moreover, a researcher could ask other people to provide data for them by, for example, asking the ball boys/ girls to write a report about their experiences, or ask the young children

Remember that you will see 'data' referred to in both plural and singular forms. Generally, the plural is used for referring to several pieces of data, typical of quantitative research, and the singular form is used for a set of data, typical of qualitative research.

present among the spectators to draw a picture. Alternatively, a researcher could collect samples of writing and reports that have not been produced specifically for research purposes, such as newspaper articles, blogs and tweets which offer opinions on the match.

So, the range of potential qualitative data sources is vast. In summary, qualitative data can be:

- *audio*; for example, a recording of a prime minister's speech or a popular song (this type of data is often, but not always, transcribed and transformed into text)
- *textual*; for example, words in a diary, print in a newspaper, or a transcribed interview
- *visual*; for example, photographs, videos, drawings and paintings, or maps and diagrams
- *observations*; for example, a researcher's own understandings and descriptions of observed behaviour and interactions.

You may have noticed that the categories of qualitative data above are not mutually exclusive. For example, a prime minister's speech can be written down and its verbal delivery recorded in both audio and video formats. The delivery could also be photographed, depicted in a drawing or written about in a poem. A researcher's descriptions of the delivery of the speech, the tone, the context of the occasion, etc., are themselves a form of verbal data. These different ways of representing the same event all point to the fact that researcher have a choice; they have to decide which kinds of data to collect and how to use them to respond to their own particular research question.

Figure 6.1   Qualitative data come from many different sources such as diary entries, video footage, children's drawings and the text in newspapers

Activity 6.1

Can you think of any other sources of qualitative data? Take a few minutes to jot down some ideas.

You will see in the reference list at the end of this chapter that Brownlow (2012) refers to Chapter 6 of *Investigating Psychology*.

During Activity 6.1 you may have remembered other types of qualitative data that you have come across in this module. For example, Damon (cited in Brownlow, 2012) used interviews with teenagers to explore their thoughts on friends and friendship. Corsaro (cited in Brownlow, 2012) used methods from **ethnography**, making extensive observations of young children and taking part in activities with them to see how they behaved with the other children. He observed what kinds of things they said and did, in order to work out what friendship might mean to these younger children.

Ethnography
A research approach where the researcher carries out extensive observations of a group through being involved in their activities over a period of time.

Also, part 1 of the interview with Carly Butler (The Open University 2014) described the audio data generated by her recordings of children in the playground. You may have thought of other examples too.

1.2   Investigating friendship – choosing qualitative methods?

The interview with Carly Butler is available on the module website.

Imagine that you are a researcher who is interested in young people's friendships. Your research question is: 'What is the role of friendship in the life of a 13-year-old?' You have decided to carry out a study using qualitative research methods and you know that there is a wide range of qualitative research methods that you could choose from. How would you decide which method(s) to use?

Activity 6.2

In Table 6.1 you will see a list of four different sources of qualitative data (diary, blog, ethnographic field notes and interviews). For the first part of this activity, try to complete the second column yourself by saying what type of data each data source could provide. Keep the research question in mind while you are thinking about this: 'What is the role of friendship in the life of a 13-year-old?' The first row has been completed to help you.

Spend a few minutes completing the blank cells in the table. The activity will help you to think about some of the questions researchers ask themselves when making choices about their data sources.

For the second part of this activity, consider which data sources you would choose to help answer the research question.

Table 6.1 Deciding on suitable ways to generate appropriate data

Data source	Data it provides
Diary	Private written accounts which may say something about the person's experiences and thoughts about their friendships
Blog	
Ethnographic field notes made while spending two months with a group of friends during school lunch breaks	
Semi-structured interviews	

As part of Activity 6.2, you might have thought about how semi-structured interviews can be used to give participants an opportunity to express their views in depth, in their own words. In fact, both blog posts and diary entries would probably also represent the participants' views in their own words. In this case, the researcher needs to think carefully about the strengths and weaknesses of each type of data. In qualitative research, it is common for more than one method of data collection to be used as each type of data provides different types of details about the participants' experiences. A blog, for example, is likely to represent details of a participant's life that they want to share with a wide audience (possibly the world!), whereas diary entries may be more private. In the example in Activity 6.2, a researcher could use the blog posts and diary entries to help create follow-up semi-structured interviews; they could read the blogs and diaries first and then generate some interview questions which would prompt the participants to elaborate further on interesting points or discrepancies. So, it is important for a researcher to think very carefully about how each type of data can be used to answer their research question and, in some cases, how multiple types of data can be used together to build up a rich picture of the participant's experiences.

Figure 6.2 Interviews are one way of giving participants an opportunity to express themselves in their own words

All of these research methods will give rise to qualitative data that can shed light on different aspects of friendship, and the choice of method will depend on how well each method can help researchers to answer their research question. Overall then, which data source do you think you would want to use for this kind of study?

Box 6.1 Qualitative research: implications for generalisation

In Chapter 2, you were introduced to the concepts of sampling and generalisability. Qualitative research raises different questions about sampling and generalisability. Qualitative research does not begin with the assumption that findings should generalise to the wider population. For example, diary entries by six unemployed youths in Wales will be personal to those participants, and reveal details of their lives that are unlikely to be generalisable to the experiences of unemployed youth in, say, South Africa. However, if the research question is about the details of the lives of unemployed youths in Wales then a relatively small sample size might be a sensible decision. This would mean that the researcher has time to conduct detailed, in-depth interviews with each participant and generate data which is appropriate for addressing the particular research question being investigated. So, whereas one of the priorities for quantitative research is to discover universal psychological properties, qualitative research tends to prioritise more socially and culturally specific psychological properties. While the findings of qualitative research are not imagined to apply universally, they do combine to add depth of knowledge around particular research topics.

The different types of qualitative data that you have come across above lend themselves to different types of analysis, depending on the questions the researcher is trying to answer. For example, some psychologists are concerned with attempting to explain life and culture from the insider's perspective, so they take part in activities alongside their participants, closely observe what they are doing or saying, and take rich detailed field notes, a process that the ethnographer Geertz (1973) described as 'thick description'. These are used to help explain why people think and behave in particular ways in light of their broader circumstances; for example, their culture, relationships, personal histories or social circumstances. Other psychologists, however, may be concerned with what people say and how talk unfolds in naturalistic settings; for example, student–teacher interactions in a classroom, or a political speech. They could then carry out a form of analysis called discourse analysis. This approach is concerned with understanding language as social action, in other words, how language can be used to create versions of the truth, to declare peace, or to establish and enact power and control, for example. Alternatively, other psychologists might be interested in interviewing people about their experiences and opinions. In this case, a thematic analysis of the interview transcripts might be most appropriate as it helps the researcher to look for commonalities across lots of accounts from different people. Thematic analysis is a popular analytic approach in psychological research and will be described in more detail in the following sections, using data from semi-structured interviews as an example.

1.3 Introducing thematic analysis

In 2006, Braun and Clarke published a now well-known academic paper about **thematic analysis**. I will draw on their paper here when introducing you to thematic analysis. Let's start by considering the types of data it can be used to analyse.

Braun and Clarke (2006) describe thematic analysis as 'a method for identifying, analysing, and reporting patterns (themes) within data'

Thematic analysis
A qualitative method used to identify, analyse and report patterns (themes) in qualitative data.

(p. 79). So, the main aim of thematic analysis is to make sense of the data by looking for patterns or themes across the whole data set.

What might this data look like? Thematic analysis can be used to analyse a wide variety of qualitative data types that are *written or spoken*, such as interviews, newspaper reports, television programmes and open-ended questionnaire responses. Where recordings of audio data are used they are generally transcribed and transformed into written data for analysis. Thematic analysis is very flexible. For example, if a researcher is interested in how young people communicate with friends using different media, they might collect audio recordings of face-to-face conversations, SMS (text) messages and audio recorded telephone calls. A thematic analysis could then be carried out to identify patterns in the data resourced from different types of communication media. Alternatively, a researcher may decide to conduct interviews only; a thematic analysis could then be carried out to identify patterns across this single source of spoken (or transcribed) data.

Thematic analysis does not require any quantification of data. By this I mean the data is not collected in numerical form, nor is data turned into numbers. Therefore, calculations such as the mean and standard deviation do not (indeed, cannot) feature in thematic analysis (or in any other type of qualitative data analysis), nor is data presented in tables of numbers or in bar charts. Instead, the data is described in words. However, there has to be some kind of data reduction involved in reporting a thematic analysis – researchers cannot just present a set of interview transcripts as their 'results'; there has to be a way of describing the data that captures its key points in a clear and succinct way.

The aim of thematic analysis is therefore the identification of the main themes or patterns in the data set, and these themes will then inform how the findings are presented in a report. How do researchers go about doing this? The answer to this question will be addressed in Section 2.

Figure 6.3 Undertaking a thematic analysis reduces a pile of qualitative data down to a single, succinct report that captures the main themes or patterns across the whole data set

Summary

- There is a vast range of qualitative data sources.
- There are many different types of qualitative data including: audio records, written text, visual records and observational notes.
- Qualitative data deals with meanings and experience.
- There are many different methods for conducting qualitative analyses.
- Thematic analysis is one method of analysing qualitative data.

2   Doing thematic analysis

Braun and Clarke (2006) identify six phases of thematic analysis. These phases are not intended to be a set of fixed independent stages to be completed in turn; you do not start at Phase 1 and work your way through one phase at a time to Phase 6 in order. This is because the process of carrying out a thematic analysis is *iterative*, meaning that the earlier phases of the process are returned to and repeated until you are satisfied with the outcome overall. For instance, you might read a transcript and identify some themes, then read a second transcript and identify some similar themes but change your mind about some of the others. So, you might go back and code the first transcript again. This is described in more detail below using analysis of interviews as an example.

2.1   Phase 1: Familiarisation

Immersion
The process of becoming very familiar with your data by scrutinising it repeatedly over a period of time.

Thematic analysis requires the researcher to become **immersed** in their data. This process starts with transcription: there is no better way of getting to know your data than by listening carefully and typing out what your interviewees say. Transcription is a lengthy, time-consuming process and is often contracted out to speed typists, but it is very valuable for familiarisation if you have the time. Researchers then read the transcripts, reread them and reread them again and again so that they become very familiar with all of them (very often it can feel like you eat, sleep and breathe them!). Also, it is a good idea to make notes during the initial familiarisation phase, such as marking interesting parts of the transcript. It is this familiarisation process which forms the first phase of thematic analysis.

Figure 6.4   Data immersion is an important part of the familiarisation phase of thematic analysis

2.2   Phase 2: The generation of initial codes

The process of coding forms part of the early stages of thematic analysis. Researchers look carefully at their data and develop their coding scheme according to the features in the data that they think are important to their research question. This approach is known as **inductive coding**. The codes are not specified beforehand. Instead, the researchers look to see what is present in their data, and develop appropriate codes. Occasionally, researchers might apply pre-determined codes. This is a process of **deductive coding**, where researchers decide in advance what features they want to search for in the data. (This perhaps sounds like the pre-determined categories used by Prato-Previde et al. (2003) to investigate dogs' attachment to their owners. The similarity between deductive coding in thematic analysis and the study by Prato-Previde et al. is the use of existing literature to decide in advance what to look for.)

Inductive coding
Codes are generated from the data.

Deductive coding
Codes are generated from existing literature.

The study by Prato-Previde et al. (2003) was discussed in Chapter 5, Section 3, of *Investigating Methods*.

Deductive coding can be useful if you want to see if you can replicate findings from another study, or if you want to find out whether the findings from another study are generalisable to another population. For example, could the codes generated from a study carried out with participants in China be applied to a study conducted in Wales? However, you could adopt an inductive approach to your coding. In this case, you would not have any codes in mind beforehand and you may discover new things that have not been reported before. In this chapter, we are focusing on the kind of thematic analysis which takes an inductive coding approach.

Imagine that your research question is: 'What does friendship mean to 13-year-olds?' and that you have interviewed three young people individually for 20 minutes each.

Figure 6.5   A group of three young friends you have interviewed

The transcripts will contain a mass of text which, to begin with, is difficult to make sense of as a whole. But, if you work carefully, clear patterns begin to emerge. I am going to illustrate this process, first using nonsense text to illustrate the principles of coding and then by using real examples to put the principles into practice. Figure 6.6a contains nonsense text representing three fictitious 'interview transcripts' waiting to be coded.

Transcript 1	Transcript 2	Transcript 3
Ncsk fji qpfpqj fkelm cvdkal vnsjdnvs dlv nd sjlvnd wjonvd smvln csmv ncmvn cmxv, cmxn vmxc, nvm, xcnvm, x nvni owwejfp iqfjhcnc 'NCWO vns jvnsjbvfhvbf sn cvbwrj bbvv jkfdn vd skskss	Ncdme owievne jv nd sjlvnodj fkelm cvdkal vs dcigh rugh revdsnce wwv nwev nrwue wnv nvni rjovnw jvdsnv qpfpqj norug 3 ho hgr uovh wvjos csmv ncmvn cmxv jvhfso veer 8 gur 8 ugfr nvm	nvni csmv ncmvn cmxv nvm Utiep wfmd klsrnb fjsdal; nvbscm, jvow egh fjsla; vnds amlv hn fjeigr ewb gvruj oewnv; LNVDWORVU fkelm cvdkal NVBW nvjd voern brjoe bnrjbnrjbn qpfpqj rjoen bsowirn

Figure 6.6a Three fictitious 'interview transcripts' for coding

Now imagine that you are carrying out a thematic analysis of the three 'interview transcripts' in Figure 6.6a. You begin by reading the first transcript and noting down its main features. If this transcript was written in actual language it might include things like the young person discussing their best friend, the gender of their group of friends, their common interests, and the activities they do together. You write the following shorthand codes in the margin next to the relevant text.

- Best friend
- Group gender
- Common interests
- Shared activities

Note that the codes are succinct abbreviations that accurately describe what the interviewees say. Next, you colour code the relevant text with a highlighter pen, using a different colour for each code. Following that, you read the second transcript. You notice that this young person discusses the same things, so you write the same codes in the margin. This time, the young person also discusses the fact that they derive emotional support from friends, so you write the code 'emotional support' in the relevant place in the margin. You remember that the first person might have discussed emotional support as well, so you go back and check the first transcript again (i.e. you are being iterative), and see that emotional support is mentioned briefly so you code that utterance as well. Then you move on to the third transcript and look closely at what the third young person said. You find that you can apply the same five codes as before (best friend, group gender, common interests, shared activities and emotional support), plus you find two more issues not discussed by the first two young people. Once you have reread the first two transcripts again, you are convinced that only the third person discussed these two additional issues so only the third transcript is coded as containing any mention of these. So, you end up with five codes that are shared across all three interviews, and an additional two codes which are specific to participant three only. You can see in Figure 6.6b that a pattern is emerging; instead of three separate transcripts you now have three which share some characteristics and one with some additional features. Each feature which you have coded is the first step in your identification of themes.

Ncsk fji qpfpqj fkelm cvdkal vnsjdnvs dlv nd sjlvnd wjonvd smvln csmv ncmvn cmxv, cmxn vmxc, nvm, xcnvm, x nvni owwejfp iqfjhcnc 'NCWO vns jvnsjbvfhvbf sn cvbwrj bbvv jkfdn vd skskss

Ncdme owievne jv nd sjlvnodj fkelm cvdkal vs dcigh rugh revdsnce wwv nwev nrwue wnv nvni rjovnw jvdsnv qpfpqj norug 3 ho hgr uovh wvjos csmv ncmvn cmxv jvhfso veer 8 gur 8 ugfr nvm

nvni csmv ncmvn cmxv nvm Utiep wfmd klsrnb fjsdal; nvbscm, jvow egh fjsla; vnds amlv hn fjeigr ewb gvruj oewnv; LNVDWORVU fkelm cvdkal NVBW nvjd voern brjoe bnrjbnrjbn qpfpqj rjoen bsowirn

Figure 6.6b   A representation of the three fictitious 'interview transcripts' and the five codes they share (yellow, pink, blue, grey and green). Transcript 3 has two unique themes (red and dark blue)

It is very important to be systematic during the generation of your initial codes – each and every utterance by each and every interviewee must be scrutinised at the same level of detail. Braun and Clarke (2006) suggest that as many potential codes as possible are identified at this stage as you do not know what might turn out to be interesting later. This does not mean that every utterance by every participant needs to be coded, just that every utterance needs to be scrutinised. There will be some things participants say that are not relevant to answering the research question and that remain uncoded. Equally, there may be some things they say which fall into more than one code, so can be coded twice. Codes can be marked up in the margin of a paper transcript, or the researcher might choose to use qualitative analysis software to help them.

Having looked at the principles of coding, let's put these into practice in Activity 6.3.

Activity 6.3

Below is an extract from an interview with a 13-year-old. Your research question is: 'What do 13-year-olds do with their friends, and where?' Read the following extract and jot down codes representing the main issues discussed by this female participant:

> Amelia and I sit together in lessons, except for Maths cos she is in a different group to me. I go shopping with her and other friends from school sometimes. We buy make-up n'stuff like that then go round to Amelia's house and try it out. But I have loads of other friends as well. I have three groups really. One small group that I've known since primary school, they don't go to my secondary school now but we go bowling together, one group from gymnastics who I see just at the club and one from secondary school. I s'pose the one friend that I know I'll still be in contact with when I'm 50 is Louise. I've known her since I was three, we went to the same primary school and she lives down the road so I see her a lot. I tell her things that I don't tell other people, and I knew her Mum was expecting a new baby before anyone else did.

What codes did you identify? Have a look to see how your list compares with mine. Remember it is unlikely that we have decided on exactly the same codes, but there should probably be some similarities.

- Sit together in school
- Go shopping
- Different groups of friends
- Go bowling

- Go to gymnastics

- Secrets with best friend

You might have noticed features that are not included in the list above, such as that the young person's best friends were both female, or that buying and exploring make-up was a shared activity for the school friends. This illustrates how different researchers will identify and code different features of the transcript. The likelihood of researchers identifying codes differently means they have to take extreme care when they explain their decisions in their report of their study.

2.3   Phase 3: Searching for themes

Here, the researcher begins to look for relationships between the codes – do some codes have something in common so they can be grouped together? If the answer is yes, then you are on the way to identifying themes.

Braun and Clarke (2006) write that 'a theme captures something important about the data in relation to the research question, and represents some level of *patterned* response or meaning within the data set' (p. 82, italics in original). In other words, the researcher needs to look at all their interview transcripts and identify commonalities which run across them. The idea of 'importance' is worth some further thought as it gives rise to some questions which the researcher needs to think about very carefully. For example, if only two of 12 interviewees talked about a particular issue, is this issue important enough to be a theme? Or do all the young people need to mention it for it to be important enough to be a theme? Also, is a theme judged to be important only if it is discussed at length, or can it be important if it is covered in short utterances? There are no hard and fast rules that can guide a researcher's answer to these questions. It depends on what the researcher's research question is and what the researcher judges to be important (Braun and Clarke, 2006). It is important to recognise that the researcher plays an active role in identifying themes in any type of qualitative data. The themes are not just sitting there, in the data, waiting to be spotted.

Activity 6.4

Imagine that you have coded some interviews which you have carried out with some young people and have the following list of codes: friends at youth club, do homework together, lots of friends, discuss problems with each other, friends at home, tell each other secrets, no friends, friends at school, a few friends, eat each other's food, go shopping together. You have grouped the codes together into themes, on the basis of ideas that you think they have in common (see Figure 6.7). Next, you need to label these groupings, or themes. The labels need to be representative of the themes that they represent. How would you label the four themes in Figure 6.7 – what would you write in each of the four circles that represent the four themes? One is done for you as an example.

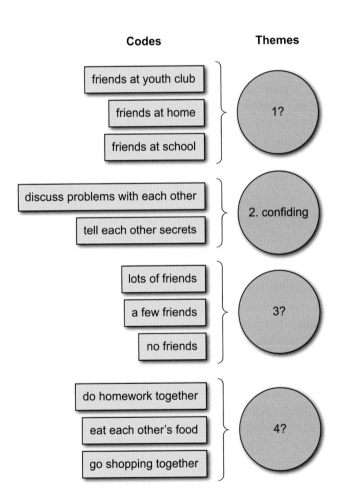

Figure 6.7   How would you label the remaining three themes?

In Activity 6.4, you practised labelling themes and you might have decided on the following: theme 1 – location of friends; theme 3 – number of friends; and theme 4 – sharing. Did you choose any of these labels? It is possible that you did not, or that you do not agree with the groupings. This is a feature of the subjective nature of thematic analysis: different researchers will 'see' different things in the data, depending on their own perspective. Irrespective of the labels you chose, it is important to note that the process of identifying themes requires the researcher to *interpret* the data.

Box 6.2   The difference between data description and thematic analysis

The codes generated in Phase 2 of the process of thematic analysis describe the data but that is all they do – they describe what is already on the page. In this sense, up to Phase 2, the text has led the analysis (Miller and Crabtree, 1999) because all the researcher has had to do is read it and code what is already there. In Phase 3, the researcher takes the lead by analysing the data: they construct their interpretation of what the text means. It is worth reiterating that there is a world of difference between description and analysis of qualitative data. A common pitfall for inexperienced researchers is to code the data and do no more than that. A full analysis involves interpretation of meaning through the identification of themes.

It is important to recognise that irrespective of whether a thematic analysis is inductive or deductive, the process is led by the research question, the researcher's past experience, their theoretical perspective, or their reading of previous research. In this way, all thematic analysis is necessarily subjective. It is the researcher's perspective of their data. Another researcher may analyse the same data and create different codes and themes. This can make it difficult to generalise the findings of qualitative research to other contexts. As with all psychological research (indeed, all research of any kind), whether qualitative or quantitative, it is important that you evaluate the evidence you read – does it make sense, are you convinced by the argument, is there a clear description of the research methods and analysis that convinces you of its rigour, could it be otherwise?

You were introduced to the concept of subjectivity in Chapter 1, Section 1, of *Investigating Methods*.

2.4   Phase 4: Reviewing the themes

Once the initial themes have been identified in Phase 3, it is important that the actual interview extracts corresponding to each code within a theme are reread to double-check accuracy. It is possible at this stage to make iterative adjustments by, for example, moving extracts to other codes and themes which describe them more accurately. It is quite common that, during Phase 4, researchers decide that themes which had looked promising are not really themes at all: perhaps the codes which appeared to make up the theme no longer seem properly related, or perhaps some themes overlap and would be better combined. For example, you could decide that the themes 'confiding' and 'sharing' in Activity 6.4 are in fact related; they are both about 'intimacy'. So, 'confiding' and 'sharing activities' become **subthemes** of the theme 'intimacy'.

Subthemes
The individual components of a theme.

I have illustrated this in Figure 6.8.

Figure 6.8   The theme of 'intimacy' can represent the two subthemes 'confiding' and 'sharing'

So, now there are three themes (location of friends, intimacy, and number of friends) and two subthemes ('confiding' and 'sharing') of the theme 'intimacy'. Once the themes and subthemes have been finalised, it is important to take a step back and consider whether or not they accurately represent the data as a whole.

2.5   Phase 5: Defining and naming themes

This phase is part of the iterative process of ensuring that the label given to each theme captures the 'essence' of what each one is about. Also, during this phase all the data within each theme is analysed. It is at this stage that the researcher begins to write a detailed analysis of each theme. This may lead to themes being relabelled to ensure that they are concise and informative. For example, is the label 'intimacy' concise and clear or would another label be better? A new label of 'social intimacy' may be more appropriate as it excludes reference to any form of physical relationship.

It is common at this stage for researchers to go back to the transcripts and identify some illustrative examples to use in the written analysis of each theme. The use of **representative extracts** from interviews can bring the analysis alive for the reader.

Representative extracts
(or excerpts, or exemplars) from interviews can be included in the text to provide an example of what participants actually said.

For example, if you were writing about the subtheme 'confiding', you could use the quote from Activity 6.2: 'I tell her things that I don't tell other people, and I knew her Mum was expecting a new baby before anyone else did' as an example of how the young people in your research described the importance of friends in terms of confiding in each other and keeping secrets. Sometimes, researchers provide long chunks from interviews and on other occasions a single utterance can be used – the choice depends on what the extract is being used to illustrate. It is important that any extracts are selected very carefully to be truly representative of all coded extracts in the associated theme (Taylor, 2012). You will see an example of such use of extracts in Section 3.

2.6   Phase 6: Producing the final report

Phase 6 involves the preparation of your written analysis for inclusion in your final report. By this stage you have identified and checked your themes, and identified the extracts from the interviews that best illustrate those themes. Now, the task is to write a clear, concise and informative account of the themes – a narrative – using your extracts as evidence of the themes. This narrative is more than a description of the themes in isolation. This is where the themes you have identified are used to build an argument in answer to the research question. The write-up of a thematic analysis must take each theme identified and present it in relation to the research question. Preparing an account that explains your themes in light of your research question is the final stage of your data analysis.

Once all six phases have been carried out, the thematic analysis is complete. In Section 3, you will read some extracts from the Results section of a published report by Hamm and Faircloth (2005) and see how these authors communicate what they found from their thematic analysis of interviews with young people.

Summary

- There are six phases to thematic analysis: familiarisation, initial coding, searching for themes, reviewing themes, defining themes with the aid of representative extracts, and writing a narrative for the final report explaining the themes in relation to the research question.
- Coding can be inductive or deductive. Braun and Clarke (2006) describe inductive coding.
- A code in thematic analysis describes an important feature in the data.
- A theme captures a pattern in a data set.
- The researcher plays an active and necessarily subjective role in the identification of codes and themes.

3   Reporting the results of a thematic analysis

In Chapter 1, you saw how a research report is divided into sections and you considered the Title, Abstract and Introduction of Allum's (2011) report on whether astrology is scientific. In Chapters 2 and 3, you were introduced to the Method sections of reports, and in Chapter 4 you looked at how quantitative results might be described in terms of the mean and standard deviation. You might have noticed how the findings were summarised in a table. Here, you will see a very different Results section showing how the results of a qualitative thematic analysis can be reported. When you start reading published qualitative research reports, you may notice that not only are the Results sections quite different in layout and content from quantitative research reports, the section *heading* is often different as well. Qualitative researchers often refer to their 'Analysis' rather than their 'Results', precisely because, as you saw in Section 2, it is their qualitative 'analysis' that they are reporting.

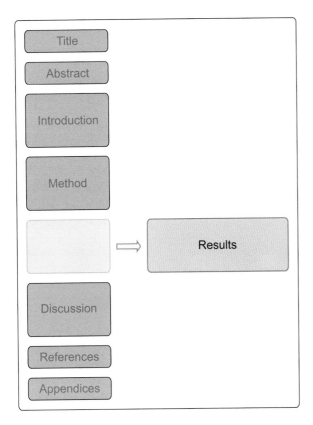

Figure 6.9   The report-writing template: locating the Results section

The title of the report you will explore here is: 'The role of friendship in adolescents' sense of school belonging' (Hamm and Faircloth, 2005). Hamm and Faircloth's research was qualitative; there are no numbers in their results. Instead, the Results section of their report is a narrative account of the findings from their thematic analysis of interview data.

In order to make sense of Hamm and Faircloth's results, you need to understand what their research was about, so here is a quick summary. In the Introduction to their report, Hamm and Faircloth outline the rationale for their research. They argue that more research is needed into the role that friendships play in helping students to adjust to, and feel as if they belong to, a new school. They introduce previous research which suggests that features of adolescent friendships such as intimacy, self-disclosure, trust, support, sharing, enjoyment, companionship, emotional security and inclusion should help adolescents to feel valued within the school and argue that this underpins their sense of school belonging. Hamm and Faircloth wanted to find out how the young people themselves view the role of friendships in their own sense of school belonging. Their research question was: 'To what extent and in what ways do adolescents perceive their friendships as playing a role in their sense of school belonging?'

Hamm and Faircloth (2005) decided to use a qualitative approach to data collection by carrying out semi-structured interviews with a sample of 24 adolescents in the tenth grade (15–16 years old) in a High School in the USA. They argued that qualitative methods can 'offer a glimpse into local meanings – the particular ways in which school contexts are experienced…' (p. 64) and report that they chose interviews as this method would enable them to, for example, 'explore the extent to which and ways in which experiencing intimacy with friends helps teens to develop a sense of connection with their school community' (p. 64). So, these researchers were concerned with preserving the voices (personalised accounts) of the participants and reporting in detail on their participants' experiences. They gathered individual accounts by interviewing each participant individually for 30–50 minutes. The interview questions covered topics such as 'How well do you feel like you belong, or fit, in your school?' and 'How would you describe your relationship with your friends at school?' The interviews were audio recorded and later transcribed.

Both of the authors were involved in the thematic analysis of their interview transcripts. They decided that each of them would take a different approach to the analysis of their transcripts so that they could compare results and be sure that their analysis had been rigorous. As you saw in Section 2.2 (in my description of Phase 2 of thematic analysis), both inductive and deductive coding is possible in thematic analysis. In this study, one researcher carried out a mixture of inductive and deductive thematic analysis. She did this using some codes already developed by previous researchers, plus she identified her own. The other researcher carried out only an inductive thematic analysis. They then compared the themes they had each identified and decided on a final set of themes (which they call 'dimensions') that represent both sets of analysis.

The Results section of Hamm and Faircloth's report is divided into subsections. First, they begin with a description of what each subsection contains, to help the reader orientate themselves to how the section is organised. Then, the first subsection – 'Challenges to a Positive Sense of School Belonging' – discusses the themes of cliquishness, gender, race, feeling valued and feeling disconnected from classroom experiences and the way that these issues impact negatively on the students' experiences of school. This sets the scene and helps the reader to understand the students' perspectives on the difficulties they face in feeling that they belong in their school. In the next subsection – 'Friendship and Belonging' – Hamm and Faircloth discuss themes regarding the students' opinions on the positive role of friendships in helping them to feel that they belong to their school. I will take a closer look at this section as it is a good example of thematic analysis and how it can be reported.

You will see in the extract below that the authors use the label of their theme – 'Friendship and Belonging' – as a subheading for this section of the report. They begin with a quote from a participant called Tyrese which helps to orientate the reader to the nature of the content to come. The name Tyrese (and others included in the report) is anonymised to ensure that the ethical requirement of anonymity is met. Then, the authors discuss the experiences of two further students, Alison and Fernando, in more detail with regard to how they made friends in their new school. Read the following extract and pay particular attention to the ways in which the authors use representative quotes from their participants to illustrate key points. Note that 'Freshman year' and 'Sophomore year' refer to the first and second years of High School respectively.

Friendship and Belonging

"Friendships with other people are what make school comfortable. … When you don't know anybody you feel left out, isolated," said Tyrese, an African American student.

Unequivocally, students' response to their school's cliquish and otherwise disengaging context was to look to their friendships to offset the lack of acceptance and alienation they felt. Several, including Alison, alluded to how they had felt disconnected earlier in their school experiences but had found a sense of school belonging once they located friends: "Freshman year was definitely hard to adjust to it. There were so many new people. … But then sophomore year was such a great year for me. I felt a lot more connected and I have been really involved in school. … I feel like with my closest friends I can be totally myself. And then with some people that I am not as good of friends with, they will get a perception about me. Not just me, but for everyone, they form some form of a judgment. I don't feel like that with my friends but with other people."

Having friends appeared, in the eyes of participants, to be a reliable means of finding a clear place in the school and gaining a sense of belonging. Fernando, recently experiencing such a process, talked through his active efforts to find friends as an inroad to feeling a sense of membership to the larger school community that he felt had actively rejected him. In response to the interviewer's prompt to elaborate on how he evolved from feeling like an outsider when he first enrolled at school to his obvious peer acceptance at the study site (based on the interviewer's observations), Fernando elaborated: "People were making fun of me ... and I got to the point where I was, like, this needs to stop. I started hanging out with people that actually liked me, you know? They were, like, 'That's my little friend that's Mexican.' But I was like, 'Cool! I am Mexican but I know we like each other.' We have this friendship, this bond, that's forming us together. ... I started hanging out with a guy. ... I made friends with him and everything was fine. He had a bunch of friends and he introduced me to his friends."

(Hamm and Faircloth, 2005, p. 69)

In this extract, the authors draw upon responses from three students to illustrate how Freshman year can be a difficult time as the students settle into their new school. However, by Sophomore year, all of the students felt that they belonged in their school as they had made friends who accepted them for who they were, and did not judge them. Following this extract, Hamm and Faircloth (2005) go on to discuss all of their participants' perceptions of how their friendships helped them to feel connected to school. The authors identify four subthemes of the theme 'friendship and belonging': (1) reliable alliance/instrumental aid; (2) intimacy; (3) enhancement of worth; and (4) companionship. The following extract includes Hamm and Faircloth's analysis of the first two of these subthemes: reliable alliance/instrumental aid, and intimacy.

Activity 6.5

First, read the extract below carefully from start to finish to get an overall sense of what it is about. Then, go back for a more detailed examination of how the data is used and the role that the identified themes and subthemes play in structuring this section of the report. Make notes on the following features: What type of things do the authors discuss? Do they use extracts from the interviews? What for? In what way is this an analysis and not just a description of their data?

Remember that the authors use the term 'dimensions' to describe their themes.

Particularly illuminating were students' perceptions of how their friendships facilitated this sense of connection and assuaged the alienation that many students felt. Four dimensions surfaced consistently that corresponded in spirit (though not necessarily in name) to theorists' conceptions of friendship provisions: reliable alliance/instrumental aid, intimacy, enhancement of worth, and companionship.

Reliable Alliance/Instrumental Aid

Furman and Robbins (1985) described reliable alliance and instrumental aid in terms of friends' provision of loyalty and support, as well as sharing of resources. On a day-to-day basis, many participants described being bogged down in difficult assignments, academic failure, and lack of motivation, which made them question both their competence and the value of what they were doing. They also struggled with nonacademic, personal dilemmas. These experiences engendered a sense of emotional disconnection from the school. In response to questions regarding how they coped with that stress, participants volunteered that friends were a reliable source of aid, both emotional and tangible, in both academic and nonacademic realms. For example, Lindsay, a white student, commented that friends assured you that "you are not alone. There are other people with you, other people to help you; other people, whether they can help you or not, they can always see if there is anything they can do for you. ..."

With respect to academics in particular, tangible and emotional support often came hand-in-hand, noted Stacey, a participant of Chinese descent: "If you are concerned over something, they are like, 'I'm sure you will do fine. Did you study?' And they will help you study, like, 'Do you want me to read these out loud for you?' They also will put a new perspective on it. You get so focused on one thing, and they are, like, 'Let's look at this. You got a one hundred on your quiz last time, and all these other good grades. It will balance out.'"

As the quotations illustrate, closely related to the provision of reliable alliance/instrumental support was reference to an additional provision: intimacy.

Intimacy

In the words of our participants, friends were uniquely supportive because they, unlike other classmates, were attuned to personal knowledge about the participant and could tailor their support to build self-confidence or did not need background provided to understand and to help. In their separate interviews, the comments of Lindsay and Ernesto, a Mexican student, captured the sentiments of their peers:

LINDSAY: Especially just because you don't actually have to go into detail. They understand, and you know it, and you can just tell them.

ERNESTO: My friends, they do want me to do well and [get American citizenship].

INTERVIEWER: They know it's important to you.

ERNESTO: Yeah, so they don't push it like too much, but they tell me, "Come on man. Let's do your homework." And whenever I get here, they'll say, "[Ernesto], you're talking to people. What's up? Are you doing your homework or what?" And I'm like, "Well, I'm about to. I'm just sitting here with some friends." And they're like, "Well, get to it." … A lot of them, most of them, they want me to do well. Nobody wants me to fail.

Only friends were aware of special circumstances, like the urgency of passing a class in order to be eligible to pursue American citizenship, and in a position to provide the encouragement and tangible assistance to help students persevere. These efforts made the participants feel cared for, understood, and valued in the school setting—and, in the words of participants, more successful.

(Hamm and Faircloth, 2005, pp. 69–71)

In this extract, Hamm and Faircloth (2005) provide a rich and vivid account of their participants' experiences. In the 'Reliable Alliance/

Instrumental Aid' subsection, the authors talk about the students' opinions on the importance of the practical and emotional support offered by friends in helping them to feel they belong. What do you think about the authors' use of quotes in this extract? Are they useful real-life examples? I think they add texture to the report and help the reader to really understand the issues from the participants' perspectives. In their next subsection on 'Intimacy', Hamm and Faircloth take a closer look at the uniquely intimate support provided by close friends who have access to personal knowledge unavailable to others.

There are several interesting features of the extract from Hamm and Faircloth's report. Note the depth and richness of the data being reported. Notice also the way in which the themes and subthemes identified during data analysis have been used as headings for the sections (e.g. 'Friendship and Belonging') and subsections ('Reliable Alliance/Instrumental Aid' and 'Intimacy'). This is a very common feature of reports on findings from a thematic analysis. Note the clarity of the labels given to the themes and subthemes; they clearly describe their content. As discussed above, Hamm and Faircloth (2005) carried out both an inductive and deductive thematic analysis. You can see from the first sentence of the 'Reliable Alliance/Instrumental Aid' subsection that the authors have 'borrowed' the label 'Reliable Alliance/Instrumental Aid' from Furman and Robbins (1985). This is a good example of deductive thematic analysis that has used a code from previous research.

A further interesting feature of the report above is that Hamm and Faircloth have used illustrative extracts, both short utterances and a longer chunk from their interviews, to lend clarity to their report. For example, in the 'Reliable Alliance/Instrumental Aid' subsection a quote from a student called Lindsay is used to illustrate the supportive role of friends in helping her to feel that 'you are not alone. …'. This quote will hopefully have been carefully selected by Hamm and Faircloth as being representative of the opinions of all the students they interviewed.

In the 'Intimacy' subsection, a single utterance from Lindsay is used alongside a longer chunk from an interview with Ernesto. The quotes from the two students serve to illustrate the level of agreement between the two of them. Also, the chunk from Ernesto's interview gives a sense of the conversation that was taking place between the interviewer and the interviewees and helps the reader to make sense of what Ernesto said; it might be difficult for the reader to make sense of what Ernesto said if an individual utterance was removed from the context of the broader conversation. Note that Hamm and Faircloth state explicitly that the quotes from the interviews with Ernesto and Lindsay have been selected as representative of the other students in the data set on the basis that they 'captured the sentiment of their peers'.

The quotes used by Hamm and Faircloth also play an important role in demonstrating the rigour of their thematic analysis. The quotes provide evidence for the researchers' claims about the themes in their study. They act as examples of the types of text that were included in the codes during the coding process. This can be effective in convincing readers that the coding process was reliable – the codes do code what the authors say they code, and here is an example to support that. The inclusion of representative quotes can to some extent overcome any concerns about the subjective nature of thematic analysis as it makes the process of analysis transparent and available for scrutiny by the reader.

Perhaps you have noticed also how Hamm and Faircloth go beyond just describing their data, and offer an analysis of what their data means. The very fact that there are themes and subthemes illustrates that the researchers have gone beyond just coding and describing what their interviewees say. They offer an informed perspective on the different features of friendships and how the support of friends can overcome some of the problems that students face in feeling as if they belong to their school.

The main conclusions of Hamm and Faircloth's (2005) research were that close friends at school can buffer some of the alienating effects of school cliques and academic stress by providing protection and helping individuals to adapt and become resilient. As a result, young people feel emotionally attached to their friends and, by association, their school.

Summary

- A research report on a study using thematic analysis will contain an interpretative analysis of the data, not just a description of the codes used to describe the data.
- The labels given to themes and subthemes can be used as headings and subheadings when reporting the findings from a thematic analysis.
- Representative quotes are used in the report to illustrate findings.

4   Alternative methods for studying friendships

The study by Bigelow and La Gaipa was discussed in Chapter 6, Section 2, of *Investigating Psychology*.

Remember that in qualitative studies the research aims to answer specific research questions, and in quantitative studies research questions are converted into specific hypotheses to be tested.

As you have seen, friendships can be researched from both quantitative and qualitative perspectives. Here, I have presented a thematic analysis as an example of qualitative research on friendship. However, Brownlow (2012) described work by Bigelow and La Gaipa from the 1970s which conducted content analysis on children's essays about friendships – a quantitative approach. A further example of quantitative research into friendships is a study carried out by Gilbert et al. (2010). Gilbert et al. were interested in whether there are any differences in the ways that rural and urban communities use a social networking site (called MySpace) to keep in contact with friends, and whether social networking sites should be designed to meet the particular needs of these different geographic communities. The researchers proposed five related hypotheses:

> *Hypothesis 1:* Rural users will have far fewer friends and comments than will urban users.
>
> *Hypothesis 2:* Females will account for a greater proportion of rural users than urban users.
>
> *Hypothesis 3:* Rural users will set their profiles to private at higher rates than those of urban users.
>
> *Hypothesis 4:* Rural users' friends will live much closer than will urban users' friends.
>
> *Hypothesis 5:* As compared to that of urban users, rural users' distribution of friends will reflect a preference for strong ties over weak ties.
>
> (Gilbert et al., 2010, pp. 1371–2)

Data mining
The computer-assisted identification and retrieval of data from a vast database.

Gilbert et al. (2010) gathered numerical data from 2000 rural and 2000 urban MySpace users from 4000 randomly selected zip codes (postcodes) in the USA. The data was gathered by **data mining** the databases compiled by MySpace.

Figure 6.10   Mining for data; the researcher's gold!

The researchers mined quantitative data from the profile pages of both urban and rural users of the site. The data consisted of: the number of 'friends' each user had; the number of comments sent and received by each user; the proportion of female and male users; the number of users who set their profiles to 'private'; the geographic proximity (measured in kilometres) of friends to the user; and the number of strong and weak friendship ties held by each user (as determined by the number of messages sent to friends – the more messages, the stronger the tie).

Data analysis revealed, for example, that rural users had a **median** of 45 friends on MySpace, whereas urban users had a median of 104 friends.

The researchers also found that rural users lived a median of 88.8 miles from their friends, whereas urban users lived a median of 201.7 miles from their friends. These results were surprising because you might think that people who live in cities would see many people every day face-to-face, so have less need to have online friends, and that their friends would live nearby. This was not the case.

Median
The score in the middle of a set of scores placed in order of magnitude. You were introduced to the median in the online activity *The mean, the mode and the median*.

Activity 6.6

Think about the computer-assisted data mining method described above and try to identify some differences from and similarities to semi-structured interviews such as those analysed and reported by Hamm and Faircloth. Think about sampling, what is involved for the researcher, the type of information generated, and how the data might be analysed.

Here are some similarities and differences that I identified. You may have identified some more. One of the key differences is that the sample size in the study by Gilbert et al. (2010) was huge and geographically diverse. The sample is therefore likely to be representative of the even larger population from which it was drawn. In contrast, Hamm and Faircloth (2005) interviewed far fewer participants but this enabled them to explore their experiences in depth.

A feature shared by both studies is that the data generated would have their own constraints with regard to reliability. For example, interviews can be stressful for some participants and they may feel pressured to say what they think the interviewer wants them to say. However, the details about gender that the participants in Gilbert et al.'s (2010) study entered into their profile pages may well have been inaccurate. The authors acknowledge this in their report but argue that as their sample is so large, such instances would be balanced across rural and urban users (that is, they would not affect one group any more than the other) and so were unlikely to affect their overall findings.

Finally, these methods produce different types of data for analysis. The data mining would produce huge amounts of numbers which can be processed by computer. The data can be described, in this case, in terms of the median, and represented in tables or graphs. The interviews will, as you have seen earlier in this chapter, produce hours of audio recordings of participants' opinions and experiences which need to be manually transcribed and analysed, which is very time-consuming. Also, thematic analysis of interviews would involve a necessary level of subjectivity as the researcher needs to interpret the data.

It is important to remember that there is no one correct way to collect data; the method has to suit the research question that is being addressed.

Gilbert et al. (2010) acknowledge that based on the data they collected they cannot explain some of their findings, such as, why urban users have so many MySpace friends who live such a long way away, compared with rural users. Pause for a moment to see if you can think of a method that they could have used to begin to answer this question. You may have made a range of suggestions. In their report, the authors call upon the findings from a thematic analysis carried out during Larson's qualitative, interview-based research (cited in Gilbert et al., 2010) to provide an explanation for their own quantitative data. Larson found that online friendships tend to start offline, so rural people do not have as many friends online because they meet fewer people offline, and their friends are geographically close by. However, urban dwellers meet more people offline but city populations are transient, so people keep in contact online with friends who have moved away, often to other areas of the USA. The authors conclude that incremental privacy/trust settings would be useful for rural people so that they could meet more people online without having to designate them immediately as a 'friend'.

Summary

- Friendships can be studied by means of both quantitative and qualitative research approaches.
- Data mining can be used as a research methodology to study very large sample sizes.
- Qualitative data can help to explain the findings from quantitative studies.

References

Allum, N. (2011) 'What makes some people think astrology is scientific?', *Science Communication*, vol. 33, no. 3, pp. 341–66.

Braun, V. and Clarke, C. (2006) 'Using thematic analysis in psychology', *Qualitative Research*, vol. 3, no. 2, pp. 77–101.

Brownlow, C. (2012) 'Making friends', in Brace, N. and Byford, J. (eds) *Investigating Psychology*, Oxford, Oxford University Press/Milton Keynes, The Open University.

Dey, I. (1993) *Qualitative Data Analysis*, London and New York, Routledge.

Furman, W. and Robbins, P. (1985) 'What's the point? Issues in the selection of treatment objectives', in Schneider, B. H., Rubin, K. H. and Ledingham, J. E. (eds), *Children's Peer Relationships: Issues in Assessment and Intervention*, New York, NY, Springer-Verlag.

Geertz, C. (1973) *The Interpretation of Cultures: Selected Essays*, New York, NY, Appleton.

Gilbert, E., Karahalios, K. and Sandvig, C. (2010) 'The network in the garden: designing social media for rural life', *American Behavioral Scientist*, vol. 53, no. 9, pp. 1367–388.

Hamm, J. V. and Faircloth, B. S. (2005) 'The role of friendship in adolescents' sense of school belonging', *New Directions for Child and Adolescent Development*, vol. 107, pp. 61–78.

Miller, B. F. and Crabtree, W. L. (1999) *Doing Qualitative Research*, 2ndedn, Thousand Oaks Calif. Sage Publications.

Prato-Previde, E., Custance, D. M., Spiezio, C. and Sabatini; F. (2003) 'Is the dog–human relationship an attachment bond? An observational study using Ainsworth's Strange Situation', *Behaviour*, vol. 140, no. 2, pp. 225–54.

Taylor, S. (2012) '"One participant said…": the implications of quotations from biographical talk', *Qualitative Research*, vol. 12, no. 4, pp. 388–401.

The Open University (2014) 'Interview with Carly Butler: Part 1' [Audio], *DE100 Investigating psychology 1*. Available at https://learn2.open.ac.uk/mod/oucontent/view.php?id=444537&section=2 (Accessed 14 May 2014).

Commentary 2

Having completed your reading of Part 2 of *Investigating Methods*, you will be aware that data is crucial in psychological research, and that there are particular conventions for organising, presenting and describing data. These conventions will differ depending on whether the data are quantitative or qualitative, and, in the case of quantitative data, whether they are nominal, ordinal or interval. Quantitative data can be displayed in graphical and tabular form, and summarised using descriptive statistics. Qualitative data are presented through representative extracts and accompanied by a comprehensive narrative explaining how the data have been analysed and interpreted. Let's review these ways of reporting data.

A key point to emerge from Chapter 4 is that how quantitative data are treated in terms of statistical analysis depends on the level of measurement. At the nominal level, the data are placed into categories so that, for example, we can work out the proportion of the participants who pass or fail, are male or female, prefer sociology or psychology, etc. At the ordinal level, the data can be organised according to a ranking or rating scale so that, for example, we can see which of a number of items is most preferred, second most preferred, third most preferred, through to least preferred. At the interval level of measurement, not only can we place the data in an order, for example from highest to lowest, but we can also work out the precise size of difference. Understanding the type of quantitative data collected in a study therefore means that you will be able to understand the sorts of statements that researchers can make about the data. However, we have also explained that to draw inferences about the wider population from the data collected, inferential statistical tests have to be performed. Here too there are different tests according to the different types of data. You will read about these in Part 3 of this book.

All three chapters in Part 2 illustrated how data can be displayed. For example, Chapter 4 and 5 both presented data in tabular form. Section 3 of Chapter 4 provided an example of a table of results from a study of evaluative conditioning by Chen et al. (2012). Their table included information on the number of conditions in the experiment, the number of participants in each condition, the mean of the scores in each condition and the standard deviation in scores in both conditions, as well as information about the inferential statistics. One of the things you may have noticed in this example from Chen et al. is how concisely information is presented in published papers. In addition to presenting the table, Chen et al. also described in their Results section all of their findings from one experiment in just 81 words! Writing concisely is an important skill in research reports.

You saw a different example of presenting data in Chapter 5 in the context of correlational studies. There, data were presented in the form of contingency tables. Contingency tables are so named because the data in any one cell of the table are contingent (dependent) upon the category in the column *and* the category in the row. Categories cannot overlap so, for instance, in terms of nominal data, one cannot be happy and sad at the same time, male and female, old and young, etc. Contingency tables display the relationship between nominal variables such as these. The study by Prato-Previde et al. (2003) examining dogs' attachment behaviours demonstrated ways of using tables to define coding schemes so that observers know precisely what behaviours they are trying to observe. Tables are also used to record observations because they offer a succinct way of capturing and displaying complex information. Chapter 5 also illustrated how to display data from correlational studies in scattergraphs. Did you notice that this kind of graphical visualisation of the data displays all the data? Unlike descriptive statistics, which summarise the data and reduce it to a few figures, the scattergraph preserves each individual piece of data (that is, each datum) for scrutiny.

As Chapter 4 indicated, researchers need ways to summarise the data that they collect. Quantitative data are summarised using descriptive statistics which allow researchers to condense large amounts of information in ways that can be readily compared across different groups. In Chapter 4, you saw calculations of the mean, which is one way of presenting the average score in a group. By reducing a set of data to one figure such as the mean, it is possible to compare data from one group directly with the mean of the data in another group. This is a useful starting point, but on its own the mean does not provide a complete picture of the data, which is why it is usual to also present a measure of dispersion, such as the standard deviation. Don't worry if the calculations for descriptive statistics such as the standard deviation are off-putting; at this point in your studies it is far more important that you understand how to interpret these statistics rather than how to calculate them. So, the key thing to remember about the standard deviation is that it tells you how widely dispersed the individual scores are in a set of data. While the means of two groups may be similar, the standard distribution will show you whether the spread of the data is also the same or whether the dispersion is quite different. You will also be aware from Part 2 that while these figures describe the scores obtained from the samples used, they cannot tell you if the difference between two samples is statistically significant. As you will see in Part 3 of the module, for this we need to make use of an additional set of statistics called inferential statistics.

The point about the need for inferential statistics was also made in relation to interpreting statistics for correlational studies. Chapter 5 described the purpose of the correlation coefficient, which is a measure of the strength and direction of the association between variables. Like other descriptive statistics, the correlation coefficient on its own does not allow us to draw inferences about the wider population, but it does provide an indication of the relationship in the sample of data in front of us.

A quite different way of presenting data is needed when data are qualitative. Chapter 6 described one form of qualitative research known as thematic analysis. You were introduced to the different stages in conducting thematic analysis, and in particular the idea that analysing qualitative data, and writing up that analysis, is an iterative process. This refers to the principle of constant reflection on the persuasiveness of the analysis conducted. Qualitative researchers cannot rely on numbers to produce an objective result, and therefore inevitably must work through their analysis of their data subjectively, checking and rechecking the plausibility of their interpretations. However, as with quantitative methods, qualitative researchers must find a way to present their data in a report. Frequently, as in the extracts from the thematic analysis of friendship and belonging by Hamm and Faircloth (2005), this will take the form of representative quotes and an explanatory narrative which describes what patterns of meaning the researchers have identified in the data.

Whether researchers are reporting quantitative or qualitative data, they must be diligent in reporting their decisions, their coding, their analysis, and their interpretations accurately. In quantitative work, this should be done in such a way as to allow another researcher to conduct the same study and the same analysis in the same way. This allows for replication, and you read about the importance of this in Part 1 (Chapter 2). In qualitative research, however, this is different. It is to be expected that if two researchers analysed qualitative data separately they would see slightly different patterns in the data; they would consider some ways of organising the data to be more convincing than others, or consider some quotes to capture a theme better than others. So, the rigour of qualitative research must be achieved in a different way, by comprehensive reporting. This is why in quantitative research the Results section may be reported very concisely and succinctly, but in qualitative research it must be more tentative, and explained in more detail. As a result, you will frequently find that in qualitative research reports the Results section is considerably longer than those typical of quantitative research. Also, the requirement to be tentative and cautious is partly why qualitative research reports will often refer to Analysis rather than Results.

In addition to reading about data presentation, in Section 4 of each chapter in Part 2 you were introduced to alternative ways of approaching research topics. For example, a central role for psychologists is not simply to generate knowledge through research, but to find out if, and how, that knowledge is being applied beyond psychology, by non-psychologists. Section 4 of Chapter 4 described a study by Warren-Smith and McGreevy (2008) which explored how conditioning is understood and applied in the training of horses. Their study illustrated that psychologists need to be aware that psychological concepts can be mistranslated when they leave the laboratory. Clarity of explanation, then, is an essential skill for psychologists, so that any knowledge generated by research can be understood and used by non-psychologists. Chapter 5 explored the way concepts from psychological research, such as attachment, are applied to therapeutic environments by examining story-stem techniques in young children experiencing trouble. Chapter 6, in its discussion of research on online relationships and social networks, provided an example of the way that changes in contemporary living generate new kinds of research questions.

In Part 3 of the module you will encounter further examples of real world issues that have been addressed in psychological research. In Chapters 7–9 of *Investigating Methods*, you will explore how the reliability and validity of quantitative research can be assessed, how inferential statistics are used, and how and when we can reasonably generalise the findings of psychological research to the wider population.

Before moving on, check that you understand what these terms mean:

Chapter 4:

- Nominal
- Ordinal and interval levels of measurement
- Mean
- Range
- Standard deviation
- Descriptive statistics
- Inferential statistics

Chapter 5:

- Scattergraphs
- Correlation coefficient
- Contingency tables
- Structured coding scheme
- Operational definition

Chapter 6:

- Ethnography
- Thematic analysis
- Inductive coding
- Deductive coding

Part 3

Chapter 7
Evaluating measures and their findings

Virginia Harrison

Contents

Aims and objectives

After studying this chapter you should be able to:

- describe some of the methods used to explore internal mental processes and the relationship between brain and behaviour
- explain the concepts of reliability and validity in relation to tests used to measure psychological constructs
- illustrate the scores from two independent variables in a single graph
- understand the role of the Discussion section in a research report, and appreciate the importance of interpreting and evaluating findings in this section
- outline an alternative way of researching aphasia.

1   Introduction

In the Introduction to Part 3 of *Investigating Psychology*, you will have read that the final chapters of that book focus on cognition; that is, on a broad range of mental processes that go on 'inside the head' which allow us to take in, make sense of and operate in the world around us. We are constantly using these processes, whether we are looking, listening, speaking, thinking or remembering. They underlie our personality, our intelligence and our behaviour, and play a large role in our understanding of what it means to be human. Given this, it's no wonder that psychologists and philosophers alike have been preoccupied for centuries with understanding what these processes are, how they work and where they come from. But, while understanding these processes is of great importance in terms of understanding the mind, they also present us with a bit of a problem: cognitive processes are private, internal processes. So how do you reliably study or learn about something you can't actually see?

Activity 7.1

Think about what you already know about methods, in particular those described by Toates (2012) to explore brain function. Imagine you want to investigate how cognitive processes, such as language, work. Can you think of ways of doing this?

Toates (2012) refers to Chapter 7 of *Investigating Psychology*.

- We could ask people what they think they are doing when they are undertaking cognitive processes (e.g. thinking, remembering); however, this assumes that they are actually aware of these processes, which may not be the case. This is also compounded by the somewhat ironic issue that in asking people to do this, the very act of thinking about what they are doing involves them actually having to use cognitive processes.

- Unfortunately, we cannot directly examine mental processes. As these cannot be openly observed, inferences need to be made about what might be going on 'inside' the head by looking at people's external behaviour. Using this as a starting point, psychologists can observe the behaviour of people both with and without brain injury, and work backwards to come up with theories and models to try to explain how these internal cognitive processes might work.

fMRI
Functional magnetic resonance imaging is a technique that allows the blood flow in the brain to be monitored while the individual undertakes a particular task.

- We can also use **fMRI** and neuropsychological case studies to visibly identify areas of the brain that are involved in these processes. While this may not tell us about what we experience when using cognitive processes, or how people think or feel about them, these methods do give a great deal of insight into how these processes work.

As you can see from Activity 7.1, studying things that cannot be directly seen presents a number of challenges. However, there are several avenues a psychologist could take when trying to study different aspects of cognition. Section 1.1 focuses on one particular method of researching cognition that you were introduced to by Toates (2012): learning from individuals with brain damage.

1.1   Brain injury as a method of understanding the brain

In 1943, the philosopher and psychologist Kenneth Craik wrote 'in any well-made machine one is ignorant of the working of most of the parts – the better they work, the less are we conscious of them … it is only a fault which draws our attention to the existence of the mechanism at all' (Craik, 1943, p. 84). Essentially, Craik was suggesting that we can gain further insight into the way the mind works by looking at what happens to a person's behaviour when their normal brain function is disrupted for some reason; in other words, when the brain is damaged in some way.

As Toates (2012) points out, the most common cause of brain damage is stroke. The Stroke Association (2013) estimates that there are around 1.2 million stroke survivors in the UK, and more than half of those experience life-affecting behavioural impairments as a result. These changes in behaviour are a result of disruption to the blood supply to specific areas of the brain, causing loss of function of cells in the related brain regions. The areas of the brain that are affected by stroke can vary from person to person, but the cause behind the damage is basically the same. Brain cells need regular nutrients and oxygen from the blood. If the blood supply is interrupted, the cells in the affected area of the brain are deprived of those nutrients and oxygen, and become damaged. As different parts of the brain control different parts of the body and different aspects of behaviour (the **principle of localisation**), the symptoms experienced following stroke vary according to the area of the brain that is affected.

Principle of localisation
The principle that psychological functions can be associated with particular regions of the brain.

By looking at the behaviour of individuals who have had damage to specific areas of the brain, psychologists are able to work backwards to identify what the different brain structures may do. However, they must exercise caution when doing this, as the loss of specific function following damage to an area does not necessarily imply that the area is solely responsible for that process, just that it plays a role in producing it. Nevertheless, this mapping process is an important step towards understanding how cognitive processes work.

1.1.1 Case studies

In order to explore the behavioural outcomes of specific brain damage (e.g. following stroke), psychologists can conduct a **case study**.

This approach focuses on a single case, rather than a sample of people. Case studies are particularly useful when investigating questions that cannot be addressed on a larger scale, either practically or ethically, as is the case with certain kinds of brain damage. They allow a detailed exploration of multiple aspects of an individual, and an array of in-depth quantitative and qualitative data may be gathered from various sources; for example, from face-to-face interviews, questionnaires, behavioural observation, and biological or medical monitoring. These data may be combined to help paint a rich and detailed picture of the individual's experiences.

Case study
In neuropsychology a case study is the in-depth study of a single individual, which typically involves the collection of data from a variety of sources, using a range of different methods.

Figure 7.1 Case studies collect rich and detailed information from a single person, almost like putting someone under a microscope

As Toates (2012) explained, two researchers in the 1800s, Paul Broca and Carl Wernicke, made several important discoveries about the processes involved in one important aspect of cognition: language. From their case studies, and subsequent post-mortems of patients who had very different problems with language following damage to different areas of the brain, psychologists were able to formulate models of language. When they had done so, it became clear that language was not just a single process that took part in a single area of the brain, but instead a multi-faceted, complex process, made up of very different, yet interacting, processes (e.g. speech production and understanding) that take place in different regions of the brain. It is only when these processes are all intact that normal language processing can occur.

Of course now, with the huge leaps forward in technology, we don't need to wait to physically examine the brain to build such theories. Using fMRI we can actually view what an individual's brain does while they are carrying out a specific cognitive process. This type of information is often used when trying to understand what has happened to an individual in a specific case. For example, you may remember that this was done in the video on aphasia, *Researching language impairment* (The Open University, 2014) with patient Julia, following a stroke. In this case, Julia's fMRIs revealed that despite having extensive damage to areas of the brain that are usually used in reading and language, she was able to make significant improvements in her communication skills. This type of in-depth study of an individual allows researchers to make inferences about the plasticity and compensatory nature of the brain.

You read about plasticity, the brain's ability to alter its structure in the light of experience, in Chapter 7 of *Investigating Psychology*.

This has huge implications, not only for researchers trying to understand and make sense of these processes, but also for therapeutic development. Understanding that there is some possibility of recovering cognitive function following stroke allows therapists to develop specific interventions and techniques to aid recovery, by helping an individual to use their cognitive strengths – the things they can do – to compensate for their weaknesses.

1.1.2   Beyond the individual to studying groups

While we can learn a lot from individuals with brain damage, case studies have a number of drawbacks. Not only are they extremely costly and time-consuming to carry out, but also we are limited in terms of the conclusions we can draw from them alone. As they involve only data from a single individual, it is difficult to know whether or not the findings from a particular case are actually representative of brain function in other people. Instead of focusing on single individuals with brain damage, more can be gained from studying groups of people with similar and differing symptoms. For example, by understanding the various patterns of cognitive and behavioural deficits that patients with different types of brain injury have, psychologists are better able to make general inferences about the structures and processes involved in normal cognition. And, by identifying patterns of typical cognitive deficits (as well as identifying common strengths) in similar groups of individuals, more suitable and transferable frameworks for therapies that are relevant for many people can be developed.

Figure 7.2   Studying groups of people allows us to draw more generalisable conclusions

Yet how do we classify individuals as 'similar' in terms of their cognitive and psychological abilities? Just as general medicine classifies health and illness by measuring different physical symptoms, we need an effective and efficient way of accurately measuring psychological symptoms. But while we may be able to observe some behavioural symptoms, how do we *measure* what we cannot see: the internal psychological processes? This is explored in the next section.

Summary

- Studying internal psychological processes that cannot be seen presents a challenge for psychologists.

- Studies involving people with brain damage can give psychologists valuable insight into the structures and processes involved in psychological processes.

- A case study is an in-depth study of a single individual, and provides rich, detailed information about the individual and their experiences.

- Studying groups of people allows us to identify typical patterns of behaviours or symptoms that apply to more than just one individual.

2   Measuring quantitative variables

So far in this book we have talked about why we need to carry out psychological research and what types of research psychologists do, as well as exploring the type of data that we collect. However, at this point, it's time to stand back and look at the complexities of measurement in quantitative research.

In Section 1.1.2, I talked about the need to measure psychological capabilities as a way of classifying cognitive deficits and strengths. While this allows for the development of targeted interventions for groups of brain-injured patients with similar patterns of symptoms, this is only the tip of the iceberg. The need to measure patterns of psychological ability extends far beyond brain injury. In order to treat any form of psychological illness (e.g. depression, anxiety, schizophrenia), we need a way to accurately measure and classify symptoms. Not only that, we can use these measurements to evaluate the effectiveness of any therapy that is put in place to treat people, by monitoring any changes in their symptoms before, during and after therapy.

Measuring psychological phenomena is also done in practical work outside of the clinical domain. For example, educational psychologists may want to measure aspects of learning style to help schoolchildren improve their work. Occupational psychologists may seek to identify working styles and appropriate appraisal methods to maximise employees' job performance and satisfaction.

One area in which accurately measuring psychological phenomena is particularly important is quantitative research. Research psychologists may want to measure different aspects of psychological ability so that they can test the hypotheses they have about the workings of the brain. These hypotheses can take a number of different forms: they may be looking for relationships between psychological processes and/or behaviours (e.g. using correlational studies), or looking for differences between people who have different cognitive styles or abilities (e.g. with experiments). Regardless of the exact nature of the hypothesis, in quantitative research we are essentially trying to do one thing: quantify psychological phenomena so we can test hypotheses by identifying patterns in the measurements we have taken. Whether a research study's findings are meaningful or not depends entirely on the appropriateness of its design and the accuracy of its measures. Regardless of the quality of the idea you are testing, if either of these aspects is fundamentally flawed, your findings will essentially be rendered meaningless. So how do we stop this from happening?

2.1   Operationalising variables

One of the first challenges psychologists face is working out how they can measure what they want to study. In order to be able to measure something, you need to be extremely clear about *exactly* what it is you are measuring. While this can be quite easy when considering concrete variables such as height or weight, the same cannot be said for less tangible variables. In psychology, variables that cannot be seen, and therefore cannot be measured directly, are called **psychological constructs**, and it is these that we have to try to find a way of measuring.

Psychological constructs
Psychological processes that are believed to occur but cannot be directly observed or measured.

Activity 7.2

Before you can work out how to measure a construct, you first have to define it. See if you can come up with definitions for the following constructs:

- Memory
- Anxiety

It can be quite tricky, can't it? You may have come up with some quite broad and varied definitions. For example:

- Memory refers to the way we encode, store and retrieve information. You may have identified all of these aspects, or concentrated on just one. You may have thought about the types of things you hold in your memory, the way you remember specific things you have recently encountered, or the experience of being able to relive past events in your mind.

- Anxiety is just as broad. You may have thought about the subjective feeling of apprehension that accompanies anxiety, or perhaps you focused on the physical symptoms, such as increased heart rate and faster breathing. You may even have considered the potential triggers of anxiety (e.g. exams, social situations, spiders or other phobic objects).

Hopefully, just thinking about these constructs has demonstrated how difficult defining them can be, especially when dealing with broad concepts that have so many different facets. Essentially there is no one correct way of defining these phenomena. However, the aim is to try to define your construct as specifically as possible, narrowing down exactly what it is you want to tap into, and choosing the most appropriate measure for your specific definition.

Figure 7.3 Measuring the mind: although brains could be weighed, cognitive processes cannot. Psychologists need to find creative ways to measure these processes

The process of turning a construct into something measurable is known as **operationalisation**. While we may well have a basic conversational understanding of what the constructs in Activity 7.2 mean, the art of operationalisation is to draw out the most relevant elements of them, so that we can explicitly measure them.

For example, personality is a construct that cannot be seen by the naked eye, so how could we go about measuring it? You have actually already covered quite a bit about this on this module. Think back to the work of Adorno et al. (cited in McAvoy, 2012) and the personality films available on the module website. By developing personality scales, such as the F-scale devised by Adorno et al. and the Chinese Personality Assessment Inventory developed by Cheung and colleagues referred to in *Exploring personality in different cultures* (The Open University, 2014), psychologists are able to investigate certain aspects of personality.

You also learned about measuring another aspect of psychology in the introductory section of this module: intelligence (Byford et al., 2014).

Operationalisation
This is the process of devising an operational definition. You were introduced to the concept of operational definition in Chapter 5, Section 3.2, of *Investigating Methods*.

You were introduced to the Wechsler Adult Intelligence Scale in Chapter 1, Section 4, of *Investigating Intelligence*.

Standardised test
A test that is designed to capture a specific psychological construct and is administered, scored and interpreted in a standard manner. Standardised tests have usually been rigorously tested for reliability and validity on a large number of individuals in an array of different situations and contexts.

Validity
Validity is the extent to which a measure or study is measuring what it set out to measure.

Reliability
Reliability refers to the consistency, or stability, of a measure or study. In other words, it is the extent to which it can produce the same results under similar circumstances.

There, you were introduced to the Wechsler Adult Intelligence Scale (WAIS), one of the most common tests of intelligence used today. The WAIS is a type of **standardised test** that has been developed as a result of defining what intelligence is composed of, and combining different subscales that assess these dimensions to produce an overall IQ score (Wechsler, 2008).

In deciding to measure somebody's IQ using the WAIS, we can be said to have operationalised the construct 'intelligence'. We could use the WAIS to measure people's intelligence, which will result in interval data. Or, we could categorise people according to different groups (as a nominal variable); for example, low versus high intelligence. Again, standardised tests such as the WAIS are valuable here, as they often classify an individual's performance in comparison with how the 'normal' population would perform, allowing us to categorise them accordingly.

Tests become standardised through a process of applying and modifying them over and over again using a variety of different populations to ensure that they are, and remain, valid and reliable (concepts I will discuss in Sections 2.2 and 2.3). Standardised tests are particularly helpful in the field of clinical psychology, where they are used as clinical tools to measure and diagnose symptoms. Nevertheless, it is worth noting that their usefulness outside the clinical environment in predicting behaviour in domains such as academic success or employment suitability is a subject of much unresolved debate.

Using pre-existing, tried and tested standardised tests can be a great way of maximising the likelihood that you are accurately measuring the constructs you have set out to explore. However, sometimes you may want to create your own way of measuring things. This is not a problem, but in order to do this reliably, you must be clear and explicit in how you define what you are measuring as well as justifying your measures. This is very important, as the principles of validity and reliability are fundamental cornerstones of quantitative research.

So what do I mean by **validity** and **reliability** in this context?

They are both terms that you probably use in everyday language, but let's take a moment to explore their meaning in the context of psychological research.

2.2   Validity

At the heart of validity is the question of whether a researcher is measuring what they think they are measuring. This is a relatively straightforward question when talking about objective measures such as reaction time or heart rate. However, when it comes to more subjective measures that tap into psychological experience or cognitive processes, it can be a bit trickier. Can we ever really be certain that we are measuring psychological phenomena that we cannot see? Perhaps not. But there are a number of different things psychologists should consider to ensure their measures are as valid as possible.

- **Face validity**. At the most basic level, we need to use our common sense to establish whether our measures and design are likely to be appropriate. Does it seem likely that the measure we are using makes sense? For example, if we want to measure a psychological experience such as anxiety, does it look as though the information collected is really related to anxiety? Think back to Activity 7.2. Asking questions about feeling tense or fearful are likely to have face validity for measuring anxiety. However, asking seemingly unrelated questions about a person's hobbies or interests may not appear to be a directly relevant way of finding out about anxiety levels.

- **Construct validity**. While face validity relies purely on common sense, construct validity takes this idea one step further. In this case, a new measure is compared with previous research and existing measures that are thought to be *associated* with or *unrelated* to the psychological construct you want to quantify. The idea is that if your new measure is really representing the construct you think it is, then it should correlate well with the related measures, but not with the unrelated ones. For example, if you wanted to try to measure happiness, you would expect your measure to correlate highly with satisfaction or optimism scores, but not show a strong correlation with intelligence. The use of accepted standardised scales in your research can really help to ensure construct validity, as they have been thoroughly tested in this way.

- **Internal validity**. This concept is only really relevant in study designs trying to establish cause and effect. It is the extent to which you can be confident about the causal inferences you are drawing in a study, rather than the result being due to an alternative cause (or confounding variable). Establishing cause can often be tricky as it is difficult to separate out the behaviour (or process) we want to study

Correlation is covered in Chapter 5 of *Investigating Methods* and in the online activity *Interpreting correlation*.

from all of the other behaviours (or processes) that happen along with it. Being human, we know that things seldom happen in isolation. The aim is to minimise any possible confounds that may have found their way into our study design by keeping everything but the variable we are manipulating constant. For example, imagine you want to study whether a three-hour meditation workshop can help reduce feelings of anxiety. You measure participants' anxiety levels both before and after the class and find that symptoms are lower after attending meditation. You might then conclude that the workshop was successful. Yet consider this: your participants all drank coffee in the morning. As caffeine is known to increase heart rate and can induce certain symptoms of anxiety, it could be that these findings were simply due to the effects of caffeine wearing off. Controlling for factors known to influence feelings of anxiety, such as caffeine, would have increased the internal validity of this study.

- **External validity**. This is primarily concerned with the **generalisability** of our findings. There are two main things to consider here: environment (ecological validity) and population (population validity). I will look at them in turn.

Generalisability

The extent to which research findings can be applied to people or settings beyond those included in the original study.

  - **Ecological validity**. This is a phrase you have already come across a number of times: it is the extent to which a study (or testing environment) reflects what happens in real life. Laboratory experiments, for example, may not reflect what happens in everyday/naturally occurring situations as well as studies that are conducted in the home or work environment. However, they do give psychologists considerable control over possible confounding variables, as they are more able to isolate specific behaviours or variables, keeping everything else as constant as possible. In this way, there is a bit of a trade-off between internal and external validity, so it's important to take this into account when deciding how to carry out psychological research.

Population validity

A type of external validity that indicates how well a study's findings can be applied to the wider population.

  - **Population validity**. This is another type of external validity which describes the extent to which we can extrapolate from the study sample to the entire population. This can often be problematic if we haven't chosen our sample appropriately, or if our sample size is small. Using an example from Section 1.1.1, it can often be difficult to generalise from individual case studies, as we don't know how representative they are of other people. However, that doesn't mean that case studies are of no value. Converging evidence from many case studies or domains can give us a great deal of insight into what is going on.

2.3 Reliability

We use the word 'reliable' in everyday language to refer to something that is consistent and dependable. It has much the same meaning in psychology. Inherent in the concept of reliability are the notions of stability and replication, that is, the extent to which a measure or test used by researchers will produce the same set of results if repeated under the same conditions. In this sense, reliability means that any important and meaningful finding must be more than a 'one-off' and therefore allows us to say something useful about human behaviour. As discussed in Chapter 2, the reliability of a study is essential if a finding is going to be accepted by the wider scientific community, because replication of findings allows conclusions to be strengthened and to stand up to scrutiny.

This idea of stability and repeatability is something that standardised measures are rigorously tested for. In this sense, the term reliability refers to the accuracy of your measures. Some measures are likely to be more reliable than others: while a stopwatch is likely to produce accurate and consistent measurements for response time, indirect measures like those used to measure psychological constructs (such as the F-scale) are more vulnerable to error as they may be influenced by other factors. For example, a person may be inclined to respond to controversial items on measures like the F-scale in a way that they believe is more socially acceptable, as opposed to answering in line with their actual beliefs – something known as **social desirability bias**. Taking the example of anxiety again, a reliable measure should be able to consistently distinguish between highly anxious and non-anxious people, as well as be able to produce similar scores for people who are similarly anxious.

Social desirability bias
The tendency for people to respond to questions in a way they believe would meet the approval of others.

2.4 The relationship between reliability and validity

Reliability is an important component of validity. If a measure you are using is not reliable, then the validity of your study will also be compromised. For example, if people score very different results on a measure every time they take it, the measure is unlikely to be tapping into anything stable or specific. However, just because a test is reliable does not necessarily mean that it is also valid. For example, if you weigh yourself every morning on a set of bathroom scales that is out by 3 pounds, it will consistently report the same weight every day (as long as you don't lose or gain weight!). It would be reliable. However, this reading won't be valid as it is not actually giving you your true weight.

Reliable but   Reliable   Unreliable and
not valid   and valid   hence not valid

Figure 7.4   Hitting the target for both reliability and validity

Summary

- Before psychological constructs can be measured, they first have to be defined and operationalised.
- It is important to establish whether a measure is valid and reliable.
- Validity refers to the extent to which a researcher is measuring what they think they are measuring.
- Reliability refers to the accuracy and stability of a measure.
- A strength of standardised tests is that they have been through extensive reliability and validity checks.

3   Researching aphasia: an example

In Chapter 3, you were introduced to the experimental method. As a reminder, here are the key features of an experiment:

- The researcher deliberately manipulates something (the independent variable, IV) in order to see what effect this might have on something else (the dependent variable, DV).
- The DV is measured in some way to explore the effect of the IV.
- The researcher tries to control the experiment/situation in certain ways.

Sometimes it is not ethical or possible to manipulate your IV in a direct way. For example, while it may be interesting to see what impact damage to a certain part of the brain might have on language ability, it would of course be unethical (and illegal) to lesion people's brains for experimental purposes. Instead, a researcher can study the effects of brain damage by grouping participants according to naturally occurring differences (e.g. the different types of post-stroke language deficits). In this way, participants in a study are allocated to an experimental condition as a result of having an existing characteristic (a naturally occurring difference), rather than being randomly assigned to a group, and the experiment is referred to as having a **quasi-experimental design**.

Using naturally occurring differences as conditions of an IV has a number of advantages. It allows you to study real world issues as they naturally occur and investigate variables that cannot be practically or ethically manipulated otherwise. However, a degree of caution needs to be exercised when using variables like this. For example, as the researcher is not actively manipulating the IV, they have to be tentative about any causality claims that they are making, as they have less control over confounding variables compared with experiments involving random allocation of participants to conditions. This, of course, does not only apply to researching brain damage. There are several other (common) cases where natural manipulation occurs (e.g. when using factors such as gender or age as an IV).

In this section we are going to consider a study by Bakheit et al. (2007) that has used both standardised tests and naturally occurring differences to explore the recovery of participants following a stroke. Throughout this chapter I have described how studies investigating the relationship

Quasi-experimental design
A design where the experimenter assigns people to a condition based on naturally occurring characteristics, such as sex, age, height, IQ or a personality trait.

between brain and behaviour can give us insight into how cognitive processes work. Not only that, but in studying people's behaviour following a stroke, we are also able to develop specific therapies for particular people to maximise their recovery.

Aphasia affects approximately a third of people who have suffered a stroke (Pedersen et al., 1995). However, different types of aphasia have different recovery rates and trajectories. A better understanding of these differences may allow us to design more carefully targeted treatments. A number of standardised tests have been developed to allow psychologists to identify specific communication deficits among aphasic patients. Using standardised tests like this also allows psychologists to track and measure the course of language recovery following stroke and to assess the appropriateness of different types of therapy used to aid recovery. The study described next sought to measure aphasia and recovery rates in exactly this way.

3.1   Study overview and objectives

Bakheit et al. (2007) sought to investigate the recovery of language function as a result of therapeutic intervention in the first year post-stroke. In this study, the authors used a standardised and validated test of language function called the Western Aphasia Battery (WAB) (Kertesz, 1982) to identify participants with post-stroke aphasia. This consists of five subscales to assess the degree and type of aphasia: verbal fluency, language information content, comprehension, repetition, and naming. The scores on these subscales are then combined to form an overall WAB score, which can range from 0 to 100. As with other standardised scales, patients can be classified into different diagnostic groupings according to meaningful points on the scale. For the WAB, scores of less than 93.8 are taken to indicate the presence of aphasia. As such, participants who scored in this range were classed as aphasic and included in the study. In addition to measuring the overall severity of aphasia, the WAB also classifies the type of aphasia a participant has according to their scores on individual subscales of the measure. In total, 75 participants (50.6 per cent male) were recruited into the study, with a mean age of 71.0 years. While this study actually identified five different subgroups of aphasia, I'm only going to consider three of those groups in this chapter – Broca's aphasia, Wernicke's aphasia and anomic aphasia – just to make the findings easier for you to follow.

Participants in the study were all given a 12-week speech and language therapy intervention course, designed to improve their ability to communicate with others through verbal and non-verbal means. The type of therapy each patient received was varied and tailored to their individual needs. Therapy exercises targeted improvement in understanding and expression both of spoken and written language in order to improve communication in everyday life. Speech and language therapy was delivered by qualified therapists of comparable experience as part of a multidisciplinary, goal-directed rehabilitation programme.

Participants' language abilities were measured at several points through their recovery by a speech and language therapist who was not involved in the patient's treatment. WAB assessments were made at 4, 8, 12 and 24 weeks to track changes in language function, and the initial WAB score at study entry formed the participants' pre-treatment baseline aphasia score.

Activity 7.3

Think about what you learned about experimental design in Chapter 3. What do you think the variables in this study were?

You may have worked out that the DV in this study was patients' language ability, as measured by the WAB. There were also two IVs. When trying to work out what these are, we need to think about what the language scores (the DV) were likely to depend on.

IV1. In this example, Bakheit et al. (2007) wanted to look at the language function of participants with different types of post-stroke aphasia. This means the first IV (grouping variable) that they were interested in was 'type of aphasia'. As participants were classified as either having Broca's, Wernicke's or anomic aphasia, each participant belonged to only one group for this variable. This is an example of a between-participants group: the different groups contained different people, allowing the researchers to compare language abilities between groups. This IV resulted from a naturally occurring difference and so was not directly manipulated by the experimenters.

IV2. As well as looking for differences between the groups, Bakheit et al. also wanted to see how the participants' language abilities changed over time. We could therefore call this second IV 'time'. They tested

You read about between- and within-participants designs in Chapter 3 of *Investigating Methods*.

participants at baseline (before they received any therapy) and then at weeks 4, 8, 12 and 24. This means that each participant took part at all five time point conditions, *repeating* the task. This allows the researcher to see changes within participants over time.

3.2   Graphing complex data in the Results section

When collecting data from two IVs, your findings might be quite complex. One of the best ways to gain a better picture of the patterns in your data is to illustrate them by producing a graph in the Results section of your report. This allows you to make quick visual comparisons in a much easier way than looking at numbers alone.

Activity 7.4

Think back to the online activity *Bar charts*. How might you best represent your data in a chart?

It's a bit tricky when you have more than one IV to think about, isn't it? If we just had one IV, it would be much easier. And this is a good place to start. In this example, imagine we only wanted to look at the improvement of all participants' language abilities over the five time points (baseline and weeks 4, 8, 12 and 24). What information would you need to explore this?

The median is introduced in the online activity *The mean, the mode and the median.*

You may have figured out that in order to graph our data, we first need to be able to summarise and describe our data in some way for each of the time points used in the study. As you learned in Chapter 4, we can do this using descriptive statistics. While the mean is the most commonly reported measure of central tendency, Bakheit et al. (2007) summarised their data using the median. This is because the median is less affected by extreme scores at either end of a measure (which you often get in clinical data), making it a more accurate reflection of the 'average' value. The median scores for all of the participants in this study at the different time points are shown in Table 7.1.

Table 7.1 Median Western Aphasia Battery scores for all participants in Bakheit et al. (2007)

	Baseline	Week 4	Week 8	Week 12	Week 24
Median WAB scores	33.6	60.3	68	71.8	75

(Source: Bakheit et al., 2007, p. 944)

When constructing a graph, we tend to use the horizontal axis (x axis) for the IV (in this case, time) and the vertical axis (y axis) for the DV (in this case, WAB scores). A good graph should always be labelled, so hopefully this should be clear. The descriptive statistics are then graphically represented using bars to illustrate the scores in each condition. If we do this for Bakheit et al.'s data, we can produce a graph that looks like Figure 7.5.

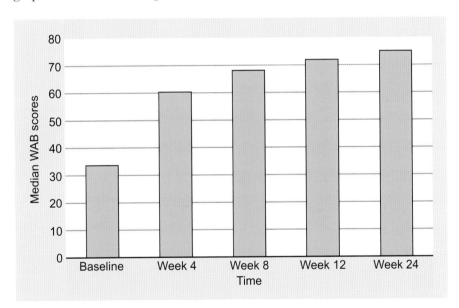

Figure 7.5 A bar chart illustrating the changes in all of the participants' WAB scores over time (Source: Bakheit et al., 2007)

By simply looking at the pattern of results, we can easily interpret what we can see by saying that, overall, participants' WAB scores appeared to improve over time, with the biggest improvement occurring in the first four weeks. However, it is important to note that at this point we are just describing the data pattern. While this progress is very encouraging in real world terms, we do not know if this pattern of improvement is statistically significant or not. We'll come back to this notion shortly.

You read about 'statistically significant difference' and inferential statistics in Chapter 4, Box 4.2.

Turning our attention back to the graph, we still have the question of how to illustrate data when you have multiple groups to represent at each time point.

The online activity *Bar graphs* introduced a couple of different types of graphs, one of which was particularly useful when looking at changes in measures over time: the line graph. Here, we would not represent the data as bars on a chart, but as single data points (at the same level as the top of the bars in Figure 7.5). We can then join up the individual points to better illustrate the changes in score over time. This would still give us the same information as the bar chart; however, it would look a little different (see Figure 7.6).

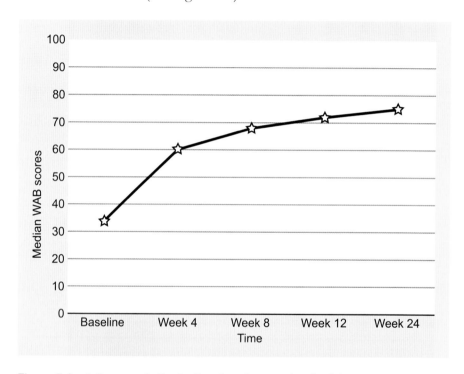

Figure 7.6   A line graph illustrating the changes in all of the participants' WAB scores over time (Source: Bakheit et al., 2007)

As I mentioned at the beginning of this section, Bakheit et al. (2007) were interested in the recovery rates of different aphasia groups: their between-participants IV. At the moment, the graphs in Figures 7.5 and 7.6 are only showing the rate of recovery for all of the participants together for the within-participants IV, 'time'. To plot the scores for both of the IVs together, we would follow the same process as above, but at each time point we would have a different data point representing the WAB scores for each aphasia group. The medians for the three groups we will consider are shown in Table 7.2.

Table 7.2   Median Western Aphasia Battery scores for three aphasia groups in Bakheit et al. (2007)

	Baseline	Week 4	Week 8	Week 12	Week 24
Broca's aphasia	29.2	54.3	65.2	68.1	72.5
Wernicke's aphasia	48.4	58.7	64.2	66.0	60.5
Anomic aphasia	80.2	89.4	94.2	95.1	95.0

(Source: Bakheit et al., 2007, p. 944)

Just as there is a different row of data for each group of participants, you would plot a separate corresponding line for each group on a chart. To allow the viewer to easily distinguish between groups, each group would need to be represented by a differently coloured or textured line, producing a graph that looks a little like Figure 7.7.

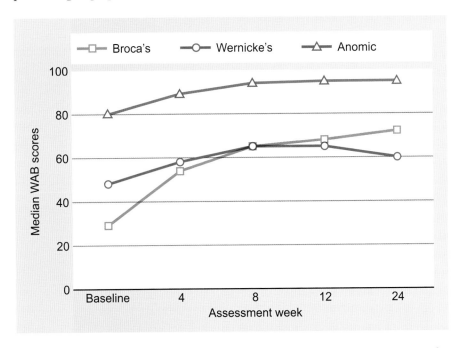

Figure 7.7   A line graph illustrating the changes in WAB scores over time for the three different aphasia groups (Source: adapted from Bakheit et al., 2007, p. 946)

Graphically representing your data in this way allows you to visually summarise your data and hopefully makes it easier for you to describe what is going on. In Figure 7.7, you can now inspect the recovery for each of the three groups by looking at their individual lines. The top line in blue represents the data from the anomic patients. Below that is a red line showing the data for the Wernicke's aphasics and a green line for the Broca's aphasics. Note how these two lower lines cross at Week 8. This is because Broca's patients show lower scores than Wernicke's until Week 8, after which they show higher scores.

Displaying the data in graph form allows us to inspect how the shapes of the lines compare, and to see whether any rise or fall across weeks is steeper for one group than another. There are two things to note here. Bakheit et al. (2007) draw attention to Broca's aphasia patients showing the most improvement, followed by Wernicke's, and then by anomic aphasia patients. They also point out that the most marked improvements occur in the first four weeks. But the authors do not draw any firm conclusions here. This is really important as you must remember that graphs are only displaying descriptive statistics. While we might visually be able to see trends or group differences in our graphs of descriptive statistics, we do not know whether these patterns are significant or meaningful until we have calculated inferential statistics. In order to draw conclusions about their data in this way, Bakheit et al. (2007) conducted a number of inferential statistical tests, which they describe in their Results section. The authors found some significant differences between the amount of progress the different aphasia groups made as a result of therapeutic intervention. While patients with Broca's aphasia recovered more language ability than anomic aphasia patients at all time points, patients with Wernicke's aphasia only showed significant gains compared with the anomic group in weeks 12 and 24. They do not report a significant difference between Broca's and Wernicke's aphasics.

Box 7.1   Interpreting graphs the 'Catchphrase' way

Sometimes graphs can look a little daunting, but essentially you just need to use the 'Catchphrase' technique here: simply say what you see!

(a)   (b)

Figure 7.8   Catchphrase is a UK game show where contestants have to describe what they see in pictures to make a well-known catchphrase. Give these a go!

NB: The answers are given at the end of the chapter.

3.3   Writing the Discussion section

We are now going to look at how Bakheit et al. (2007) presented their Discussion of the results of their study.

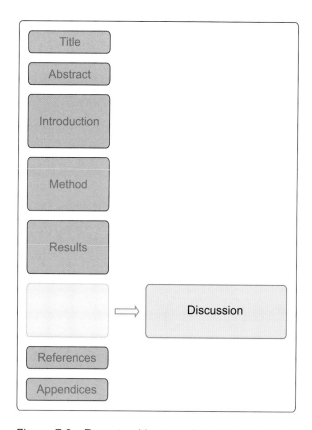

Figure 7.9   Report-writing template: locating the Discussion section

The Discussion section in your report is the place where you have to use your knowledge of the topic to interpret in plain language exactly what the results mean, without the use of numbers or statistics.

Generally, a Discussion section should:

- state the results of your experiment in plain language, without referencing the actual statistics
- provide an explanation of the results obtained
- describe how the findings compare with other research in the field (the literature you described in your Introduction)
- explain how your findings could be applied outside of the study
- critically evaluate your study, pointing out its limitations and its strengths
- make suggestions for future research.

It is common practice to begin your discussion by reiterating what you found in relation to your overarching study aims/hypotheses. Bakheit et al. (2007) stated that: 'The purpose of the present study was to examine the effect of the type of aphasia on the rate and extent of improvement of language impairment in the first year after stroke' (p. 942). In light of this, they began their Discussion section as follows.

Discussion

The findings of the present study confirm that the language function of aphasic stroke patients with ... Broca's, Wernicke's [and] anomic ... aphasia steadily improved during the 24-week observation period. The rate of improvement was fastest in the first four weeks post study entry and tended to slow down thereafter. Patients with Broca's aphasia had the largest increase and attained higher Western Aphasia Battery scores than those with Wernicke['s] ... aphasia by the end of the six months study period. By contrast, those with Wernicke [and] anomic ... aphasia showed the smallest incremental improvement from baseline.

(Bakheit et al., 2007, p. 946)

This is an important finding to start off with, as it has important real world application. Not only have Bakheit et al. (2007) found that all patients improved in terms of their language ability over the study period, but their findings also suggest that patients with Broca's aphasia may benefit more from therapeutic intervention than others. While it is good to highlight your main findings, it is also important not to be complacent about them. You should try to critically evaluate your results: are they likely to be correct? Could anything else explain them?

Try to pre-empt what a reviewer/reader might think in terms of these questions. A good place to start is by considering reliability and validity. Bakheit et al. (2007) give an example of this, defending their findings in terms of possible confounds (internal validity). They have realised that a reader may want to know whether other factors (such as age, education and handedness) could explain their pattern of results, and have defended their findings accordingly:

Our findings are unlikely to be due to differences between the study groups in their demographic and clinical characteristics. The groups were evenly matched for their premorbid level of education and cerebral dominance (as determined by hand dominance) which are considered important prognostic factors in aphasia (Geschwind, 1974). The patients' groups in this study were not closely matched for age. Patients with Wernicke's aphasia were on average older, but this cannot entirely explain the observed differences in recovery between the groups, as the relationship between age and recovery from aphasia appears to be weak (Kertesz and McCabe, 1977; Pickersgill and Lincoln, 1983; Pashek and Holland, 1988).

(Bakheit et al., 2007, p. 946)

Box 7.2   Why does handedness matter?

Knowing whether someone is right- or left-handed is important when investigating the functions of different parts of the brain. Toates (2012) mentions that the left hemisphere is dominant for language, and while this tends to be the case with right-handed individuals, it is not necessarily so for those who are left-handed. Consequently, when researchers are exploring brain function, handedness can be a factor to take into consideration.

The authors then go on to further detail their findings, specifically relating them to existing research that they had previously mentioned in their Introduction. This is good practice in academic writing as it explicitly couches the results in terms of the current academic literature and debate. Where findings are complementary, this strengthens your conclusions; however, when findings are at odds with previous work, you need to try to work out why this might be the case. To do this, you will need to think carefully and critically about both your work and the earlier study or studies to identify any issues that might help shed some light on why they produced different results. Bakheit et al. (2007) do exactly that:

Patients with Broca's aphasia in our study had the best rate and extent of improvement despite the fact that they had severe language impairment on study entry … This observation is at variance with that of a previous study (Kertesz and McCabe, 1977) that found a correlation between poor recovery from aphasia and the initial severity of the language impairment. However, the latter study did not control for the nature and duration of language therapy and included patients who did not receive any formal language therapy. Recovery from aphasia may be influenced by the intensity and duration of language therapy (Bhogal *et al.*, 2003). The effect of treatment may have mitigated the severity of aphasia in our patients with Broca's aphasia, but to a lesser extent in those with other types of aphasia. Future studies should address the possible differential effect of language therapy on the various types of aphasia.

(Bakheit et al., 2007, p. 946)

In the above extract, the authors acknowledge that they have found different results from a previous piece of work. While a previous study found that patients with initially severe language impairments had a poor recovery rate, Bakheit et al. (2007) did not. Instead, they found that the patient group with the most severe language deficit at the beginning of their study (Broca's patients) experienced the best language recovery rate. However, they also go on to try to explain this discrepancy, suggesting that patient differences between the two studies may be responsible. While Bakheit et al. (2007) provided all of their participants with a 12-week therapy intervention, therapy type and duration were not controlled for (kept constant) in the other study. As such, they suggest it may be the type of therapy employed in their study that accounted for the good recovery rate of their patients. Note how they then highlight this as a potential avenue for future research to help shed light on the subject.

You should also bring in additional research that is not mentioned in your Introduction to try to further explore and explain your findings. Bakheit et al. (2007) discuss a number of factors that may explain the different recovery rates for the different aphasia groups, and again make suggestions for future research taking these issues into account.

A number of factors may explain why the different types of aphasia improve at different rates and to a different extent. The initial severity of aphasia may have an effect. For example, Wade *et al.* (1986) have found a strong correlation between the initial severity of aphasia and the degree of improvement in the aphasia scores at six months. The type of aphasia *per se* may also be a factor. For example, clinical observations suggest that patients with Broca's aphasia tend to engage more in therapy and frequently attempt to correct their linguistic errors possibly because they usually have good insight into their language deficit. This may explain the better improvement of language function in these patients. By contrast, the unawareness of the language disorder and the inability to monitor the language output that is characteristic of Wernicke's aphasia (Marshall *et al.*, 1994) may be important impediments to functional improvement. Marshall *et al.* (1994) reported a significant correlation between the patients' competence in language comprehension and the frequency of monitoring and correcting their linguistic errors.

Other factors that influence recovery from aphasia include the size and site of the brain lesion. For example, patients with damage to half or less of Wernicke's area on CT scans appear to recover well within six months of the stroke onset. By contrast, severe language impairment is often present one year after stroke when the brain damage involves more than half of Wernicke's area (Naeser *et al.*, 1987). The location of the brain lesion also seems to influence the prognosis of aphasia. For example, aphasia due to subcortical lesions has a better prognosis than that due to cortical stroke (Liang *et al.*, 2001). Future studies of the prognosis of the different types of aphasia should include analysis of these factors on the rate and extent of recovery of language function.

(Bakheit et al., 2007, p. 947)

The above paragraphs show that the authors have really tried to understand and explain why the pattern of their results was what it was, in this case considering the nature of the aphasia's behavioural and physical symptoms. This shows careful thinking by the authors, which is one of the most important qualities of a good Discussion.

In terms of finishing your Discussion, it is a generally a good idea to provide a clear summary of your findings in light of what you have discussed in this section. What are the take-home messages that you really wish to convey? This is the final thing that the readers will read in your Discussion section – make it count. Bakheit et al. (2007) said the following:

> In conclusion, the present study examined the prognosis of the different types of aphasia in the first year of stroke in an unselected group of hospital patients. It showed that patients with Broca's aphasia achieved the best improvement during the study period. This was despite their initially more severe language impairment.
>
> (Bakheit et al., 2007, p. 947)

Summary

- Producing graphs for your Results section can be a good way of presenting your data clearly.
- The Discussion section of your report interprets and gives meaning to your results in relation to existing research and literature.
- Extracts from Bakheit et al. (2007) illustrate how to discuss the results of a study.
- Bakheit et al. (2007) found that post-stroke recovery rates were different for patients with differing aphasia types.

4   An alternative method of researching aphasia therapies

Section 3 introduced you to a study that investigated the recovery rates of patients with post-stroke aphasia. All patients received a 12-week therapy course and all showed improvements in their WAB scores following the intervention. From this study, we might conclude that the intervention was 'successful'. But is this really a fair conclusion?

Activity 7.5

Think carefully about the Bakheit et al. (2007) study – can you think of any specific limitations in terms of the method that was used here (i.e. using standardised tests to quantify recovery)? Can we really conclude that the intervention was successful? Can you think of any other way to better assess recovery? To get you started, think about what types of information we might be missing out on here.

While the Bakheit et al. (2007) study gives us some insight into the recovery trajectory of people with post-stroke aphasia, one obvious limitation is the question of whether numbers from a quantitative scale measuring language ability really translate into real world experience or recovery. While using standardised tests may increase the validity and reliability of a measure, they tell us very little about the overall well-being of the patient, the experiential aspects of aphasia and the subjective recovery of a patient, as they tend to only index symptoms.

An alternative way to carry out research into the treatment of aphasia could be to embark on qualitative work. Collecting qualitative data would allow the subjective experiences of individuals living with aphasia to be explored in a much more contextually- and data-rich manner. While this may be difficult, as the inherent communication deficits associated with aphasia may limit the information that one can garner directly from the patients, asking carers and/or family members to assist in this type of research may prove fruitful. One study by van der Gaag and colleagues (2005) did just that.

Figure 7.10   Collecting data from a variety of different sources can help to build a well-rounded picture of the topic you are exploring

Van der Gaag et al. (2005) aimed to evaluate the impact of a community-based therapy intervention on patients with post-stroke aphasia. Unlike the intervention described in the Bakheit et al. (2007) study which focused primarily on improving communication skills, the therapy assessed in this paper took into account the individuals as a whole, and not just their symptoms. As we saw from the video on aphasia (*Researching language impairment*), communication difficulties present challenges to affected individuals not just in terms of communication, but also in terms of people's self-esteem and general well-being. This is hardly surprising when you consider how important a role language and communication skills play in our day-to-day lives. It therefore may be beneficial to consider the individual's needs as a whole when developing therapeutic interventions rather than limiting work in this area to communication strategies.

In addition to focusing on a more **holistic** intervention for aphasia, van der Gaag et al. (2005) collected a wider range of data from their participants. The authors collected both quantitative data from standardised tests and qualitative data from semi-structured interviews to obtain both objective and subjective information from the aphasia

Holistic
Relating to the consideration of a person as a whole rather than focusing only on specific aspects.

patients. Not only did these measures explore communication abilities, but they also investigated the participant's overall quality of life. Participants were assessed on all measures before they started the therapy, and again six months later. In addition to collecting data from the aphasia patients themselves, similar information was also collected from their relatives in order to validate, confirm and maximise the data collected. Interviews were all transcribed, and themes were identified and compared across the transcripts.

Quantitative measures of quality of life and communication skills both showed significant improvements after therapy. This finding was supported by the qualitative data, which showed a general shift in focus from a sense of loss (e.g. of independence, sense of self, control) and frustration before the intervention, to more positive themes in the post-therapy interviews. These included reports of increased self-confidence and independence, and a desire to participate in more everyday social activities. The majority of participants also reported specific improvements in their communication abilities, as well as an increased confidence about their communication in general. Overall, the results of van der Gaag et al. (2005) suggest that their holistic community therapy not only improved communication skills for people with aphasia, but it also had a positive impact on their quality of life as a whole.

The studies by both Bakheit et al. (2007) and van der Gaag et al. (2005) explored the recovery of aphasia patients after therapeutic intervention. However, they both collected different information to assess this. Again, this brings us back to the idea of defining the constructs you are measuring and the different ways in which you can operationalise them. While Bakheit et al. (2007) took improvements in communication alone to be indicative of recovery, van der Gaag et al. (2005) took a broader definition. In psychology, there is rarely (if ever) only one correct way of exploring a question or hypothesis. Instead, it is up to you as the researcher to carefully define exactly what it is you want to explore, and to decide the most appropriate way to measure this.

Summary

- Collecting information from people with language difficulties can be challenging.
- Many psychological measures seek only to quantify symptoms; however, more in-depth information can be collected using qualitative methods.
- Collecting different types of data from a number of different sources can help to build a better, more rounded picture of the issues faced by patients with aphasia.

Answers to Figure 7.8

A: Head over heels. B: Cut a long story short.

References

Bakheit, A. M. O., Shaw, S., Carrington, S. and Griffiths, S. (2007) 'The rate and extent of improvement with therapy from the different types of aphasia in the first year after stroke', *Clinical Rehabilitation*, vol. 21, no. 10, pp. 941–9.

Byford, J., McAvoy, J. and Banyard, P. (2014) *Investigating Intelligence*, Milton Keynes, The Open University.

Craik, K. (1943) *The Nature of Explanation*, Cambridge, Cambridge University Press.

Kertesz, A. (1982) *Western Aphasia Battery*, Orlando, FL, Grune & Stratton, Inc.

McAvoy, J. (2012) 'Exposing the authoritarian personality', in Brace, N. and Byford, J. (eds) *Investigating Psychology*, Oxford, Oxford University Press/Milton Keynes, The Open University.

Pedersen, P. M., Jørgensen, H. S., Nakayama, H., Raaschou, H. O. and Olsen, T. S. (1995) 'Aphasia in acute stroke: incidence, determinants, and recovery', *Annals of Neurology*, vol. 38, no. 4, pp. 659–66.

Stroke Association (2013) *Stroke Facts and Statistics for Your Area* [Online]. Available at www.stroke.org.uk/news/stroke-facts-and-statistics-your-area (Accessed 15 July 2013).

Toates, F. (2012) 'Language and the brain', in Brace, N. and Byford, J. (eds) *Investigating Psychology*, Oxford, Oxford University Press/Milton Keynes, The Open University.

The Open University (2014) 'Exploring personality in different cultures' [Video], *DE100 Investigating psychology 1*. Available at https://learn2.open.ac.uk/mod/oucontent/view.php?id=462740&section=2.2 (Accessed 14 May 2014).

The Open University (2014) 'Researching language impairment' [Video], *DE100 Investigating psychology 1*. Available at https://learn2.open.ac.uk/mod/oucontent/view.php?id=476000&section=2 (Accessed 14 May 2014).

van der Gaag, A., Smith, L., Davis, S., Moss, B., Cornelius, V., Laing, S. and Mowles, C. (2005) 'Therapy and support services for people with long-term stroke and aphasia and their relatives: a six-month follow-up study', *Clinical Rehabilitation*, vol. 19, no. 4, pp. 372–80.

Wechsler, D. (2008) *Wechsler Adult Intelligence Scale – Fourth Edition*, San Antonio, TX, Pearson.

Chapter 8
Drawing inferences

Graham Pike

Contents

Aims and objectives

After studying this chapter you should be able to:

- appreciate the role of inferential statistics in testing hypotheses
- understand the principles underlying inferential statistics
- understand the chi-square statistic
- describe an example of published research that uses inferential statistics.

1   Testing hypotheses

In the final two chapters of this book, we will be consolidating many of the concepts you have encountered previously, and looking at how we can use these to analyse the results of quantitative psychological research. In particular, we will be looking at a number of experiments to help us explore how inferential statistical analysis makes it possible for us to infer whether results are statistically significant or not.

1.1   The cycle of enquiry

Edgar and Edgar (2012) explained that research develops in line with the principle of a 'cycle of enquiry'. For experiments, this refers to the way researchers can:

- use knowledge gained from psychological theory to form a hypothesis
- carefully design an experiment to test this hypothesis
- use the results of the experiment to modify psychological theory.

The research Edgar and Edgar used to illustrate this process was carried out by Brown et al. (cited in Edgar and Edgar, 2012) and was one of the very first studies conducted to explore the effects of using a phone while driving. The researchers tested a hypothesis similar to 'Using a mobile phone will affect performance on a driving task', by designing an experiment which had two conditions. In one condition participants drove around a test track while answering questions on a mobile phone; and in the other condition (a 'control' condition) participants drove around the same track without using a phone. In both conditions the participants had to judge whether or not they would be able to pass through gaps of varying sizes. The time taken to complete the task (in seconds) and the accuracy of the participants' judgements (whether they correctly or incorrectly estimated that the car could pass through the gap) were recorded.

The study by Brown et al. is discussed in Chapter 8, Box 8.2, of *Investigating Psychology*.

Activity 8.1

Can you work out what the independent variable (IV) and the two dependent variables (DVs) were from the above description of the experiment by Brown et al. (cited in Edgar and Edgar, 2012)?

The IV was the use of a mobile phone while driving; and the DVs were the accuracy with which a gap was judged (whether correct or incorrect), and the time taken to complete a task (in seconds).

A key step in the cycle of enquiry is designing an experiment to test a hypothesis. This raises a very important question: 'How do you know whether your hypothesis is supported or not?', and it is this question that we will explore further here.

To begin answering the question of how you know whether or not to accept your hypothesis, let's imagine it is 1969 and we are in a lab at the Cambridge Applied Psychology Unit with Ivan Brown and colleagues. After spending an exhausting, but nonetheless rather fun, few weeks at a Ministry of Defence airbase watching participants drive an Austin A40 estate car around a test track, you have collected a great deal of data to do with the judgements made by the participants and how fast they completed the test. What do you do now?

Figure 8.1   An Austin A40 estate car

You were introduced to contingency tables in Chapter 5 of *Investigating Methods.*

What you do first depends on which DV you look at, as one involves nominal data and the other interval data. Together with Brown, you decide to look at the first DV, this being the accuracy with which a gap was judged (whether correct or incorrect), which generated nominal data. You decide to display these data pertaining to how accurately the participants judged the smallest gap they were asked to drive through in a contingency table. This gap was actually 7.5 cm (3 inches) *smaller* than the width of the car! The correct response was therefore for the participant to judge that the car would *not* fit through the gap. You construct a table that shows, for each condition (telephoning or not telephoning), how many of the participants were correct and said that the car would not fit through the gap (see Table 8.1).

Table 8.1   Effect of telephoning on judging a gap 7.5 cm smaller than the car

	Driving without telephoning	**Driving and telephoning concurrently**
Judged gap correctly	72	53
Judged gap incorrectly	28	47

NB: These are not the actual data from Brown et al. but illustrate what their data may have looked like in a contingency table.

It is clear from these data that more errors were made by participants driving and telephoning than by participants who were driving without telephoning. In fact, telephoning led to 19 more participants making an incorrect judgement.

Does this mean that you can accept your hypothesis that 'Using a mobile phone will affect performance on a driving task'? To begin trying to answer this question, first have a go at Activity 8.2.

Activity 8.2

Which of the following factors do you think could have conceivably led to there being more errors in the telephoning condition than in the driving without telephoning condition?

- The drivers in the telephoning condition were less experienced.
- The drivers in the telephoning condition were more experienced.
- The telephoning condition took place in the evening and the driving without telephoning condition during the afternoon.
- The drivers in the telephoning condition were younger.
- The drivers in the telephoning condition were older.

- The safety instructions about using the telephone while driving made participants in that condition anxious about the task.
- There were more female participants in the telephoning condition.
- There were more male participants in the telephoning condition

---

The correct answer to Activity 8.2 is that *all* of the factors could have led to more errors being made in the telephoning condition than in the driving without telephoning condition. Even if the drivers in the telephoning condition were more experienced, this could have made them overconfident, or they may have had experience with a smaller car that *could* fit through the gap. The point is that *any* difference between the conditions could lead to the participants behaving differently. Those factors which bring about a difference, and are not the IV, are referred to as 'confounding variables', because they can confound the results of our experiment. In psychology, it is very important to design experiments to limit the effects of all the potential confounding variables you can think of, and researchers give a great deal of thought to the stimuli, tasks and procedures they employ. You will notice that some of the confounding variables in Activity 8.2 are to do with the design of the experiment (when each condition took place, for example) while others are to do with the participants themselves. This means we also have to take great care when recruiting participants for an experiment and in deciding to which condition they are assigned.

1.2 Random allocation to conditions

When you recruit people to participate in an experiment, you are actually drawing a 'sample' of people from the population of interest.

Sampling is discussed in Chapter 2 of *Investigating Methods* and in the online activity *Sampling.*

Psychological experiments have to be conducted using just a sample because it is simply not possible to experiment on the entire population. The problem is that people are different, and even if our sample consists of a great many people (which is also usually impractical), there is no guarantee that the sample will be a perfect match for the population. The difference that results from using a sample of people rather than testing the whole population is called 'sampling error'. It follows that two samples drawn from the same population are likely not only to differ from the population as a whole, but from one another as well.

The online activity *Sampling* demonstrated why it is so important to draw your sample as randomly as possible from the population of interest. True random sampling is very hard to achieve and rarely used in psychological experiments, as you read in Section 1 of Chapter 2. However, in conducting an experiment it is also important that participants are randomly allocated to the conditions.

Figure 8.2   You say that results showed that using your new skin cream led to much smoother skin compared with the control group? Let me explain the need for random allocation to conditions one more time …

Even if the sample cannot be drawn at random, it should be possible for the researcher to randomly allocate their participants to the conditions in the experiment. The reason random allocation is so important is that any other means of allocation could result in a difference in performance between the conditions. For example, if a researcher advertised for participants and allocated the first 20 people to respond to one condition, and the last 20 people to respond to the second condition, it could be that those in the first condition were keener, more enthusiastic or more organised than those in the second. One important exception to randomly allocating participants to conditions occurs in research that is testing the difference between naturally occurring groups, such as young and old, men and women, or people with high and low authoritarian personality scores. Obviously if you want to know if the attentional abilities of people over 65 are

You were introduced to quasi-experimental designs in Chapter 7, Section 3, of *Investigating Methods*.

different from those under 65, you cannot randomly allocate participants to conditions; instead you have to assign participants to a condition depending on their age. As random allocation is not possible, such experiments are actually 'quasi-experiments'.

Summary

- A key part of the cycle of enquiry is determining whether or not to accept a hypothesis.
- When designing experiments in order to draw cause and effect conclusions, it is important that participants are randomly sampled and randomly allocated to conditions.

2   Inferential statistics

2.1   Descriptive and inferential statistics

Let's return to our key question about whether or not we can accept our hypothesis: in our experiment on telephoning while driving, we found that driving while using a telephone led to an increase in the number of participants making an error compared with driving without using a phone. Does this mean we can accept our hypothesis that 'Using a mobile phone will affect performance on a driving task'?

We cannot answer this question simply by looking at the contingency table (Table 8.1). This is because although there was a difference between our conditions, we should expect there to be some difference simply because people are different. What we need to know is whether the difference between our conditions is large enough for us to conclude that it is unlikely to have arisen by chance alone, and instead was caused by our IV. Imagine a room with 20 people in it and splitting them into two groups of ten, and then asking everyone to complete a general knowledge quiz. Would you expect the average score for both groups to be identical? Common sense tells us that it is very unlikely that the average scores would be precisely the same, because we know different individuals will get very different scores and that therefore the scores of the two groups are also likely to differ and so their mean scores will differ too. In other words, just through chance alone we expect the two groups to differ. Now imagine that you wanted to test the effects of alcohol on cognitive function and so had asked one group to drink 3 units of alcohol before completing the quiz. The alcohol group's average score does turn out to be lower, but how do you know if this was because of the alcohol or if the score for that group would have been lower anyway even without the alcohol?

To answer this question, we need more powerful statistics that are able to assess the likely effects of sampling error, and so decide whether the differences we see in the results of our experiment were caused by the IV or were just the sort of differences we should expect because people are different. We call these more powerful statistics 'inferential statistics'. Descriptive statistics describe our data and inferential statistics allow us to draw inferences from them. We will not be looking at the mathematical calculations involved in using inferential statistics in this module, but instead will concentrate on interpreting what they mean and what they reveal about our data.

You read about the distribution of data in Chapter 1, Section 3, of *Investigating Intelligence*. You may remember that one very common way that data can be distributed is known as the 'normal distribution'.

The calculations involved in inferential statistical analyses are based on knowing how data are distributed, and therefore how likely it is that any particular value might occur.

For example, our knowledge of how IQ is distributed in the population allows us to (quite) accurately state what the likelihood is of selecting at random someone with an IQ of 100 or someone with an IQ of 95. Note that I specified 'selecting at random'. If I selected someone from a very *specific* population of people, for example, colleagues teaching at a university, then it is very likely that the IQ scores of those people will have a different mean and distribution from the population as a whole. As many inferential statistical tests are based on assumptions of normal distribution, for these tests to provide reliable results it is important that any sample is selected at random from the group it is supposed to represent, and not from just one part of that group. Furthermore, those in your sample will then need to be randomly assigned to the conditions in your experiment.

2.2   Testing for differences

Earlier in the module we introduced you to different descriptive statistics, such as the mean, mode and median (**measures of central tendency**), the standard deviation and the range (**measures of distribution**).

Measures of central tendency
The mean, median and mode tell you what score sits at the 'middle' or 'centre' of a sample.

Measures of distribution
The standard deviation and the range tell you about the variability and spread of scores in a sample.

Just as there are different kinds of descriptive statistics, there are also different inferential statistical tests, and the choice about which to use will depend in part on the type of data collected. Next I will look at two of these statistical tests: one suitable for experiments with two conditions and interval data, and one that is used to analyse nominal data.

Two inferential statistical tests that are frequently used in psychological research are the chi-square and *t*-test. 'Chi' is a Greek letter, written as χ, which is pronounced as if the 's' was missing from 'sky'. It is usual to report it as χ^2; the superscript ^{2} is the mathematical notation used to indicate 'square', which means multiplying a number by itself.

- The *t*-test is used to analyse interval data and is based on comparing means and standard deviations. For example, we could use a *t*-test to see if there is a difference between the number of words 15-year-old children and 10-year-old children can recall after studying a list of 30 words for 1 minute. From the data, we could calculate the mean number, and standard deviation, of words remembered by the two age groups (as shown in Table 8.2). A *t*-test could then be used to determine whether there is a statistically significant difference between the two groups or whether the difference is the sort you would expect to find just because no two groups (of any age) are likely to remember exactly the same number of words on average.

Table 8.2   Mean number of words recalled by children in the two age groups

Condition	Mean	Standard deviation
15-year-olds	18.6	4.3
10-year-olds	10.2	5.7

- The chi-square test is used to determine whether a difference is statistically significant when the data are nominal. For example, we could use a chi-square test to see if there is a difference between whether 15-year-old and 10-year-old children can spell the word 'piece' correctly. From the data (which are shown in Table 8.3 in a contingency table), we could calculate the frequency of correct and incorrect spellings for the two age groups, and then use chi-square to determine whether the difference between age groups is statistically significant.

Table 8.3   Number of correct and incorrect spellings by age

	15-year-olds	10-year-olds
Number correct	25	18
Number incorrect	5	12

So, the type of quantitative data you collect determines what descriptive *and* what inferential statistical tests you conduct and report. In this module we will be concentrating on the chi-square inferential statistical test. The project that you have already been working on involves collecting nominal data, so it will be the chi-square test that you will use to analyse the data. We will show you some of the steps involved in calculating chi-square, as it can help you to understand what the test is doing, but please be reassured that for your TMA we have provided an online activity *Chi-square calculator* that does the calculations for you. Your job is therefore to concentrate on *interpreting* what this statistical test tells you.

2.3 Chi-square

There is one important difference between the chi-square and *t*-test. In Chapters 3 and 5 you read about two broad types of quantitative research, these being experimental and correlational studies. The *t*-test can only be used to analyse data from an experiment. This is because it analyses the effect of a single IV on a single DV. However, chi-square is more flexible and can be used for both experimental and correlational designs because it analyses two variables. These two variables can be one IV and one DV and chi-square will tell you if there is a statistically significant difference. Alternatively, they can be the two variables of interest in a correlational study, displayed in a contingency table, and chi-square will tell you if there is a statistically significant association. Essentially, the chi-square test works out what we would *expect* the contingency table to look like if the values were distributed at random and compares these *expected* values with the ones actually *observed*. If the difference between the expected and observed values is sufficiently large, the test will give a statistically significant result. So, chi-square could be used to look for an association between two variables, but it can also be used to test for a difference. In the rest of this chapter and in Chapter 9, we will focus on the chi-square inferential statistic. The online activity *Chi-square* contains detailed instructions which show you how to calculate chi-square and how to work out whether it is statistically significant or not. The calculations are not complex as there are essentially three steps and these involve only addition, subtraction, multiplication and division. You can find out more about chi-square by completing the online activity. When doing so, try to keep in mind the overall aim of the chi-square test, which is explained in Box 8.1.

Box 8.1   Chi-square

Chi-square analyses data that has been presented in a contingency table and tells us whether there is a statistically significant difference between the observed values (which are based on the data collected) and the expected values (which are those you would expect by chance alone). The observed values correspond to the data you collected in your study, while the expected values need to be calculated.

Table 8.4a is a contingency table containing the data from a (fictitious) experiment to see whether there is a difference between conducting a conversation with a passenger physically present in the car (passenger condition) and conducting a conversation using a mobile phone while driving (mobile phone condition). The experiment involved 20 participants, ten in each condition. Each participant was asked to drive up to a pair of cones, stop, and say whether their car would be able to pass safely through. The cones were spaced so the gap was 20 cm narrower than the width of the car.

Table 8.4a   Accuracy of judgement by condition (observed values only)

		Condition	
		Mobile phone	**Passenger**
Judging the size of the gap	Incorrect	9	4
	Correct	1	6

In Chapter 5 you saw how a contingency table is constructed. For our current example, you would work out how many people in each condition were 'correct' in their judgement and how many were 'incorrect'. These would be the 'observed' values, as they relate to the data collected in our experiment, and these are shown in Table 8.4a. You will see how to calculate 'expected' values yourself in the online activity *Chi-square*, but the basic idea is that you work out the total number of observations in each row and each column. For each observed value you multiply that row and column total and divide by the total number of observations (usually the number of participants in the study), and that will give you the expected value associated with that observed value. For example, to work out the expected value for the cell corresponding to incorrect judgements in the mobile phone condition, we would multiply the column total of 10 by the row total of 13 (which equals 130), and then divide this by 20, which is the total number of observations, to give an expected value of 6.5. Rather than you having to spend time doing this for every cell now, I have entered these values for you in Table 8.4b.

Table 8.4b   Accuracy of judgement by condition (observed and expected values)

		Condition	
		Mobile phone	**Passenger**
Judging the size of the gap	Incorrect	Observed = 9 Expected = 6.5	Observed = 4 Expected = 6.5
	Correct	Observed = 1 Expected = 3.5	Observed = 6 Expected = 3.5

Looking at the observed and expected values, it is clear that when using a mobile phone the observed value for incorrect judgements (9) was higher than the expected value (6.5), while for correct judgements it was lower (observed = 1 and expected = 3.5). This tells us that when using a mobile phone participants made more incorrect and fewer correct judgements than we would expect by chance alone. You can see that the opposite pattern is true for the passenger condition. The question we now need to ask is whether the difference between the observed and expected values is large enough, and that is exactly the question that the chi-square test will answer.

Figure 8.3   When I said you should ask for directions, I didn't mean phone a friend!

2.4 Probability

Rather than simply providing an answer such as 'yes, this is a real difference', the output of inferential statistical tests (including the chi-square) is a 'probability value'. Probability is, as it sounds, to do with how probable something is. You might be aware that gambling is based on calculating probability. In a casino, for example, the owners can easily calculate the probability that the ball will land on a particular number on a roulette wheel. If there are 38 numbers on the wheel, then the probability that the ball will land on any particular number is 1 in 38. Likewise, the chance that a flipped coin will come down as 'heads' is 1 in 2, or the chance that a rolled dice will show a '4' is 1 in 6. In research, it is usual to express probabilities as a 'proportion'. Just like a percentage is a score expressed as being 'out of 100', a proportion is a score expressed as being 'out of 1'. This means that a chance of 1 in 1 would be expressed as a percentage of 100 per cent or a proportion of 1. Table 8.5 shows how a variety of different probabilities would be expressed as a percentage and as a proportion.

Table 8.5 Expressing probability as percentages and proportions

Chance	Percentage	Proportion
1 in 1	100%	1.0
1 in 2	50%	.5
1 in 5	20%	.2
1 in 10	10%	.1
1 in 20	5%	.05
1 in 100	1%	.01

Inferential statistical tests tell us the probability that the results of our experiment were due to sampling error; in other words, the probability that our results happened by chance alone. Psychologists have decided that any result that has a probability equal to or lower than .05 (i.e. a 1 in 20 chance, or a percentage chance of 5%) should be considered 'statistically significant'. In other words, psychologists are saying that if the result is more than .05, it is too likely that the result could have happened by chance alone. It is important to remember that the result of the inferential statistical test is simply telling us how likely it is to get that particular pattern of data. It does not tell us anything about how well the research was designed and conducted. For a result to be meaningful, the research must have been carefully designed and rigorously conducted; the participants need to have been randomly sampled and allocated; and the result of the inferential statistical test must be lower than .05. When we judge a piece of quantitative research, therefore, we have to consider the whole study, not just the outcome of the statistical tests.

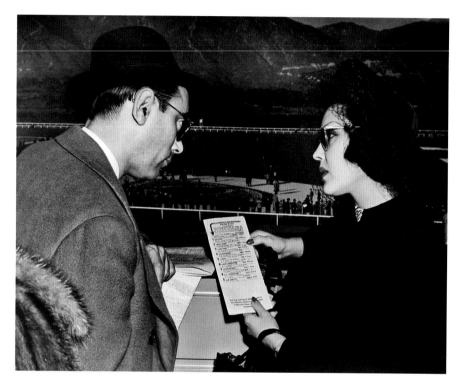

Figure 8.4   'How's your horse doing?' 'Well, he went out at 5 to 1.' '5 to 1? Those are really good odds.' 'The problem is that all the other horses went out at half past twelve!'

Rather than use the words 'lower than' or 'greater than' when reporting the results of an inferential statistical test, it is standard practice to use the symbols '<' and '>'.

- '<' means 'less than'. For example, '4 < 5' means '4 is less than 5'. Note that the symbol looks like an arrow that is pointing at the smaller value. If you see '$p < .05$' in a research report, it means 'the probability was less than .05'.

- '>' means 'greater than'. For example, '5 > 4' means '5 is greater than 4'. Note that again the symbol looks like an arrow that is pointing at the smaller value. If you see '$p > .05$' in a research report, it means 'the probability was greater than .05'.

If the results of the inferential statistical analysis reveal a probability value of .05 or smaller, we can conclude that they are statistically significant. This means we can accept our hypothesis (in other words, what we predicted did indeed happen). However, if the results of our inferential statistical test reveal a probability value of more than .05 (even if it is .06), we conclude that they are not statistically significant. This means we must reject our hypothesis (as our predicted outcome did not happen).

Let's look at an example from Bakheit et al. (2007) (described in Chapter 7). They report their key result by saying 'There was very strong evidence of overall differences between the groups in the median percentage increase in the Western Aphasia Battery scores at all assessment weeks ...' (Bakheit et al., 2007, p. 945). They follow this statement by explaining what inferential statistical test they used, and reporting its result as:

$p < .001$

Is this result statistically significant? All you have to do is determine whether '.001' is greater or less than '.05' – as .05 is the level that researchers have decided constitutes a statistically significant result. In this case, .001 is less than .05, so the result is statistically significant.

> Another way to remember the direction of the symbols '<' and '>' is that the bigger side of the symbol goes next to the bigger number, the smaller (pointed) side goes next to the smaller number. So, in $p > .05$, the bigger side of the symbol is next to p so p must be bigger than .05. In $p < .05$, the smaller side of the symbol is next to p so p must be smaller than .05.

Activity 8.3

Which of the following probability values are statistically significant? Hint: if the value is less than .05 then it is statistically significant.

A $p > .05$

B $p < .001$

C $p > .1$

D $p < .025$

E $p > .25$

F $p = .055$

G $p = .99$

The answer is that only B and D are statistically significant. You may have been tempted to say that answer F was statistically significant, but as .055 is greater than .05 (in the same way that 55 is greater than 50), it is not statistically significant. If you found this confusing, you might find it helpful to revisit the online activities *Chi-square* and *Working with numbers.*

In Activity 8.3, you may have noticed that the less than symbol '<' was used when the result was statistically significant, and the greater than symbol '>' and equals symbol '=' were used when it was not statistically significant. This is the convention used in most academic journals.

Box 8.2   Testing for differences – the null hypothesis

Throughout this book you have been reading that quantitative research tests hypotheses. This is done, though, by testing something called the 'null hypothesis'. Remember that a hypothesis makes a prediction about results, be that a prediction about a difference caused by the effect of the IV on the DV, or a prediction about an association – a correlation – between variables. Inferential statistical analyses are conducted to see whether, in fact, that prediction is supported by the data.

These inferential tests all follow the same principle: they calculate the likelihood of these particular results occurring *if there was no difference or correlation.* In other words, inferential tests start with the premise that there is no meaningful difference or association, and then they calculate how plausible it is that you would get the results you did, if that was the case. This starting point, that there is nothing going on between the variables, is known as the null hypothesis. Therefore, the inferential statistics actually test the null hypothesis. Don't worry if this is confusing at the moment; you will be able to return to these concepts later in your studies. For now, you might find it easier to think of inferential statistics as calculating how likely it is that a particular set of results will occur by chance. If the probability that they would occur *by chance* is less than .05, then you have a statistically significant result.

2.5   Effect size

The probability value is extremely important when conducting quantitative psychological research, and researchers certainly wait with bated breath to find out if their results are statistically significant or not. However, whether a particular result is statistically significant or not does not tell you anything about the 'size' of the result. The size of a result does not have to be 'big' to be significant. For example, if you have a sufficiently large sample and those in one condition consistently perform better than those in another condition, then even a difference of 1 per cent between the groups can be statistically significant. In other words, a result might be *statistically* significant but be quite insignificant in reality. Imagine, for example, that you have been asked to invest a lot of time and money in a reading project that would improve reading speeds because studies have found a statistically significant effect. You would want to know the *size* of the effect, in this case by how much reading speeds were increased, before you decided whether it was a valuable investment. Therefore, if your result is statistically significant, it is important to also report the size of the difference between your conditions. This is done by reporting both the probability value and an estimate of what is known as 'effect size'.

Effect sizes can be very useful when evaluating the practical importance of research findings. For example, imagine that a school is producing a new curriculum and it is reviewing recent research to help design the lesson plans. There are likely to be many studies describing new teaching techniques that have had statistically significant results. Should the school simply choose the technique that has the most statistically significant result? The answer is that the school really wants to know not only whether the new technique will work, but by how much it will improve learning. This is exactly what effect size is used for. By looking at both statistical significance and effect size, the school can select a technique that has been shown to be likely to work, and also one that will benefit its students the most.

You can find out more about effect size in the online activity *Chi-square*.

In Section 3, we will explore a piece of research that was analysed using the chi-square test and look again at how to understand and report what the test tells us.

Summary

- Inferential statistics make use of knowledge of how data are distributed (such as the normal distribution) and produce a probability value that tells us the likelihood that the results could have occurred by chance alone.

- There are different inferential statistical tests to accommodate the different types of studies and data.

- For each inferential test there is also a measure of effect size, which describes the magnitude of the difference between the conditions.

3 Reporting the results of an experiment

In this section, we will look at a study on change blindness, but first I will explain what this means. Change blindness is the term used to describe a situation in which someone fails to notice that a key element of their surroundings (such as the identity of the person right in front of them) has changed. One of the most important experiments on change blindness was conducted by Simons and Levin (1998), who designed a study in which one researcher initiated a conversation with the participant. After about 15 seconds, two other researchers carrying a door pushed between the first researcher and the participant so that their view of one another was blocked. While the view was blocked, the first researcher swapped places with one of the researchers carrying the door. Once the door had passed, this other researcher then continued the conversation with the participant. Only seven of the 15 participants noticed that the person they were having a conversation with had changed; the other eight participants continued the conversation with this other researcher as if nothing had happened! In other words, those eight participants were 'blind' to the 'change' that had taken place.

Figure 8.5   Frames taken from a video of one person participating in the Simons and Levin (1998) study. Frames a–c show the sequence of the switch. Frame d shows the two experimenters side by side (Source: Simons and Levin, 1998)

Box 8.3   Inattentional blindness

A further aspect of attention which powerfully demonstrates the limitations of the human mind is something known as 'inattentional blindness'. This is demonstrated in the film *Researching attention* (The Open University, 2014) on the module website. If you haven't seen the film yet, it is worth having a look now before reading any further: the tasks in studies of inattentional blindness are quite fun to do and the effect can be ruined once you know what is going on.

If you have seen the film, you will know that inattentional blindness is the term used to describe a situation in which someone fails to notice something that happens right in front of them. In other words, although they can perceive what is happening perfectly well, they do not attend to it. Probably the most famous demonstration of inattentional blindness is known as the 'gorilla in the midst'. Simons and Chabris (1999) conducted a study in which participants watched a film that began with two teams of players (one wearing white shirts and the other black) each passing a ball between the members of that team. The participants were asked to count how many times the members of one of the teams passed the ball. About 45 seconds into the film, a woman wearing a gorilla costume enters the scene from the left, walks through the teams of players and exits to the right. Overall, just 44 per cent of participants noticed the woman in the gorilla suit. This means that over half of the participants must have seen the gorilla (in that they were looking at the screen when she appeared) but failed to attend to it to the extent that they did not even notice it!

Figure 8.6   A single frame showing the gorilla walking across the scene (Source: Simons and Chabris, 1999. Figure provided by Daniel Simons)

3.1   Nelson et al. (2011): an experiment on 'change blindness' and eyewitness identification

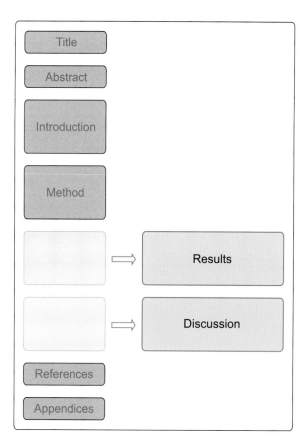

Figure 8.7   Report-writing template: locating the Results and Discussion sections

Let's now look at the study on change blindness by Nelson et al. (2011). I will focus on how inferential statistics are presented and discussed in a research report. Before I do that, it is important to understand what was done in the experiment.

So, prior to looking in detail at extracts from the Results and Discussion section, we will begin by looking at how the experiment was conducted, and at an extract from the Method (the Design subsection).

The experiment consisted of showing 717 participants one of four videos. All four videos consisted of a female student, who ceases studying in a student lounge and leaves to purchase a drink. While she is out of the room, another woman (Actor A) enters, picks up a book and heads towards the exit, only to stop by the student's table. After looking around to see if anyone can see her, she takes some money from the student's table, puts it inside her own book and leaves the room. In two of the videos the amount taken by the woman is just $5 (a low severity crime), while in the other two it is $500 (a high severity crime). Two different endings were also filmed: in the first, involving 'no change', Actor A leaves the room, turns a corner and walks through an exit; and in the other, involving a 'change', when Actor A turns the corner she is replaced by a second woman of similar appearance (Actor B). Table 8.6 shows how the four films used in the Nelson et al. study were constructed.

Table 8.6   How the four films in Nelson et al. (2011) were constructed

Film		Severity of crime		Change or no change
1	Actor A leaves the room and turns a corner	Actor A takes $5	Female student leaves the room and Actor A enters	Actor A is seen leaving
2		Actor A takes $5		Actor B is seen leaving
3		Actor A takes $500		Actor A is seen leaving
4		Actor A takes $500		Actor B is seen leaving

Activity 8.4

From the description in Table 8.6, can you work out what the IVs were in this experiment? It might be a little more complicated than usual because there are two IVs. See if you can identify them, and also state what the conditions were.

The four films were created by making adaptations at two points:

- Actor A either took $5 or $500 – this IV is called 'crime seriousness'
- Either Actor A or Actor B was seen leaving – this IV is called 'no change vs. actor change'.

So, in this study, the researchers were manipulating the seriousness of the crime and whether a change in actors was made. Below is the Design section from the Nelson et al. (2011) article, which describes the IVs. Note that the authors refer to participants as 'subjects'. You may remember that Banyard (2012) explained that this is now uncommon in psychological reports. Note also that the authors do not refer explicitly to 'independent variables'. Instead, they use a different way of describing an experiment that has more than one IV – a 2 × 2 design – this term is commonly used in psychological research. If you go on to study psychology at a higher level, this will be explained in detail, but for now just note that the two IVs are provided in parentheses, and these follow a statement of how many conditions were part of that IV.

Design

In a 2 (crime seriousness) × 2 (no change vs. actor change) design, subjects were randomly assigned to view one of four different 2-min videos of a confederate committing a crime. Half the videos depicted a relatively more serious crime (theft of $500), and half a relatively less serious crime (theft of $5). Further, half (the two 'no change' videos) depicted only one actor (Actor A) in the vicinity of the crime, whereas the other half (the two 'actor change' videos) depicted two actors. In the actor change videos, Actor A turns a corner after stealing the money and is out of sight for 1 s, whereupon Actor B replaces Actor A. In the no change videos, Actor A turns a corner after stealing the money and is also out of sight for 1 s.

(Nelson et al., 2011, p. 66)

In the extract, the abbreviation 's' refers to seconds.

Did you spot anything missing from the Design section above? As well as not stating explicitly whether the design was between-participants or within-participants, the authors also did not mention what the DV was. Instead, they included details of the DVs (there was also more than one DV) in the Results section.

Between-participants and within-participants designs are explained in Chapter 3 of *Investigating Methods*.

This is a good example of the way in which experienced researchers often do not abide by standard reporting conventions, but instead move information around to fit the particular study being reported. Although this happens a lot in published articles, it is rather annoying when you are searching an article for a particular piece of information – which is one good reason why psychology students are taught to stick as rigidly as possible to the report template they are given.

3.2 The results of Nelson et al. (2011)

Let's look at what the DVs were. In this experiment, the DVs corresponded to the questions that the researchers asked the participants after they had watched the film.

The first set of questions was to see whether the participant was able to identify Actor A, who they had seen take the money in the film. A line-up was constructed containing pictures of six women of similar appearance. Pictures of Actor A and Actor B were included in the line-up along with pictures of four other women not seen in the film (known as 'foils'). The second set of questions was aimed at discovering whether participants in the 'change' condition had noticed that the woman seen walking through the exit was not the same woman who was seen taking the money. In addition, the participants were asked questions to make sure that they did not know any of the people in the film or anything about the phenomenon of change blindness.

We will be looking at two aspects of the results of Nelson et al. (2011). First, we will look at the results from the participants allocated to the 'actor change' condition, where Actor A was replaced with Actor B, to see how many participants detected the change. Second, we will look at the results from participants in both conditions (change and no change) to see how well they performed when asked to do the line-up test.

The part of the Results section we will look at first concentrated on the questions that explored whether participants detected the change in the actor. The results of the inferential statistical tests conducted have been reported according to the standard convention, and look like this, '$\chi^2(1, N=516) = 5.07, p=.02$'. Figure 8.8 indicates what each part of this result relates to and we will look in more detail at how to interpret this information in Chapter 9 (including the term 'degrees of freedom'). For now, don't worry if it seems confusing as you can ignore the symbols and numbers and instead concentrate on the text that precedes them and which states in (fairly) plain English whether the results of the inferential statistical test were statistically significant or not.

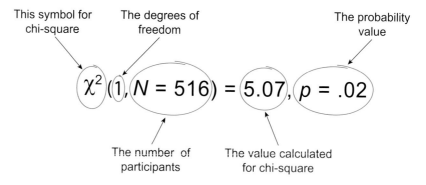

Figure 8.8   Interpreting the results of a chi-square test

Results

Change detection

Of the 374 people in the actor change conditions, only 17 (4.5%) detected a change when Actor B took the place of Actor A (a much smaller proportion than that found in previous studies of change blindness). Therefore, 95% of the subjects in the actor change conditions did not detect the change in actors. Although 17 subjects is too few to carry out many of the statistical comparisons used in previous change blindness research, we note that six of these subjects said that the perpetrator was not in the lineup, nine (82%) of the remaining subjects accurately identified the perpetrator (Actor A), and just one (9%) incorrectly identified the distracter (Actor B). If we compare the accuracy (correct or not, which includes 'I *don't know*' responses) of the 11 participants who noticed the change (and made a selection from the lineup) to the 505 who did not, then, as expected those participants who noticed the change were more likely to select the perpetrator from the lineup, $\chi^2(1, N = 516) = 5.07, p = .02$.

...

Crime severity did not affect whether or not subjects noticed the change. Six percent of participants in the low severity actor change conditions noticed the change, while 3% in the high severity actor change conditions noticed the change, $\chi^2(1, N = 374) = 1.93, p = .16$.

(Nelson et al., 2011, p. 69)

Your first impression of the Results section above might have been that it contains a great deal of information that is packed into a small space. This was my impression too, and I found myself wishing that the authors had included a table of the results, so that I could more clearly see what they found. To help, so that you can see all the relevant figures together in one place and make comparisons between them easily, I've constructed Table 8.7.

Table 8.7 The decision made about the line-up by participants in the 'Change' condition

Did the participant notice the change in actor?	Chose Actor A	Chose Actor B	Chose a foil	Said they didn't know	Said the person wasn't in the line-up	Total
Yes – noticed change	9	1	1	0	6	17
No – didn't notice	92	98	65	18	84	357

The table makes it much easier to see how many participants noticed, and did not notice, the change in actor, and also what decisions they made when shown the line-up.

The extract from Nelson et al. (2011) starts by telling us that there were 374 participants in the conditions where a change in actor took place and only 17 of these people noticed the change (which is just 4.5 per cent of 374). This is a much lower percentage than most previous change blindness research. For example, Simons and Levin (1998) found that 7 of the 15 participants (or 47 per cent) noticed the change in researcher. Nelson et al. (2011) explain that having such a low number of participants who noticed the change precludes them using the statistical analyses employed in previous change blindness research. They then go on to describe the data in the first row of Table 8.7, which shows that these participants tended to either correctly identify Actor A as the perpetrator (9 participants) or say that they didn't think the perpetrator was in the line-up (6 participants).

The authors then focus on those participants who identified someone from the line-up, meaning those who chose Actor A, Actor B or a foil. Using a chi-square test, they compared the 11 participants who both noticed a change and chose someone with the 505 participants (across all conditions) who did *not* notice a change but did choose someone. The results showed that the 11 participants who noticed the change were statistically significantly ($p = .02$) more likely to choose the correct person (Actor A) from the line-up than the 505 participants who did not notice the change.

The final analysis, also using chi-square, explored whether the severity of the crime had an effect on whether or not participants noticed the change in actor. The results were not statistically significant ($p = .16$).

Activity 8.5

The authors do not explicitly state any hypotheses, but based on the results they report, would you accept or reject the following hypotheses?

1   Participants who notice the change in actor will be more likely to select the perpetrator from the line-up.

2   The severity of the crime will affect the participants' accuracy of identification.

Remember that to accept the hypothesis the results of the inferential statistical test must be statistically significant, which means the probability value reported must be less than .05.

In answer to hypothesis 1, the relevant section of the results says 'those participants who noticed the change were more likely to select the perpetrator from the line-up, $\chi^2(1, N = 516) = 5.07, p = .02$'. As the probability value is less than .05 (it is actually equal to .02), then this result is statistically significant and the hypothesis can be accepted.

For hypothesis 2, the report of the chi-square test of whether crime severity affected identification accuracy was '$\chi^2(1, N = 374) = 1.96$, $p = .16$'. As the probability value is greater than .05 (it is actually equal to .16), then this result is not statistically significant and the hypothesis must be rejected.

The final part of the Results section tackles a worrying type of error that a real eyewitness might make, which is whether it is possible to make a misidentification, i.e. to identify an innocent person. Nelson et al. (2011) looked to see if people confused the identity of the perpetrator with someone else they saw at the crime scene.

Misidentification

In the no change conditions, 29% of subjects misidentified someone in the lineup and a further 7% selected 'I don't know if the perpetrator is pictured in the lineup' ... In the actor change conditions, the misidentification rate rose to 58%, and a further 6% stated that they didn't know who the perpetrator was. In the no change conditions, the proportion of subjects who misidentified each foil varied, from just 0.4% ($N = 1$) to 13% ($N = 30$), but the distracter (Actor B) was not the most popular foil (selected by 9 per cent of participants; $N = 21$).

In the actor change conditions, subjects were as likely to identify the innocent actor (Actor B; 35%) as the actual perpetrator (Actor A; 36%). Subjects in the actor change conditions were also more likely to pick Actor B (the distracter) from the lineup than any other foil, by more than two to one (35% of subjects chose Actor B, 15% chose the next most common foil). Crime severity did not contribute significantly to whether those in the actor change condition picked the innocent Actor B: 21% versus 25% for the high and low severity conditions, respectively, $\chi^2(1, N = 516) = 1.41, p = .24$.

(Nelson et al., 2011, p. 70)

The first two sentences of the extract above report the number of misidentifications made by participants in the no change condition and those in the actor change condition. A smaller percentage (29 per cent) of participants in the no change condition made a misidentification compared with participants in the actor change condition (58 per cent). Of those who said they didn't know if the perpetrator was pictured in the line-up, the numbers were similar in both conditions (7 per cent in the no change condition and 6 per cent in the actor change condition).

The authors then looked at which specific photo was being chosen when the participants made a misidentification. In the no change condition, Actor B was not the photo most often chosen. Remember that participants in the no change condition had never seen Actor B before, so for them she was just another foil. Although this may seem like an odd thing to have looked at, the reasons the authors did so was to show that there was nothing distinctive about Actor B that might make participants choose her. In the actor change condition, where the participants had seen her, Actor B was not only by far the most chosen of the foils, but was chosen (35 per cent) nearly as often as Actor A (36 per cent). In other words, the participants in the actor change condition did seem to be confusing the identity of the actual perpetrator with someone else who had also been present at the crime scene, even though she was innocent.

In the final sentence of the extract, the authors used chi-square to test whether crime severity affected the decisions made by participants in the actor change condition. The results showed that 21 per cent of participants in the high severity condition picked Actor B, while 25 per cent of participants in the low severity condition picked Actor B – this difference was not statistically significant ($p = .24$).

From the 'Misidentification' subsection of the Results section we can, therefore, tell that:

- participants in the actor change condition were less likely to identify the perpetrator than those in the no change condition
- participants in the actor change condition were as likely to identify the innocent actor (Actor B) from the line-up as they were to identify the perpetrator (Actor A)
- crime severity did not affect whether participants in the actor change condition picked the innocent actor (Actor B) or not.

3.3 Discussing the results of Nelson et al. (2011)

Let's have a look at how Nelson et al. (2011) discussed these results. Below, the first part of the Discussion section from the article has been reproduced. The extract has been divided into paragraphs, with some additional explanation between them. The Discussion makes reference to something called 'unconscious transference', which in this context is a phenomenon whereby a witness (unconsciously) identifies an innocent person because they have seen them somewhere else. For example, Deffenbacher et al. (2006) showed that witnesses can select someone from a line-up not because they saw them commit the crime, but because they had previously seen their face in a mugshot album. They had unconsciously transferred the memory of the face from the mugshot album into their memory of the crime.

Discussion

Misidentification and identification accuracy

Although only 17 people detected a change in actors in the actor change conditions (about 5% of people who were exposed to this change), more than a third of subjects in the actor change conditions identified the second actor (which was equivalent to the proportion of subjects who correctly identified the perpetrator). It is clear that unconscious transference, as a result of change blindness, is a problem when identifying perpetrators of a crime. In situations where a witness does not notice that an innocent person has replaced a perpetrator in a visual scene, he or she is likely to (incorrectly) identify that innocent person. Because Actor B was not the foil most often chosen by subjects in the no change conditions, we conclude that the higher misidentification rate for Actor B in the actor change conditions was not the result of Actors A and B appearing too similar.

(Nelson et al., 2011, p. 70)

This first paragraph of the Discussion describes the main findings of the study, namely that just 17 participants noticed that the actor seen at the end of the film (Actor B) was not the same person as was seen taking the money (Actor A). Even though only about 5 per cent of the participants in the actor change condition actually noticed the change, over a third of participants chose Actor B from the line-up. The authors suggest that this was because of unconscious transference – these participants were not conscious of the change, nor that they had seen Actor B previously but not committing the crime. This could be a problem in real life where a witness confuses an innocent person with the perpetrator at or near the scene of the crime. For example, if the perpetrator runs into a crowd and the witness loses sight of them for a second, they might then see an innocent person and think they were the perpetrator. Another potential explanation for the large number of participants picking Actor B in the current study could be that Actor B looks very similar to Actor A. However, it is very unlikely that this is the case as Actor B was not chosen by participants in the no change condition more than the other foils.

Another critical finding is that while more than half of subjects in the no change condition were accurate in their identifications of the perpetrator (64%), when Actor B replaced Actor A in the actor change conditions, this accuracy rate dropped significantly (to 36%). Subjects in the no change conditions were exposed to Actor A for a longer period of time than the subjects in the actor change conditions (40 s compared to 30 s). This might be one reason why more people correctly identified the perpetrator in the no change conditions. Another possible explanation is that the phenomenon of unconscious transference was in play. Subjects in the actor change conditions were exposed to an innocent actor (Actor B) immediately after they witnessed a crime committed by a guilty actor (Actor A). Because these subjects subsequently claimed that there were only two individuals in the video that actually contained three people (the victim, the guilty Actor A, and the innocent Actor B), there is evidence that they likely inferred that the perpetrator and the innocent actor were the same person, and as a result, identified the innocent actor rather than the actual perpetrator.

(Nelson et al., 2011, p. 70)

The paragraph above looks at the result that although 64 per cent of participants in the no change condition correctly identified Actor A as the perpetrator, only 36 per cent of participants in the actor change condition did so. The authors point out that Actor A was seen for a longer period of time in the no change condition (40 seconds) compared with the actor change condition (30 seconds) and that this could explain the difference in correct identifications. However, they suggest that unconscious transference is a more likely explanation, because 95 per cent of participants in the actor change condition were not aware of the change. In other words, they thought that Actor A and Actor B were the same person. Hence Actor B was selected as often as Actor A.

So, the experiment conducted by Nelson et al. (2011) found an interesting result that has important implications for a real world situation, as it shows that eyewitnesses are capable of identifying an innocent person just because they see them at the crime scene. In *Investigating Psychology*, Chapter 9, we will explore applied research on eyewitnesses further and see how psychology can help us understand, and even improve, the evidence they provide.

3.4   Writing the Results section

We have already seen that the Nelson et al. (2011) article deviates from the standard reporting template. For example, I noted in Section 3.1 that the DVs were reported in the Results section rather than in the Design subsection of the Method section. Their Results section also deviates from the norm; for example, by structuring the results to deal with one DV at a time. While it is still the case that most of the information we would expect to see in a Results section is present, it was difficult in places to identify that information. Therefore, when you are writing a Results section for your own research reports, you should follow the standard template, as follows.

- Restate the hypothesis.
- Describe the data that was collected.
- Report descriptive statistics (as either a table or a graph).
- Describe what the descriptive statistics tell us about the data.
- State what inferential statistical analysis was conducted.
- Report the results of the inferential statistical analysis in the conventional form.
- State whether the result was statistically significant or not.
- State whether the hypothesis can be accepted or rejected.

Summary

- 'Change blindness' is a phenomenon whereby a person sees a change in their environment but does not notice it.
- Nelson et al. (2011) conducted an experiment that used change blindness to study eyewitness identification. They found that many participants failed to notice that the identity of a perpetrator had changed, and so this could lead to an innocent person being picked out of a line-up.
- The extracts from Nelson et al. (2011) highlight how the results of inferential statistics are reported.

4 A different type of inferential statistic: the *t*-test

Previous chapters in this book have concluded by looking at a different way of researching the area of psychology explored in that chapter. Rather than do that here, we are going to stick with the Nelson et al. (2011) study and look at a different inferential statistical test. In Section 2.2, we saw that there are different inferential statistics, and that each one has been designed for a particular situation. In determining which statistical test to use for analysing data from experiments, two of the most important questions to answer are:

- What type of quantitative data were collected?

- How many IVs and conditions were there?

As you saw in Section 3, the inferential statistical test used by Nelson et al. (2011) was the chi-square test. This statistical test was employed because nominal data were collected, and chi-square is the appropriate inferential test to use when analysing nominal data.

Remember that the nominal data collected were the identification accuracy data, where participants could either be 'correct' or 'incorrect', and the noticing change data, where they could either 'notice it' or 'not notice it'. We can assign numerical values to these outcomes ('1' for correct and '2' for incorrect, for example), but the numbers are simply being used as labels – and it really does not matter what number we assign as the label. Instead, what matters is how many participants end up in each category, as this constitutes the observed values. The chi-square test then compares these observed values with the expected values ('observed' and 'expected' values were explained in Section 2.3).

However, in addition to questions regarding which person in the line-up was the perpetrator and whether the participant noticed the change in actor, Nelson et al. also asked those participants who selected someone from the line-up how confident they were that they had made a correct decision (with a higher score indicating greater confidence). These data required a different inferential statistical test than the chi-square. This is because the data collected in answer to this additional question are not nominal, as the numbers represented an actual quantity. For example, a value of '7' would indicate *more* confidence than would a value of '2'. This means that the data are ordinal and so the chi-square test cannot be used. Nelson et al. (2011) reported that the mean confidence of those participants who correctly identified the perpetrator was 5.01 (with a standard deviation of 1.38), and 4.24 (with a standard deviation of 1.68) for those participants who identified the wrong person. This meant that those participants who correctly identified the perpetrator were more confident in their decision than participants who identified the wrong person or who said the perpetrator was not in the line-up. In order to decide whether this difference was statistically significant, the authors needed to conduct an inferential statistical test suitable for ordinal data, and one which was also suitable for an IV with two conditions (confidence when correct identification made, and confidence when incorrect identification made). The authors analysed these data using a *t*-test (introduced in Section 2.2), which gave a probability value of '$p < .001$', meaning the difference between the conditions was statistically significant.

Some statisticians argue that a t-test is not a good test to use with ordinal data but, as you can see, some researchers do use it in this way. For now, just remember that the t-test cannot be used with nominal data.

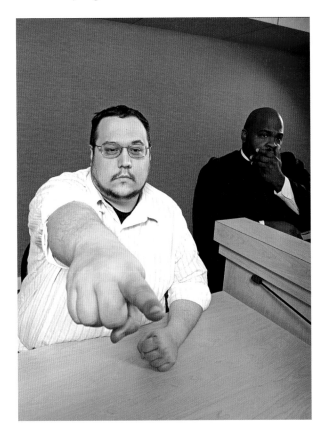

Figure 8.9 It was you!

Even though a different inferential statistical test was used, it was reported in a very similar fashion to the chi-square test you saw in the extract of the Results section: $t(496.59) = 5.64, p < .001, r\mathrm{pb}_2 = .07$

(Nelson et al, 2011, p. 69). To aid comparison, the results of this *t*-test are shown in Figure 8.10, along with the results of one of the chi-square tests from Nelson et al. (2011), and what each part means.

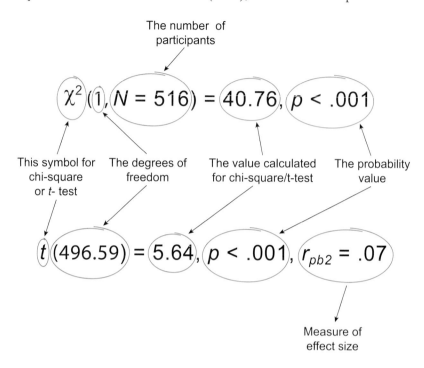

Figure 8.10   Interpreting the results of chi-square and a *t*-test

Both results in Figure 8.10 start with a symbol indicating which test was used (χ^2 and *t*). They then have some numbers in brackets, which indicate something called 'the degrees of freedom' that we will explore in Chapter 9, and then, following an equals sign (=), another number which is the value calculated by the statistical test. Next there is a '*p*', which stands for probability, followed by a 'less than' symbol (<) and then another value. This value indicates the probability that the results were due to chance. This value is the one that must be .05 or less for the result to be considered statistically significant. Lastly, the *t*-test has a final symbol (r_{pb2}) and value (.07), which provide a measure of effect size – the chi-square should really have one of these too but it wasn't reported!

As you can see, although the convention for reporting inferential statistics can seem very complex, essentially the same information is provided for all tests. We will come back to this in Chapter 9.

Summary

- The chi-square statistical test can be used to analyse nominal data collected from either a correlational study or an experiment.

- The *t*-test statistical test is commonly used to look for a difference between two conditions when the data are not nominal.

References

Bakheit, A. M. O., Shaw, S., Carrington, S. and Griffiths, S. (2007) 'The rate and extent of improvement with therapy from the different types of aphasia in the first year after stroke', *Clinical Rehabilitation*, vol. 21, no. 10, pp. 941–9.

Banyard, P. (2012) 'Just following orders?', in Brace, N. and Byford, J. (eds) *Investigating Psychology*, Oxford, Oxford University Press/Milton Keynes, The Open University.

Deffenbacher, K. A., Bornstein, B. H. and Penrod, S. D. (2006) 'Mugshot exposure effects: retroactive interference, mugshot commitment, source confusion, and unconscious transference', *Law and Human Behavior*, vol. 30, no. 3, pp. 287 307.

Edgar, H. and Edgar, G. (2012) 'Paying attention', in Brace, N. and Byford, J. (eds) *Investigating Psychology*, Oxford, Oxford University Press/Milton Keynes, The Open University.

Nelson, K. J., Laney, C., Fowler, N. B., Knowles, E. D. and Loftus, E. F. (2011) 'Change blindness can cause mistaken eyewitness identification', *Legal and Criminological Psychology*, vol. 16, no. 1, pp. 62–74.

Simons, D. J. and Chabris, C. F. (1999) 'Gorillas in our midst: sustained inattentional blindness for dynamic events', *Perception*, vol. 28, pp. 1059–74.

Simons, D. J. and Levin, D. R. (1998) 'Failure to detect changes to people during a real-world interaction', *Psychonomic Bulletin and Review*, vol. 5, no. 4, pp. 644–9.

The Open University (2014) 'Researching attention' [Video], *DE100 Investigating psychology 1*. Available at https://learn2.open.ac.uk/mod/oucontent/view.php?id=476360&section=2 (Accessed 14 May 2014).

Chapter 9
Reporting experiments

Graham Pike

Contents

Aims and objectives

After studying this chapter you should be able to:

- explain how inferential statistics are reported
- understand the concept of degrees of freedom and how to work out the degrees of freedom for reporting a chi-square analysis
- interpret inferential statistics in a published research report
- appreciate the relationship between one- and two-tailed hypotheses
- read and understand an entire published research report
- explain how a research report is structured.

1 Reporting inferential statistics

This final chapter will have a slightly different structure to the previous ones. In this chapter you will have the opportunity to read an entire report, and to reflect on the way reports are structured. First, we will revisit some of the concepts you have been learning about, especially those concerned with reporting and interpreting results from experiments.

1.1 The reporting convention for inferential statistics

We saw in Chapter 8 that in order to tell whether there is a difference between two conditions, and therefore whether we should accept or reject our hypothesis, we need to employ an inferential statistical test. We also saw that it is usual to report this statistical analysis in the Results section of a research report.

Regardless of which inferential statistical test you use, you will find that when it comes to reporting the results, you need to provide the same basic set of information. Unfortunately, the convention in research reports is not to describe the results of the inferential statistical test using plain English, but rather to use a shorthand comprising symbols and numbers. The advantage of this method is that it means all researchers report inferential statistics in the same basic fashion and that quite complex concepts are reported very economically.

Essentially, all inferential statistical tests are described by reporting five basic pieces of information. These are:

- the particular test that was used
- an indication of the sample size and/or the number of conditions (known as 'degrees of freedom')
- the 'value' that the inferential statistical test calculated
- the probability that the result occurred by chance
- an indication of the size of the result (known as 'effect size').

The specific symbols and numbers will vary depending on which inferential statistical test was used, but the report should still follow the principle of reporting these five pieces of information. By now you should be aware that many published research reports do not follow the same conventions, and reporting inferential statistics is no exception to this. For one thing, including an indication of 'effect size' was only added to this list fairly recently, so it is rare to see this in older articles – and indeed many researchers still do not report it today. So, when reading articles you will see deviations from the ideal of showing five pieces of information, but the point is that the seemingly complicated symbols and numbers are just an efficient method of reporting the same information, regardless of the actual statistical test that was used.

Box 9.1   Why is *p* not enough?

The way all inferential statistics work is that the data collected is run through a series of equations. These equations calculate a single value. This value, together with an indication of the sample size and the number of conditions in the experiment, is used to work out a probability value. You might be thinking to yourself, why not simply report the probability value, as that is all you need to know in working out whether to accept or reject your hypothesis? Indeed, you will see in many journal articles that some researchers do just that, particularly when they are reporting lots of statistical tests. However, remember that the report of your research should allow other researchers to replicate your experiment. As well as replicating your methodology, they also need to be able to replicate your analyses, so it is important to include all the details.

In this chapter, we are going to focus on how to understand the results of an inferential statistics test. We will first look at degrees of freedom, which we have not yet properly introduced you to in this book, and then we will look at examples of how inferential statistics are reported in published reports.

1.2   Degrees of freedom

The second piece of information on the reporting convention list in Section 1.1 was:

- An indication of the sample size and/or the number of conditions (known as 'degrees of freedom').

Your response to this item might have been to think, what does 'an indication' mean, why not just list the actual sample size and the actual number of conditions, and what are 'degrees of freedom'? These are very good questions. The answer to why we report the 'degrees of freedom' is a little complicated, and we won't get too bogged down here with the details. However, while degrees of freedom might seem an odd concept at the moment, when you use more complex inferential statistics it makes reporting the results much easier. The reason *why* we need to know the degrees of freedom is that they will affect the probability value (the fourth piece of information on the reporting convention list in Section 1.1).

Degrees of freedom refers to the number of values (the data) in a calculation that are free to vary. For instance, imagine that we have a set of data that is comprised of four values and that we know has a mean of 6.5. In other words, the sum of the values is 26, and this is then divided by 4 to give a mean of 6.5. How many of the values would we need to know before we could say for certain what any remaining values would be? If your instinct is that we would need to know all but one, then well done! In this example, then, the data have three degrees of freedom, as three values can vary. You can think of degrees of freedom as being a bit like cracking a safe where you have worked out what four numbers are needed for the combination lock, but still have to work out what order to enter them in. When you put in the first number, it could be any one of the four. Likewise, you cannot know for certain what the second and third numbers are. However, once you have got the first three correct, you *can* know for certain what the last number is.

The online activity *Chi-square* explains that to work out probability values you need to know the value calculated by the particular statistical test you are using (e.g. chi-square) and the degrees of freedom associated with your study.

Degrees of freedom
A feature of reporting inferential statistics which indicates sample size and/or number of conditions.

Figure 9.1   Cracking degrees of freedom

Let's look in more detail at the example where we have four values with a mean of 6.5. We know the mean of the four values is 6.5, and therefore the total sum of the values must be four times 6.5, which equals 26. So if I told you that the first value was 10, could you say for certain what any of the remaining three values were? You couldn't, as there are many, many combinations of three numbers that when added to 10 would produce a total of 26 and therefore a mean of 6.5. What about if I told you that the first two values were 10 and 5, could you say for certain what the remaining two values were? Again, you couldn't. For example, the remaining two values could be 2 and 9, or 3 and 8 and the mean of all four values would still be 6.5. Okay, so what if I told you the first three values were 10, 5 and 4, now could you say for certain what the remaining value is? This time the answer is 'yes', as there is only one value that would produce a mean of 6.5 if the other values were 10, 5 and 4, and that value is 7. You should be able to imagine that changing the 7 to any other value would also result in the mean being different. So, in this example three of the values are free to vary before the remaining value is fixed. This means the degrees of freedom for these data would be 3.

Another way of saying this is that all but one of the values in a set of data are free to vary – and this can be expressed as $N - 1$ (where N denotes the number of values in the data). Calculating the degrees of freedom in an experiment is sometimes as simple as working out $N - 1$, but the calculation becomes more complicated the more complicated the experiment gets!

If you find the concept of degrees of freedom confusing, then you are not alone. A lot of psychology students struggle with degrees of freedom as a concept, and certainly with how to calculate them. You will not be required to calculate degrees of freedom by hand as part of the assessment on this module, and indeed it is now standard practice in psychology to use a computer programme to analyse quantitative data, and this programme calculates all of the information you need, including degrees of freedom. So, don't worry if you find the concept confusing, just remember the key points that (a) knowing the degrees of freedom is necessary for calculating the probability value (if you have to do it by hand), and (b) degrees of freedom need to be stated when reporting the results of an inferential statistic.

1.3   Degrees of freedom for chi-square

As chi-square deals with nominal data, it would be inappropriate to use a descriptive statistic such as the mean to summarise the data. For example, if I used the number '1' to represent the category of 'Dog owner' and the number '2' to represent 'Does not own a dog', calculating that the mean equalled 1.5 would not be a useful thing to do – it would imply participants were halfway between owning a dog and not owning a dog! Instead, the way we describe the data used in a chi-square test is through a contingency table. Table 9.1 is the contingency table we used in Chapter 8 (Table 8.4a) for the (fictitious) experiment to see whether there is a difference in driving judgements when conducting a conversation with a passenger physically present in the car (passenger condition) compared with conducting a conversation using a mobile phone while driving (mobile phone condition).

Table 9.1   Accuracy of judgement by condition (observed values only)

		Condition	
		Mobile phone	Passenger
Judging the size of the gap	Incorrect	9	4
	Correct	1	6

Imagine that you know there are ten participants in each condition, but you do not know any of the values in Table 9.1. How many are free to vary before the remaining values are fixed? You might be tempted to answer that until you add in three values you could not be certain what any of the remaining values were, but unfortunately it is not that simple. Say that we know that the top left-hand cell (incorrect judgements in the mobile phone condition) contains a 9, don't we then also know for certain that the bottom left cell (correct judgements in the mobile phone condition) must contain a 1? After all, we know that there were ten participants in this condition, so if one cell has a 9 the other must have a 1.

In fact, the calculations for the degrees of freedom in chi-square are based on both the row and column totals being known. In other words, to make the calculations we would start with a contingency table that looks like Table 9.2.

Table 9.2 Accuracy of judgement by condition (row and column totals only)

		Condition		Row total
		Mobile phone	Passenger	
Judging the size of the gap	Incorrect			13
	Correct			7
Column total		10	10	20

In Table 9.2, the moment we know any of the values, the remaining values also become fixed. For example, if we know that the top left-hand cell contains a 9, then the one below it must contain a 1 as the column total is 10 and the value to its right must be 4 as the row total is 13 – and because we then know that the top right-hand cell contains a 4, the bottom right must contain a 6 as the column total is 10. If you have ever done puzzles like Sudoku, then this process will be very familiar to you!

Figure 9.2 Just like some movies, making it in 3D does not make it any better!

So, for a contingency table that contains two rows and two columns, the degrees of freedom are '1'. Say we added a third condition to the experiment consisting of drivers having a conversation alone (i.e. talking to themselves). Now the contingency table looks like Table 9.3.

Table 9.3   Accuracy of judgement with three conditions (row and column totals only)

		Condition			Row total
		Mobile phone	Passenger	Talking to themselves	
Judging the size of the gap	Incorrect				18
	Correct				12
Column total		10	10	10	30

Can you work out how many values are free to vary before the remaining values are fixed? As there are more than two columns, knowing just one value means the other value in that column would be fixed (e.g. knowing the top left-hand cell is 9 fixes the bottom left-hand cell as 1), but not the values in the other columns. However, if we knew one of the values in any two of the columns, then all the remaining values would be fixed – you can either take my word for it, or try placing two values in the table and seeing that you can then work out the others.

Therefore, for a contingency table that has two columns and two rows (known as a 2 ×2 design), the degrees of freedom are 1, and for a contingency table that has three columns and two rows (known as a 3 × 2 design), the degrees of freedom are 2. It turns out that you can work out the degrees of freedom for a contingency table by using the following rule:

- Minus 1 from the number of rows. Minus 1 from the number of columns. Multiply these two numbers together.

Activity 9.1

Can you work out the degrees of freedom for the following?

1 A contingency table that has four columns and three rows (known as a 4 x 3 design).
2 A chi-square with a 4 × 4 design.
3 A contingency table that looks like Table 9.4.

Table 9.4   What are the degrees of freedom for this table?

		Condition		
		Mobile phone	Passenger	Not talking
Confidence in judging the size of the gap	Very			
	Somewhat			
	Not at all			

The answers are as follows.

1   4 columns minus 1 = 3; 3 rows minus 1 = 2; and 3 multiplied by 2 = 6 degrees of freedom.

2   4 − 1 = 3; 4 − 1 = 3; and 3 x 3 = 9 degrees of freedom.

3   There are 3 rows and 3 columns, which gives 4 degrees of freedom.

In reading about degrees of freedom for chi-square and in completing Activity 9.1, you may have noticed that the degrees of freedom were based entirely on how many rows and columns there were, and had nothing to do with the number of participants. If you did, well done, that is exactly right! This poses a problem when reporting the results of a chi-square test, as the same degrees of freedom would be reported regardless of whether the study involved 10 or 10,000 participants. To overcome this limitation, it is standard practice to include both the degrees of freedom and the number of participants when reporting the results of a chi-square. An example of this was provided in Chapter 8 from the Nelson et al. (2011) study. The results of their t-test were reported like this: $t(496.59) = 5.64, p < .001, r\text{pb}_2 = .07$. The value in brackets is the degrees of freedom, and only a single value is needed as the method for reporting the degrees of freedom for the t-test does take into account the number of participants. However, the results of their chi-square were reported like this: $\chi^2 (1, N = 516) = 5.07, p = .01$. The first value in the brackets is the degrees of freedom, but the number of participants (N) has also been stated. When reporting the results of a chi-square it is important to include both the number of participants and the degrees of freedom in this fashion.

Degrees of freedom is therefore a method of reporting an important component of inferential statistics that can be used for both simple and complex designs. You will sometimes see the degrees of freedom abbreviated to 'df' in research reports, and sometimes the convention is to put them in brackets after the value of the particular statistical test.

For example, $t(28) = 7.14$ means that the value for the t-test (t) was 7.14 and there were 28 degrees of freedom. As we saw in the online activity *Chi-square*, once we know these two values we can then work out the probability that this result was due to chance – and the probability value is usually indicated by 'p'. So $t(28) = 7.14$, $p < .01$ means that the value for the t-test (t) was 7.14, there were 28 degrees of freedom and the probability that this result was due to chance alone (p) was less than .01.

Summary

- The results of inferential statistics are all reported using the same five pieces of information.
- One piece of information for reporting inferential statistics is the 'degrees of freedom', which are needed to calculate the probability value.

2   Reporting inferential statistics: a closer look

Although we have now covered all the information used in the standard reporting convention for inferential statistics, it is worth looking at this again in relation to a specific study described in a published research report.

2.1   Reporting an analysis of false memories

In Chapter 9 of *Investigating Psychology*, you read about witnessing and remembering, and particularly how the way a question is asked can lead people to remember different things. Moreover, leading questions can sometimes cause people to remember something that never happened! A study conducted by Ost et al. (2008) explored such 'false memories' further to see whether people who are prone to fantasising are more likely to form a memory about something that didn't happen than people who are less prone to fantasising. Ost and colleagues tested this suggestion by questioning participants from the UK and from Sweden about the media coverage of the terrorist attacks that took place in London on 7 July 2005. This is obviously a sensitive issue, and one that may have affected you personally. We are using the Ost et al. (2008) study here because it is an important piece of research in psychology, informing us about the fallibility of memory. Rather than focus on eyewitness accounts of the event itself, the study is concerned with people's memory of the media coverage surrounding the event.

Ost et al. (2008) explored the memory of their participants by asking them to complete a questionnaire about what they thought they could remember of:

- footage of the aftermath of the explosion
- a non-existent computerised reconstruction of the moment of the explosion
- non-existent closed circuit television (CCTV) footage of the moment of the explosion.

As the computerised reconstruction and CCTV footage did not actually exist, it is not possible that the participants could have had a real memory of them. Below is an extract from the Results section of Ost et al. (2008) which describes some of the key inferential statistical tests that were carried out:

> Of the UK sample, 40% claimed to have seen the non-existent CCTV footage, compared to 16% of the Swedish sample, $\chi^2 (1) = 7.14, p < .01, 28\%$ of the UK sample claimed to have seen a non-existent computerised reconstruction, compared to 6% of the Swedish sample, $\chi^2 (1) = 8.57, p < .01,$; while 84% of the UK sample claimed to have seen any footage of the aftermath, compared to 50% of the Swedish sample, $\chi^2 (1) = 13.07, p < .01.$
>
> (Ost et al., 2008, p. 80)

If you ignore the symbols and numbers that have been used to report inferential statistics, that is, the bits that look like '$\chi^2 (1) = 7.14, p < .01,$', this paragraph is *fairly* easy to understand. For example:

- 40% of UK participants and 16% of Swedish participants said they remembered the non-existent CCTV footage.
- 28% of UK participants and 6% of Swedish participants said they remembered the non-existent computerised reconstruction.
- 84% of UK participants and 50% of Swedish participants said they remembered footage of the aftermath.

From this, it is clear that more of the participants from the UK seem to have formed false memories than participants from Sweden, and also that more participants from the UK remember seeing some footage (regardless of whether it was real or not). I will discuss the details regarding the results of the inferential statistics in Section 2.2, but first I thought you might like to know how the authors account for their findings. Ost et al. (2008) suggest that this difference between the UK and Swedish participants probably resulted because of a phenomenon known as the 'availability heuristic' (Tversky and Kahneman, cited in Ost et al., 2008), which states that errors in memory are likely to increase if more information is available. As UK participants are likely to have been exposed to more media information about the attacks, the availability heuristic suggests that they should also make more errors when remembering.

2.2 Reporting results for inferential statistics

In the extract, Ost et al. (2008) have used descriptive statistics to describe the data they collected, and they have then used inferential statistics to test the differences observed. The particular test they have used is chi-square $\left(\chi^2\right)$, which you were introduced to in Chapter 8, and they have reported the results of the test using the usual convention; for example: $\chi^2 (1) = 7.14, p < .01$. Let's explore this reporting convention further. Remember that the five pieces of information that ideally should be reported are:

- the particular test that was used
- an indication of the sample size and/or the number of conditions (known as 'degrees of freedom')
- the 'value' that the inferential statistical test calculated
- the probability that the result occurred by chance
- an indication of the size of the difference (known as 'effect size').

In the extract above from Ost et al. (2008), three inferential statistics are reported:

- $\chi^2 (1) = 7.14, p < .01$
- $\chi^2 (1) = 8.57, p < .01$
- $\chi^2 (1) = 13.07, p < .01$

You can see that the same information has been reported each time. This information corresponds to four of the five standard parts of the convention we described earlier. No measure of effect size has been included. You will also notice that only the degrees of freedom, and not the number of participants, have been reported. This is probably because the requirement to include the number of participants when reporting chi-square is a fairly recent development in psychology that occurred after the publication of the Ost et al. (2008) study.

Let's match up the symbols and numbers to their corresponding information (see Table 9.5). Remember that is the symbol χ^2 that means the chi-square test; '<' is the symbol that means 'less than'; and '>' is the symbol that means 'more than' (assuming you are reading from left to right).

Table 9.5   The convention for reporting chi-square

Which statistical test was used?	Indicate the degrees of freedom	What value did the test calculate?	What is the probability that this result is due to sampling error?	Indicate the size of the effect
χ^2	1	7.14	$p < .01$	Not reported
χ^2	1	8.57	$p < .01$	Not reported
χ^2	1	13.07	$p < .001$	Not reported

If we were to write out the results of the first inferential analysis in plain language, we would write something like, 'The data were analysed using a chi-square test, which produced a value of 7.14. The degrees of freedom for this test were 1. This test showed that there was less than .01 (or a 1 in 100) probability that the difference between the conditions was due to chance.' You can see that following the convention allows all this information to be presented in a very concise way.

Activity 9.2

Based on the results of these inferential statistical tests, can the following hypotheses be rejected or accepted?

1   More people from the UK will have false memories of CCTV footage than people from Sweden:

$\chi^2 (1) = 7.14, p < .01$

ACCEPT OR REJECT

2   More people from the UK will have false memories of a computerised reconstruction than people from Sweden:

$\chi^2 (1) = 8.57, p < .01$

ACCEPT OR REJECT

3   More people from the UK will have any memory of footage of the aftermath of the attacks compared to people from Sweden:

$$\chi^2 (1) = 13.07, p < .01$$

ACCEPT OR REJECT

If the probability value is less than .05, then we can accept the hypothesis; if it is greater than .05, we must reject the hypothesis. As the probability value reported for each inferential statistical test is less than .05, we can accept all three hypotheses. Remember also that you need to refer back to the descriptive statistics when interpreting inferential statistics. For example, you would only accept the first hypothesis if the probability value was less than .05 *and* if the contingency table (see below) showed that more people from the UK had false memories than people from Sweden.

Table 9.6   The contingency tables for the data from Ost et al. (2008)

	CCTV	
	Yes	**No**
UK	20	30
Sweden	8	42

	Reconstruction	
	Yes	**No**
UK	14	36
Sweden	3	47

	Any footage	
	Yes	**No**
UK	42	8
Sweden	25	25

As can be seen from the contingency table (Table 9.6), more UK participants than Swedish participants reported having a memory of the CCTV and reconstruction footage, as well as any footage of the events.

So, although it can look a little confusing, the convention for reporting inferential statistical tests allows for a great deal of information to be summarised with just a few symbols and numbers. The test used above was chi-square because the data analysed were nominal. For the next part of their study, Ost et al. (2008) needed to apply a different test because they were analysing interval data.

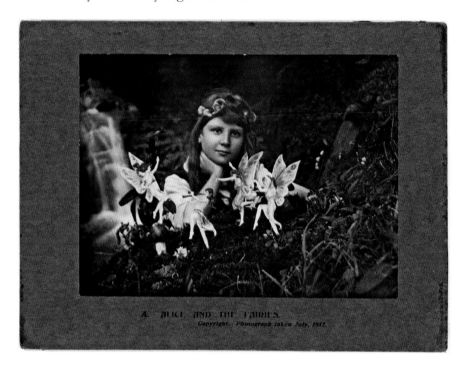

Figure 9.3 Is remembering a fantasy remembering a fantasy or fantasising about a memory?

Ost et al. also wanted to see whether people who were more prone to fantasising, from the UK sample only, would also be more likely to form false memories. They used the Creative Experiences Questionnaire (CEQ) designed by Merckelbach et al. (2001) to measure 'fantasy proneness' (but note that Ost et al. refer to it as the Creative Experiences *Scale*). Ost et al. compared the CEQ scores of participants who claimed to remember a particular detail about the non-existent footage (in this case whether they remembered seeing the bus that was attacked moving or not) with those that said they did not remember. The CEQ produces an overall score which is treated as interval data, with a higher score reflecting a higher level of fantasy proneness. As the data are not nominal, we cannot use chi-square. Instead, we use an inferential statistical test called the '*t*-test', which is commonly used when analysing the results of psychological experiments. The paragraph from the Ost et al. (2008) article describing the analysis of the CEQ data has been reproduced below (note that 'M' refers to 'mean'; and 'SD' refers to 'standard deviation'):

An effect ... was found for participants' scores on the Creative Experiences Scale, with participants who claimed that the bus was, or was not, moving scoring significantly higher (M = 13.33, SD = 4.22) than participants who claimed that they did not remember (M = 10.54, SD = 4.40) $t(31)$ = 2.39, p <. 05, *one-tailed.*

(Ost et al., 2008, p. 82)

As before, if you remove the symbols and numbers to do with the inferential statistic, this paragraph is fairly simple to understand. For example, it states the following.

- The mean score on the CEQ was 13.33 (with a standard deviation of 4.22) for participants who said they remembered whether the bus was or was not moving.

- The mean score on the CEQ was 10.54 (with a standard deviation of 4.40) for participants who said they could not remember whether the bus was or was not moving.

By now you are probably familiar with the idea that simply looking at the descriptive statistics does not tell us whether the differences between the conditions were statistically significant. So, in this case the researchers used a *t*-test to determine this. As with the chi-square, we can put the symbols and numbers reported into our table of standard information (see Table 9.7).

Table 9.7   The convention for reporting a *t*-test

Which statistical test was used?	Indicate the degrees of freedom	What value did the test calculate?	What is the probability that this result is due to chance alone?	Indicate the size of the effect
t	31	2.39	p < .05	Not reported

You can see that exactly the same pieces of information have been reported for the *t*-test that were reported for the chi-square.

On the basis of this test, should the researchers accept or reject their hypothesis that people more prone to fantasising are also more likely to form false memories? As the probability (*p*) value is less than .05, and the descriptive statistics showed that participants who formed false memories had higher CEQ scores on average than those who did not, the result is statistically significant and therefore the hypothesis can be accepted.

2.3 Inferential statistics and one- and two-tailed hypotheses

You may have noticed that the previous extract from Ost et al. (2008) finished with the term 'one-tailed', which was placed after the details of the *t*-test. Previously, you have read that a hypothesis states that the independent variable (IV) will have an effect on the dependent variable (DV). If the hypothesis states that there will be an effect, but not *what* this effect will be, then we refer to it as a 'two-tailed' hypothesis. However, if the hypothesis does state *what* the effect will be then we refer to it as 'one-tailed'.

Figure 9.4 One or two tails?

Below are one- and two-tailed versions of the hypothesis that Ost et al. (2008) would have used.

- Participants who claimed to remember whether the bus was or was not moving will have a higher CEQ score than those participants who did not claim to remember.

- Participants who claimed to remember whether the bus was or was not moving will have a different CEQ score from those participants who did not claim to remember.

The first hypothesis is one-tailed as it makes a prediction about what the effect of the IV will be on the DV– participants who claimed to remember whether the bus was or was not moving will have a higher CEQ score than those participants who did not claim to remember. In this instance, there is only *one* way in which this prediction could be supported: the 'claiming to remember' group must be the group to score higher for the prediction to be supported. To accept this one-tailed hypothesis, our probability value must be below .05 *and* the mean CEQ score for those claiming to remember whether the bus was moving or not must be higher than for those not claiming to remember. Even if the probability value was less than .05, if those claiming to remember had a *lower* CEQ score we would have to reject the hypothesis because it made the prediction that those claiming to remember would have a *higher* CEQ score.

The second hypothesis is two-tailed as it does not make a prediction about what the effect of the IV on the DV will be. It predicts a difference in scores, but not which group will score higher or lower. Therefore, there are *two* possible ways this prediction could be supported; one group could score higher, or the other group could score higher. To accept this two-tailed hypothesis, our probability value must be below .05, but it does not matter which group is higher or lower – only that there is a difference. As your two-tailed hypothesis gives you two chances of supporting your hypothesis, the probability calculations must make an adjustment to allow for this. You will learn more about this if you go on to study further psychology modules.

Summary

- One way in which psychologists have studied false memories is by asking participants to remember the media coverage of an important event, including aspects that the participant could not possibly have seen.

- As inferential statistics are used to test a *hypothesis*, it is important to consider whether the hypothesis is one- or two-tailed.

3   Reporting an experiment

Throughout this book we have covered the sections, conventions and terminology that are used to report psychological experiments in journal articles. In this final chapter, you are provided with a complete journal article to read (Figure 9.5). The article in question is by Loftus and Palmer (1974). This will hopefully be familiar to you as it was the focus of Chapter 9, Section 2, of *Investigating Psychology*. If you are not familiar with the Loftus and Palmer study, you should read that section before proceeding.

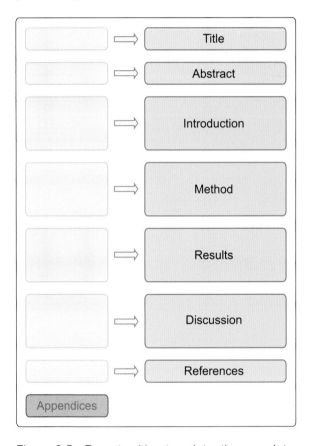

Figure 9.5   Report-writing template: the complete report

Reading journal articles is a skill that you will be developing throughout your studies, so do not worry if you find the article confusing at first. It is likely that the trickier sections will be the Method and Results, as these contain experimental and statistical terminology. Most of this should be familiar to you, and we have provided some additional help with some of the sections – but do not worry if you find yourself referring back to earlier bits of this book to refresh your understanding of terms and concepts.

3.1 Revisiting reporting inferential statistics

The report by Loftus and Palmer (1974) contains three different statistical tests so, before you try to read the whole article, let's try to clarify what tests are used and how to interpret them so that you will know what to expect.

Two experiments are reported in the article. The first experiment explores whether estimates of vehicle speed by witnesses to a crash are influenced by the wording of the question they are asked; and the second explores whether the wording of the question might also cause witnesses to a crash to misremember a key detail. For Experiment 1, Loftus and Palmer report that 'an analysis of variance was performed with verbs as a fixed effect, and subjects and films as random effects, yielding a significant quasi F ratio $F'(5, 55) = 4.65$, $p < .005$' (1974, p. 586). There is a lot of information in this sentence, and some of it (e.g. 'fixed effect' and 'random effects') refers to more advanced terminology that we will not cover in this module. However, some aspects of it might look familiar. The inferential statistical test employed here is known as 'analysis of variance' (often abbreviated to ANOVA), which is a test that is capable of analysing complex data, and is commonly used in psychology. The 'analysis of variance' test produces a statistical test known as an F ratio in the same way that the chi-square test produces a 'chi-square' value and the t-test produces a value for 't'. Like the t-test, analysis of variance is a test used to look for differences between conditions. Whereas the t-test can only be used to look for differences between two conditions, the analysis of variance test can cope with more complex experimental designs with multiple conditions. Although it is a different inferential statistic, you can see in Table 9.8 that the information provided fits the standard information we described earlier.

Table 9.8   The convention for reporting analysis of variance

Which statistical test was used?	Indicate the degrees of freedom – e.g. the size of the sample (s) and/or the number of conditions	What value did the test calculate?	What is the probability that this result is due to chance alone?	Indicate the size of the effect
F	5, 55	4.65	$p < .005$	Not reported

Is the result of this test statistically significant? As the 'p' value is less than .05 (in fact it is smaller than 0.005), the result is statistically significant and we can accept the hypothesis – in this case that the specific word used in the question about speed did affect the estimates of speed provided.

Two inferential statistical tests are employed in Experiment 2, and these are our old friends the 'chi-square' and the 't-test'. Remember that the inferential statistical test employed is based on the type of data (i.e. the level of measurement) and the complexity of the experiment. The 't-test' was used to analyse the data relating to the estimates of speed given in the different conditions. These are interval data. Again, the standard information has been provided in Table 9.9.

Table 9.9   The convention for reporting a t-test

Which statistical test was used?	Indicate the degrees of freedom – e.g. the size of the sample (s) and/or the number of conditions	What value did the test calculate?	What is the probability that this result is due to chance alone?	Indicate the size of the effect
t	98	2.00	$p < .05$	Not reported

As the 'p' value is less than '.05', the result is statistically significant, and the hypothesis can be accepted.

The chi-square was used to analyse the data presented in Loftus and Palmer's Table 2 . Their table shows you how many people answered either 'yes' or 'no' to the question about seeing broken glass, depending on which of the three conditions ('smashed', 'hit' or the control condition) they were assigned to. A chi-square test was used because these data are nominal. Although Loftus and Palmer have not reported the chi-square in the standard format, it is still possible to identify the standard information (see Table 9.10).

Table 9.10   The convention for reporting chi-square

Which statistical test was used?	Indicate the degrees of freedom – e.g. the size of the sample (s) and/or the number of conditions	What value did the test calculate?	What is the probability that this result is due to chance alone?	Indicate the size of the effect
χ^2	2	7.76	$p < .025$	Not reported

Following the inferential statistics, Loftus and Palmer go on to discuss how the probability of falsely remembering the broken glass is affected by both the specific word used in the sentence and the estimate of speed given by that participant. This might be a little confusing, but the key points are covered in Pike and Brace (2012).

When you get to the Results section of the report, try not to feel daunted by the symbols and numbers. Instead, remember that each one is simply providing the standard information given in Tables 9.8, 9.9 and 9.10, and that the key point is whether the probability value calculated by the test is greater or less than .05.

3.2   Reconstruction of automobile destruction (Loftus and Palmer, 1974)

Below is a reproduction of the research report by Loftus and Palmer (1974). The title is: 'Reconstruction of automobile destruction: an example of the interaction between language and memory'. You should now be familiar with the conventions for writing research reports, in particular experimental reports, and will have read an example of each of the individual sections by themselves. While you have read extracts of reports in the earlier chapters, this is the first chapter to include an entire article from start to finish. Don't be put off if there is a particular sentence or section that you find hard going.

Sometimes, continuing reading can be useful, as the information later on might help you to understand the section you found tricky.

Chapter 1 described the usual structure of a research report (and in Section 4 you will be provided with a template to follow when writing sections of your own report for TMA 05). You will notice that there are differences between the structure outline in Chapter 1 and the way that Loftus and Palmer have written and structured their article. Some of these differences are because of the conventions used by the *Journal of Verbal Learning and Verbal Behavior*, which published the report, and some are because Loftus and Palmer are reporting two experiments, and so have two Method, Results and Discussion sections. When completing your TMA, please stick to the template we provide rather than trying to copy the approach taken in this Loftus and Palmer article.

Reconstruction of Automobile Destruction: An Example of the Interaction Between Language and Memory

ELIZABETH F. LOFTUS AND JOHN C. PALMER

University of Washington

Two experiments are reported in which subjects viewed films of automobile accidents and then answered questions about events occurring in the films. The question, "About how fast were the cars going when they smashed into each other?" elicited higher estimates of speed than questions which used the verbs *collided*, *contacted*, or *hit* in place of *smashed*. On a retest one week later, those subjects who received the verb *smashed* were more likely to say "yes" to the question, "Did you see any broken glass?", even though broken glass was not present in the film. These results are consistent with the view that the questions asked subsequent to an event can cause a reconstruction in one's memory of that event.

How accurately do we remember the details of a complex event, like a traffic accident, that has happened in our presence? More specifically, how well do we do when asked to estimate some numerical quantity such as how long the accident took, how fast the cars were traveling, or how much time elapsed between the sounding of a horn and the moment of collision?

It is well documented that most people are markedly inaccurate in reporting such numerical details as time, speed, and distance (Bird, 1927; Whipple, 1909). For example, most people have difficulty estimating the duration of an event, with some research indicating that the tendency is to overestimate the duration of events which are complex (Block, 1974; Marshall, 1969; Ornstein, 1969). The judgment of speed is especially difficult, and practically every automobile accident results in huge variations from one witness to another as to how fast a vehicle was actually traveling (Gardner, 1933). In one test administered to Air Force personnel who knew in advance that they would be questioned about the speed of a moving automobile, estimates ranged from 10 to 50 mph. The car they watched was actually going only 12 mph (Marshall, 1969, p. 23).

Given the inaccuracies in estimates of speed, it seems likely that there are variables which are potentially powerful in terms of influencing these estimates. The present research was conducted to investigate one such variable, namely, the phrasing of the question used to elicit the speed judgment. Some questions are clearly more suggestive than others. This fact of life has resulted in the legal concept of a leading question and in legal rules indicating when leading questions are allowed (*Supreme Court Reporter*, 1973). A leading question is simply one that, either by its form or content, suggests to the witness what answer is desired or leads him to the desired answer.

In the present study, subjects were shown films of traffic accidents and then they answered questions about the accident. The subjects were interrogated about the speed of the vehicles in one of several ways. For example, some subjects were asked, "About how fast were the cars going when they hit each other?" while others were asked, "About how fast were the cars going when they smashed into each other?" As Fillmore (1971) and Bransford and McCarrell (in press) have noted, *hit* and *smashed* may involve specification of differential rates of movement. Furthermore, the two verbs may also involve differential specification of the likely consequences of the events to which they are referring. The impact of the accident is apparently gentler for **hit** than for *smashed*.

Experiment I

Method

Forty-five students participated in groups of various sizes. Seven films were shown, each depicting a traffic accident. These films were segments from longer driver's education films borrowed from the Evergreen Safety Council and the Seattle Police Department. The length of the film segments ranged from 5 to 30 sec. Following each film, the subjects received a questionnaire asking them first to, "give an account of the accident you have just seen," and then to answer a series of specific questions about the accident. The critical question was the one that interrogated the subject about the speed of the vehicles involved in the collision. Nine subjects were asked, "About how fast were the cars going when they hit each other?" Equal numbers of the remaining subjects were interrogated with the verbs *smashed*, *collided*, *bumped*, and *contacted* in place of **hit**. The entire experiment lasted about an hour and a half. A different ordering of the films was presented to each group of subjects.

Results

Table 1 presents the mean speed estimates for the various verbs. Following the procedures outlined by Clark (1973), an analysis of variance was performed with verbs as a fixed effect, and subjects and films as random effects, yielding a significant quasi F ratio, $F'(5, 55) = 4.65$, p < .005.

TABLE 1   SPEED ESTIMATES FOR THE VERBS USED IN EXPERIMENT 1

Verb	Mean speed estimate
Smashed	40.5
Collided	39.3
Bumped	38.1
Hit	34.0
Contacted	31.8

Some information about the accuracy of subjects' estimates can be obtained from our data. Four of the seven films were staged crashes; the original purpose of these films was to illustrate what can happen to human beings when cars collide at various speeds. One collision took place at 20 mph, one at 30, and two at 40. The mean estimates of speed for these four films were: 37.7, 36.2, 39.7, and 36.1 mph, respectively. In agreement with previous work, people are not very good at judging how fast a vehicle was actually traveling.

Discussion

The results of this experiment indicate that the form of a question (in this case, changes in a single word) can markedly and systematically affect a witness's answer to that question. The actual speed of the vehicles controlled little variance in subject reporting, while the phrasing of the question controlled considerable variance.

Two interpretations of this finding are possible. First, it is possible that the differential speed estimates result merely from response-bias factors. A subject is uncertain whether to say 30 mph or 40 mph, for example, and the verb *smashed* biases his response towards the higher estimate. A second interpretation is that the question form causes a change in the subject's memory representation of the accident. The verb *smashed* may change a subject's memory such that he "sees" the accident as being more severe than it actually was. If this is the case, we might expect subjects to "remember" other details that did not actually occur, but are commensurate with an accident occurring at higher speeds. The second experiment was designed to provide additional insights into the origin of the differential speed estimates.

Experiment II

Method

One hundred and fifty students participated in this experiment, in groups of various sizes. A film depicting a multiple car accident was shown, followed by a questionnaire. The film lasted less than 1 min; the accident in the film lasted 4 sec. At the end of the film, the subjects received a questionnaire asking them first to describe the accident in their own words, and then to answer a series of questions about the accident. The critical question was the one that interrogated the subject about the speed of the vehicles. Fifty subjects were asked, "About how fast were the cars going when they smashed into each other?" Fifty subjects were asked, "About how fast were the cars going when they hit each other?" Fifty subjects were not interrogated about vehicular speed.

One week later, the subjects returned and without viewing the film again they answered a series of questions about the accident. The critical question here was, "Did you see any broken glass?" which the subjects answered by checking "yes" or "no." This question was embedded in a list totalling 10 questions, and it appeared in a random position in the list. There was no broken glass in the accident, but, since broken glass is commensurate with accidents occurring at high speed, we expected that the subjects who had been asked the *smashed* question might more often say "yes" to this critical question.

Results

The mean estimate of speed for subjects interrogated with *smashed* was 10.46 mph; with *hit* the estimate was 8.00 mph. These means are significantly different, $t(98) = 2.00$, $p < .05$.

TABLE 2   DISTRIBUTION OF "YES" AND "NO" RESPONSES TO THE QUESTION, "DID YOU SEE ANY BROKEN GLASS?"

Response	Verb condition		
	Smashed	Hit	Control
Yes	16	7	6
No	34	43	44

Table 2 presents the distribution of "yes" and "no" responses for the *smashed*, *hit*, and control subjects. An independence chi-square test on these responses was significant beyond the .025 level, $\chi^2(2) = 7.76$. The important result in Table 2 is that the probability of saying "yes," P(Y), to the question about broken glass is .32 when the verb *smashed* is used, and .14 with *hit*. Thus *smashed* leads both to more "yes" responses and to higher speed estimates. It appears to be the case that the effect of the verb is mediated at least in part by the speed estimate. The question now arises: Is *smashed* doing anything else besides increasing the estimate of speed? To answer this, the function relating P(Y) to speed estimate was calculated separately for *smashed* and *hit*. If the speed estimate is the only way in which effect of verb is mediated, then for a given speed estimate, P(Y) should be independent of verb.

TABLE 3   PROBABILITY OF SAYING "YES" TO, "DID YOU SEE ANY
BROKEN GLASS?" CONDITIONALIZED ON SPEED ESTIMATES

Verb condition	Speed estimate (mph)			
	1–5	6–10	11–15	16–20
Smashed	.09	.27	.41	.62
Hit	.06	.09	.25	.50

Table 3 shows that this is not the case. P(Y) is lower for *hit* than
for *smashed*; the difference between the two verbs ranges from .03
for estimates of 1–5 mph to .18 for estimates of 6–10 mph. The
average difference between the two curves is about .12. Whereas
the unconditional difference of .18 between the *smashed* and *hit*
conditions is attenuated, it is by no means eliminated when
estimate of speed is controlled for. It thus appears that the verb
smashed has other effects besides that of simply increasing the
estimate of speed. One possibility will be discussed in the next
section.

Discussion

To reiterate, we have first of all provided an additional
demonstration of something that has been known for some time,
namely, that the way a question is asked can enormously influence
the answer that is given. In this instance, the question, "About how
fast were the cars going when they smashed into each other?" led
to higher estimates of speed than the same question asked with the
verb *smashed* replaced by *hit*. Furthermore, this seemingly small
change had consequences for how questions are answered a week
after the original event occurred.

As a framework for discussing these results, we would like to
propose that two kinds of information go into one's memory for
some complex occurrence. The first is information gleaned during
the perception of the original event; the second is external
information supplied after the fact. Over time, information from
these two sources may be integrated in such a way that we are
unable to tell from which source some specific detail is recalled.
All we have is one "memory."

Discussing the present experiments in these terms, we propose
that the subject first forms some representation of the accident he
has witnessed. The experimenter then, while asking, "About how

fast were the cars going when they smashed into each other?" supplies a piece of external information, namely, that the cars did indeed smash into each other.

When these two pieces of information are integrated, the subject has a memory of an accident that was more severe than in fact it was. Since broken glass is commensurate with a severe accident, the subject is more likely to think that broken glass was present.

There is some connection between the present work and earlier work on the influence of verbal labels on memory for visually presented form stimuli. A classic study in psychology showed that when subjects are asked to reproduce a visually presented form, their drawings tend to err in the direction of a more familiar object suggested by a verbal label initially associated with the to-be remembered form (Carmichael, Hogan, & Walter, 1932). More recently, Daniel (1972) showed that recognition memory, as well as reproductive memory, was similarly affected by verbal labels, and he concluded that the verbal label causes a shift in the memory strength of forms which are better representatives of the label.

When the experimenter asks the subject, "About how fast were the cars going when they smashed into each other?", he is effectively labelling the accident a smash. Extrapolating the conclusions of Daniel to this situation, it is natural to conclude that the label, smash, causes a shift in the memory representation of the accident in the direction of being more similar to a representation suggested by the verbal label.

References

Bird, C. The influence of the press upon the accuracy report. *Journal of Abnormal and Social Psychology*, 1927, 22, 123–129

Block, R. A. Memory and the experience of duration in retrospect. *Memory & Cognition*, 1974, 2, 53–160.

Bransford, J. D., & McCarrell, N. S. A sketch of a cognitive approach to comprehension: Some thoughts about understanding what it means to comprehend. In D. Palermo & W. Weimer (Eds.), *Cognition and the symbolic processes*. Washington, D. C.: V. H. Winston & Co., in press.

Carmichael, L., Hogan, P., & Walter, A. A. An experimental study of the effect of language on the reproduction of visually perceived form. *Journal of Experimental Psychology*, 1932, 15, 73–86.

Clark, H. H. The language-as-fixed-effect fallacy: A critique of language statistics in psychological research. *Journal of Verbal Learning and Verbal Behavior*, 1973, 12, 335–359.

Daniel, T. C. Nature of the effect of verbal labels on recognition memory for form. *Journal of Experimental Psychology*, 1972, 96, 152–157.

Fillmore, C. J. Types of lexical information. In D. D. Steinberg and L.A. Jakobovits (Eds.), *Semantics: An interdisciplinary reader in philosophy, linguistics, and psychology*. Cambridge: Cambridge University Press, 1971.

Gardner, D. S. The perception and memory of witnesses, *Cornell Law Quarterly*, 1933, 8, 391–409.

Marshall, J. *Law and psychology in conflict*. New York: Anchor Books, 1969.

Ornstein, R. E. On *The experience of time*. Harmondsworth, Middlesex. England: Penguin, 1969.

Whipple, G. M. The observer as reporter: A survey of the psychology of testimony. *Psychological Bulletin*, 1909, 6, 153–170.

Supreme Court Reporter, 1973, 3: Rules of Evidence for United State Courts and Magistrates.

(Received April 17, 1974)

This research was supported by the Urban Mass Transportation Administration, Department of Transportation, Grant No. WA-11-0004. Thanks go to Geoffrey Loftus, Edward E. Smith, and Stephen Woods for many important and helpful comments, Reprint requests should be sent to Elizabeth F. Loftus. Department of Psychology, University of Washington, Seattle, Washington 98195.

(Loftus and Palmer, 1974, pp. 585–9)

3.3 Deviating from the reporting convention

One thing that may have struck you when reading the Loftus and Palmer (1974) report is that their Method section was not divided into separate categories (such as Design, Procedure, etc.). After you have read a number of journal articles, you will realise that there is no single convention specifying how to set out the Method section, and that different journals and different authors structure the information in different ways. However, all of the relevant information should be included and at a level of detail sufficient to allow another researcher to replicate the study. When learning how to report research, it is a good idea to stick to structuring the Method section using the following subsections:

- Design
- Participants
- Materials
- Procedure

Indeed, using these subsections is a good idea even once you've gained considerable expertise in writing research reports because they ensure that you include all the information needed.

Activity 9.3

Below are some of the sentences from Loftus and Palmer's first experiment. See if you can work out which of the subsections of a Method section the sentences belong to.

Sentence	Which subsection?
Forty-five students participated in groups of various sizes.	
Seven films were shown, each depicting a traffic accident.	
These films were from longer driver's education borrowed from the Evergreen Safety Council and the Seattle Police Department.	
The length of the film segments ranged from 5 to 30 sec.	
Following each film, the subjects received a questionnaire.	
Subjects received a questionnaire asking first to, "give an account of the accident you have just seen," and then to answer a series of specific questions about the accident.	
Nine subjects were asked, "About how fast were the cars going when they hit each other?" Equal numbers of the remaining subjects were interrogated with the verbs *smashed, collided,* and *contacted* in place of ***hit***.	

The entire experiment lasted about an hour and a half.	
A different ordering of the films was presented to each group of subjects.	

Below are the answers from the module team. It is perhaps worth noting that there was not complete agreement in every instance between everyone as to what the correct answer should be. Some of the team thought that this sentence, 'Subjects received a questionnaire asking first to, "give an account of the accident you have just seen," and then to answer a series of specific questions about the accident.', should be in the Materials section, while some thought it should be in the Procedure. Not only do many research reports deviate from the convention by not including subheadings or including different subheadings, it is also common for different authors to put different information in different places. The most important thing is that all the information needed to replicate the study is included somewhere.

Sentence	Which subsection?
Forty-five students participated in groups of various sizes.	Participants
Seven films were shown, each depicting a traffic accident.	Materials
These films were from longer driver's education borrowed from the Evergreen Safety Council and the Seattle Police Department.	Materials
The length of the film segments ranged from 5 to 30 sec.	Materials
Following each film, the subjects received a questionnaire.	Procedure
Subjects received a questionnaire asking first to, "give an account of the accident you have just seen," and then to answer a series of specific questions about the accident.	Materials

Nine subjects were asked, "About how fast were the cars going when they hit each other?" Equal numbers of the remaining subjects were interrogated with the verbs *smashed*, *collided*, and *contacted* in place of **hit**.	Design This sentence could be in the Materials subsection, but it actually contains details about the IV and how it was manipulated, which is the aim of Design subsection
The entire experiment lasted about an hour and a half.	Procedure
A different ordering of the films was presented to each group of subjects.	Design This could be in the Procedure subsection, but it describes one of the experimental controls that was introduced to try to limit the impact of confounding variables

The Method section in the Loftus and Palmer report probably gave you a fairly good idea about what happened in the experiment, but do you think you could replicate the experiment on the basis of the information provided here? Can you think of any information that is missing?

Not much information is provided about the participants (referred to in the report as 'subjects'), including how old they were, what gender they were and what they were students of. But perhaps more importantly, all we are told about the films used is that they varied from 5 to 30 seconds in length and were used by the police for driver education. Although a little more information is later provided in the Results section, it would still be difficult to replicate the experiment without knowing more about the collisions.

So, when writing a Method section, you should aim to provide more information than Loftus and Palmer did in their report, and you should also make sure that you use the four subsections: Design, Participants, Material and Procedure.

Summary

- Reports of psychological experiments are written to follow a particular structure; within this, inferential statistics are also reported according to a convention.

- Many published reports deviate from the standard structure to allow for the complexities of a particular study, but they still attempt to provide the information needed for replication.

4 Report writing for quantitative studies

This final section will revisit the report template that you have encountered throughout this book and at the same time reflect briefly on what you have learned about report writing. The knowledge and skills covered in this book, and your practice in writing sections of a report as part of the DE100 project, will be invaluable to you as you progress with your studies. In later modules you will learn about how to report research conducted using methods other than an experiment, but the basic approach to writing research reports is similar regardless of the specific method employed.

4.1 The template for reporting a psychological experiment

A research report is divided into six main sections: the Abstract, Introduction, Method, Results, Discussion, and References. You also, of course, need a title. In addition, you may want to consider including an Appendix. Appendices are only rarely used in published journal articles, but are often required when you are learning how to write reports. Let's look again at each section in the research report template as we did in Chapter 1.

Figure 9.6   Your report template

- **Title**. A report should have a succinct and informative title. Don't be tempted to aim for something witty – be informative. You may want to look at some of the titles of reports listed in the references for this chapter and think about what makes some report titles more informative than others.

- **Abstract**. The Abstract is a short paragraph summarising the entire report. You saw examples of this in Chapters 1, 3 and 9 where the authors provided succinct summaries of their studies and what they found. The Abstract should state what the study was about, what method was used to carry out the research, the results obtained (in plain English without statistical jargon), and what the results meant.

- **Introduction**. The Introduction to the report must set out the background and rationale for the research. It should summarise the existing research around the topic and explain why the current study is needed. Remember you were introduced in Chapter 1 to the idea that the Introduction is funnel shaped: it should start by identifying the topic of the study, introducing relevant literature, and gradually narrow the focus to the precise issue being investigated. It should finish with a statement of the hypothesis in quantitative studies and with the research question in qualitative studies. The extracts from Allum (2011) in Chapter 1 and Hayne et al. (2003) in Chapter 3 provided clear examples of this structure. You may want to have another look now to remind yourself. Can you see how each Introduction set up the overall topic and purpose of the study, and explained the existing literature, all carefully referenced? Both of these Introductions then narrowed their focus to the study being reported. Both ended with a statement of the hypothesis.

- **Method**. You are familiar now with the idea that different journals require slightly different formats for the Method section, although they all require similar information. You have seen several examples of Method sections, or parts of Method sections, throughout this book. But, they do not all follow a conventional format. The report by Loftus and Palmer (1974) presented in this chapter is an example of that. While you should use these examples for ideas about how to express yourself, when writing your own quantitative reports in the future you should use these four subsections: *Design*, *Participants*, *Materials*, and *Procedure*.
  - The *Design* subsection must state what type of study you conducted (e.g. was it a correlational study or an experiment?) and what the variables were. For an experiment, this also means stating the IV and DV. You should also say how the

variables were 'operationalised' (i.e. how were they put into practice).

For a correlational study, this means stating how the variables were measured. For an experiment, it means stating the conditions of the IV, and how the DV was measured. This section should also include a description of any controls that were introduced (i.e. any steps taken to limit the potential effects from any variables other than those being measured).

Chapter 8, Section 3.1, provided an example of a Design section from the report by Nelson et al. (2011), but remember that Section 3.1 also pointed out what was missing from their Design section.

You read about operationalisation in Chapter 7, Section 2.1.

You read about confounding variables in Chapter 8, Section 1.1.

o   The *Participants* subsection must state how many participants took part in the study, with an indication of who the participants were, such as the number of males and females, mean age and any other relevant information. Chapter 3, Section 3.2, gives an example of what was considered relevant in the study by Hayne et al. (2003) in their investigation of infants learning through imitation. Note though that the Participants section should also say how participants were recruited, and whether they received any payment or other incentive. You would be expected to include this in your report.

o   The *Materials* subsection must give details of any stimuli used in the study, and any equipment (including computer software) used to conduct the study. This section should also give details of how data were recorded. You saw an example of this in Chapter 5, Section 3.2, in relation to the coding scheme conducted by Prato-Previde et al. (2003). Alternatively, if your study was analysing data from an existing database or archive, you would describe this instead. Allum (2011) would have done this when he described the Eurobarometer data he drew on for his study of belief in astrology which you read about in Chapter 1.

o   The *Procedure* subsection must provide a step-by-step description of how the study was conducted, and a description of all the instructions given. You saw examples of this in the study by Burger (2009) in Chapter 2, Section 3.1, which discussed the importance of giving sufficient detail not just in the Procedure subsection, but throughout the Method section, to allow other researchers to replicate your study.

Remember you have access to the complete journal articles on the module website.

- **Results**. The Results section in a quantitative report should follow a clear structure. Your Results section should begin by restating the hypothesis because this will remind your reader what is being tested. You should describe the data collected, that is, state how they were measured and whether they were nominal, ordinal or interval. You should also include details of any calculations performed on the data, once the data were collected and before statistical analysis, such as combining two or more scales, for example. Descriptive statistics should be provided: either as a table (you saw an example in Chapter 4, Section 3.2, in an extract from Chen et al., 2012); or as a graph (you saw examples of this in Chapter 7, Section 3.2, in relation to the study of aphasia by Bakheit et al., 2007). Make sure that you give the tables or graphs a caption so that your reader knows what they are looking at. You should not leave your reader to work out what is indicated by the descriptive statistics, however, so make sure you also include a statement in plain English of what the descriptive statistics show. As you now know, you should also state what inferential statistical analysis was conducted (such as a chi-square test, or a t-test). Furthermore, you must report the results of this analysis in the conventional statistical form. You saw examples of reporting the chi-square test and the t-test in Chapter 8, Section 3.2, in relation to the study on change blindness by Nelson et al. (2011). Even though your report of the statistical test will indicate the p value, you should still state in words whether the result was statistically significant or not. Don't leave it to your reader to work it out (even though they could). Similarly, you should state whether the hypothesis is accepted or rejected. This might seem to be a great deal of information but it can, and should, be presented succinctly.

Box 9.2   Qualitative research reports

You will know from Chapter 6, Section 3, that while qualitative research reports share many similarities with quantitative research reports, in the Results section in particular they take a very different format.

You saw an example of the findings from a qualitative study in Chapter 6, which presented extracts from Hamm and Faircloth's (2005) thematic analysis of friendship and belonging. You may want to take this opportunity to compare the style of the Results section you would write for a quantitative report (see Chapters 4, 7 and 8, for example) with that presented in Chapter 6 for a qualitative report.

The key difference of course is that quantitative reports present the results using numbers, such as descriptive statistics and inferential statistics, and frequently graphs and tables are included. Also included is a clear statement about whether the hypothesis is accepted or rejected. In qualitative research, the Results section takes the form of a narrative describing what was found, often including examples of data such as quotes from interviewees, and all of this is related to the research question that underpinned the study. Indeed, in qualitative reports this section is often called 'Analysis', not 'Results'. This is in recognition of the way in which qualitative research aims to present a careful account of the researcher's decisions and interpretations, which might be expected to differ somewhat from one researcher to the next. 'Results' implies that if the numerical data were analysed in the same way by any researcher, the results would always be the same. With qualitative analyses, each researcher's analysis would be slightly different.

- **Discussion**. This is the section where you explain what your findings mean. You know from Chapter 7, Section 3.3, that a Discussion section should begin by stating the results of your study in plain language. It must also provide an explanation of the results obtained. It is not sufficient to say what you found; you must also say what you think it means. Therefore, you should explain how your findings compare with other research in the field; that is, with the literature you described in your Introduction. The extracts from Bakheit et al. (2007) in Chapter 7 illustrate this well. Note that Chapter 7, Section 3.3, also suggests that you should offer suggestions for how your findings could be applied beyond the study. An important feature of the Discussion section is your critical evaluation of your research. Here you would say what the limitations of your study are. This might be an issue about your method, such as your sampling procedures, or your materials, or procedure. But, you should also point out the strengths of your study. The purpose of your critical evaluation is not to undermine everything you have done, but to assess it. The Discussion section should also include suggestions for future research. Remember that research is part of a cycle of enquiry and this is the place where you can suggest the next steps in that cycle.

- **References**. A point that has been made many times during this module is the absolute requirement to cite the sources of your evidence and your ideas. You will have seen examples throughout all the chapters, and many of the extracts too cite references for the sources that the authors drew on. As this chapter included the entire report from Loftus and Palmer (1974), you also had an opportunity to see their referencing right across the report and of course their Reference list. As you might expect by now, just as different journals require slightly different formats for the Method section for instance, so too do they require a particular format for references, and authors are expected to adapt to the requirements of the journal. You will be expected to reference thoroughly within your report (and within any essays you write), as the authors in the reports cited here have done. And, in the same way that those authors were required to format their references in a particular way, so too are you required to format your references in a particular way (using the OU Harvard referencing convention).
- **Appendix**. If included, the Appendix will typically contain examples of stimuli used in the experiment and a copy of the instructions given to participants.

Summary

- Although published research often deviates from the standard report template, it is important when learning how to write a report that you follow the template.
- Each section and subsection of a report should include specific information.

References

Allum, N. (2011) 'What makes some people think astrology is scientific?', *Science Communication*, vol. 33, pp. 341–66.

Bakheit, A. M. O., Shaw, S., Carrington, S. and Griffiths, S. (2007) 'The rate and extent of improvement with therapy from the different types of aphasia in the first year after stroke', *Clinical Rehabilitation*, vol. 21, no. 10, pp. 941–9.

Burger, J. M. (2009) 'Replicating Milgram: would people still obey today?', *American Psychologist*, vol. 64, no. 1, pp. 1–11.

Chen, C.-Y., Lin Y.-H. and Hsiao, C.-L. (2012) 'Celebrity endorsement for sporting events using classical conditioning', *International Journal of Sports Marketing & Sponsorship*, April, pp. 209–19.

Hamm, J. V. and Faircloth, B. S. (2005) 'The role of friendship in adolescents' sense of school belonging', *New Directions for Child and Adolescent Development*, vol. 107, pp. 61–78.

Hayne, H., Herbert, J. and Simcock, G. (2003) 'Imitation from television by 24- and 30-month-olds', *Developmental Science*, vol. 6, no. 3, pp. 254–61.

Loftus, E. F. and Palmer, J. C. (1974) 'Reconstruction of automobile destruction: an example of the interaction between language and memory', *Journal of Verbal Learning and Verbal Behavior*, vol. 13, no. 5, pp. 585–9.

Merckelbach, H., Horselenberg, R. and Muris, P. (2001) 'The Creative Experiences Questionnaire (CEQ): a brief self-report measure of fantasy proneness', *Personality and Individual Differences*, vol. 31, no. 6, pp. 987–95.

Nelson, K. J., Laney, C., Fowler, N. B., Knowles, E. D. and Loftus, E. F. (2011) 'Change blindness can cause mistaken eyewitness identification', *Legal and Criminological Psychology*, vol. 16, no. 1, pp. 62–74.

Ost, J., Granhag, P. A., Udell, J. and Roos af Hjelmsäter, E. (2008) 'Familiarity breeds distortion: the effects of media exposure on false reports of real life traumatic events', *Memory*, vol. 16, no. 1, pp. 76–85.

Pike, G. and Brace, N. (2012) 'Witnessing and remembering', in Brace, N. and Byford, J. (eds) *Investigating Psychology*, Oxford, Oxford University Press/Milton Keynes, The Open University.

Prato-Previde, E., Custance, D. M., Spiezio, C. and Sabatini, F. (2003) 'Is the dog–human relationship an attachment bond? An observational study using Ainsworth's Strange Situation', *Behaviour*, vol. 140, no. 2, pp. 225–54.

Commentary 3

Having read all nine chapters of *Investigating Methods*, you should now have a better understanding of the research process in psychology, from choosing a research question and a method, through data collection and analysis, to the reporting of findings. You have also learned about the different sections of a research report, and have read a complete report of the Loftus and Palmer (1974) study.

Let's revisit the main teaching points from Part 3 of *Investigating Methods*. Did you notice that the focus of this last part was on quantitative data? This is because the aim was to introduce you to inferential statistical tests, and these kinds of tests are only performed on quantitative data. Other tools are used for qualitative data, and you read about one such tool, thematic analysis, in Part 2 (Chapter 6).

Many psychology students often say they worry about whether or not they have properly understood statistics. Learning statistical analysis is a gradual process. It is not unusual to find that it is only near the end of their psychology degree, when students undertake their own independent project work, that many of the concepts associated with inferential statistical tests properly make sense to them. If you feel uncertain about whether you have properly understood everything you learned about in the module, then don't worry. As you continue with your studies you will have further opportunities to engage with project work and analyse data, and with practice you will become more confident. Importantly, many psychology students find that the experience of carrying out research is the most exciting part of their studies. So, any concern that you might feel about engaging with statistics will probably be outweighed by the excitement of designing, running and writing up your own research. This is because when you attempt to carry out research yourself, you get a clearer sense of the challenges and rewards involved in conducting psychological research. By doing research and gathering evidence yourself, you gain a better understanding of all the different elements involved, and you also begin to understand the need to evaluate the evidence properly when drawing conclusions.

One of the key points we hope you have learned is that you cannot draw conclusions about quantitative data from descriptive statistics alone. Instead, you must perform an inferential statistical test. Let's remind ourselves why. Imagine that you want to see if there is a difference in the performance on a task between two groups of participants. You collect the data, calculate the means and find that they are not identical. This suggests that there might be a difference in performance between the two groups. Inferential statistical tests will allow you to decide whether there really is a difference between the two groups, or whether what you observed may just be down to the two particular samples of people you selected. In other words, they will tell you whether the difference is a 'real' difference or simply the result of chance fluctuations. By performing an inferential statistical test, a probability value 'p' is calculated, and this value tells you how likely it is that the difference you saw in your data, and in your descriptive statistics, could have occurred due to chance. Psychologists have agreed that .05 is a reasonable cut-off point, so the calculated value of p has to be smaller than .05 to be considered 'statistically significant'. In other words, if p is less than .05 there is less than a one in 20 chance that the results occurred just by chance. If p is larger than .05 then there is just too much risk that the difference observed *could* have happened by chance alone.

There are many different types of inferential statistical tests, and we have only introduced you to two of these: the chi-square statistic and the *t*-test. However, regardless of which inferential test you use, they all provide a p value and it is this that allows you to interpret your results. Not surprisingly, then, it is essential to report the p value in your Results section. There are, in fact, five basic pieces of information that should be included in the Results section, and these are set out in Chapter 9: the test performed, for example, chi-square or *t*-test; degrees of freedom; the chi-square or t value calculated; the p value; and the effect size.

If you are concerned about how you would calculate these tests, remember that the vast majority of psychologists do not perform inferential statistical analysis by hand and instead use statistical software, and this software will calculate the value of p and all these other pieces of information. You just need to pick out the relevant bits for your report and understand what they mean. You saw examples of this in Chapters 8 and 9.

Remember, however, that finding out whether your results are 'statistically significant' simply tells you *how likely* it is that you would get that particular pattern of data. To decide whether a statistically significant result is meaningful, you also have to consider the design of the study itself and how the study was conducted. This is particularly important in psychology as often what we are measuring are psychological constructs. Measuring someone's IQ is a very different proposition from measuring someone's height! You read in Chapter 7 that many of the things that psychologists are interested in cannot be directly observed or measured. Instead, psychological constructs have to be defined in a way that allows them to be measured, and this is what is meant by 'operationalising' the variables. So, when trying to make sense of a statistically significant result relating to a psychological construct, it is important to think about how this was measured, to consider its validity (did the researcher measure what they thought they were measuring), and its reliability (the likelihood that if the researcher measures the variable in that way again, they will get similar results). Therefore, while you would report the descriptive and inferential statistics in the Results section, the Discussion section is where you need to make sense of the findings, and evaluate the study. This would include looking at how the variables were operationalised, and any limitations that might be associated with the particular operational definition chosen.

The aim of this book has been to help you acquire a basic understanding of research methods and to develop skills which will allow you to make sense of psychological research reports and to carry out research yourself. Other psychology modules will build on this and develop further both your understanding of the research process and your research skills. If you progress to Levels 2 and 3, you will be expected to engage in reading more primary sources and to demonstrate greater evaluation skills. We hope that we have instilled in you a desire to read primary sources: book chapters are a valuable and efficient way of gaining a sense of broader issues, but it is from actual research reports that you gain a greater sense of the complexity of psychological research. The Introductions to reports will provide a concise overview of the field and the Discussion sections can be very illuminating in terms of the detail and the broader issues facing those attempting to research a particular topic. Also, the more research reports that you read, the more familiar you will become with the terminology used in psychology, and this will hone your evaluation skills too.

Note, though, that conventions for reporting research have changed over the years. Older research reports may well be shorter, there may be omissions in regard to information about ethics, and the term 'subjects' rather than 'participants' might be used. You are likely to find a bias towards quantitative methods in older reports and this is because the use of qualitative methods has grown considerably over recent decades. In terms of quantitative data analysis, there is now an emphasis on reporting the effect size alongside p value. Also, whereas previously there was a requirement to write in the third person when reporting quantitative research ('it was'), it is now acknowledged that it may be more appropriate in places to use the first person ('I'). Furthermore, while inferential statistical tests used to be calculated using a calculator, the advent of computers and statistical software means that more powerful and more complex tests can now be performed.

As explained in the 'Final note' of *Investigating Psychology*, psychology is a perpetually developing body of knowledge; it is a dynamic discipline that is influenced by developments in society as a whole. While research questions are rooted in previous work, which you saw illustrated through the concept of the cycle of enquiry, they are also influenced by what is happening in society. If you read primary sources, then you will be able to see how psychological research is informed by what is happening in the broader social and political environment of the day, as well as by earlier research and theories.

Before you finish your reading of this book, check that you understand what these terms mean:

Chapter 7:

- Functional magnetic resonance imaging (fMRI)
- Case study
- Psychological constructs
- Validity
- Ecological validity
- Population validity
- Reliability
- Quasi-experimental design

Chapter 8:

- Sampling error
- Measures of central tendency
- *p* value
- Effect size
- Chi-square
- *t*-test

Chapter 9:

- Degrees of freedom

Final note

If you have been reading this book alongside your other module materials and your study guide, you will now be very close to completing your studies for DE100. We hope that you have found the study of psychology as rewarding and fascinating as we have. Perhaps you have already identified aspects of human – or non-human – psychology about which you want to understand more. Whatever you go on to study next, we hope that you will be able to take with you the skill and desire to evaluate critically, and carefully, the merits of any information presented to you. Good luck in your future studies.

Glossary

Between-participants design

Also referred to as an independent groups design. This is a term used to describe the design of an experiment where participants take part in only one condition.

Case study

In neuropsychology a case study is the in-depth study of a single individual, which typically involves the collection of data from a variety of sources, using a range of different methods.

Cognitive psychology

The study of internal mental processes such as perception, attention, memory, thinking and learning.

Confounding variable

A variable that is not controlled by the researcher but that can affect the results.

Content analysis

Involves analysing the content of written material or audio-visual material, and coding this in terms of pre-selected features.

Control condition

The 'baseline' condition, against which experimental conditions can be compared.

Correlation

An association between two events, meaning that they tend to occur together more often than one might expect by chance.

Correlation coefficient

This is a measure of the strength and direction of the relationship between two variables.

Counterbalancing

An aspect of experimental design that includes all possible orders in which participants complete tasks or conditions, or in which experimenters present stimuli – this is to control for order effects.

Cycle of enquiry

The way in which the questions that research addresses are often derived from theories or explanations, and the findings of that research then generate new questions or refinements to theory or explanation.

Data mining

The computer-assisted identification and retrieval of data from a vast database.

Deductive coding

Codes are generated from existing literature.

Degrees of freedom

A feature of reporting inferential statistics which indicates sample size and/or number of conditions.

Demand effects

The effects on behaviour when participants are aware of taking part in research and adapt their behaviour as a consequence.

Dependent variable

A variable that is expected to change as a result of the manipulation of the independent variable.

Descriptive statistics

These are used to describe features of a data set; for example, the mean and the standard deviation.

Direction of effect

Describes which of two variables is the initial cause and which is the resulting effect.

Ecological validity

The extent to which a study reflects naturally occurring or everyday situations.

Ethnography

A research approach where the researcher carries out extensive observations of a group through being involved in its activities over a period of time.

Evaluative conditioning

Liking or disliking something because it has been associated with something positive or negative.

Experiment

A research method that looks at the effect of an independent variable on a dependent variable.

Experimental condition

A condition in an experiment where participants are exposed to a specific variation in the independent variable.

fMRI

Functional magnetic resonance imaging is a technique that allows the blood flow in the brain to be monitored while the individual undertakes a particular task.

Generalisability

The extent to which research findings can be applied to people or settings beyond those included in the original study.

Holistic

Relating to the consideration of a person as a whole rather than focusing only on specific aspects.

Hypothesis

A hypothesis is a researcher's prediction about what will happen when a quantitative study, such as an experiment, is conducted. The researcher then tests this prediction.

Immersion

The process of becoming very familiar with your data by scrutinising it repeatedly over a period of time.

Independent variable

A variable that is manipulated by the experimenter to see what effect this has on another variable.

Inductive coding

Codes are generated from the data.

Inferential statistics

Statistical tests that permit conclusions to be drawn from quantitative data generated by research.

Interval level

Measurement on a scale where the differences, the intervals, between the points on the scale are the same.

Mean

An average that is calculated by adding together all the items and then dividing the total by the number of items.

Measurement

To apply a numerical measure according to a fixed, defined rule.

Measures of central tendency

The mean, median and mode tell you what score sits at the 'middle' or 'centre' of a sample.

Measures of distribution

The standard deviation and the range tell you about the variability and spread of scores in a sample.

Median

The score in the middle of a set of scores placed in order of magnitude.

Nominal level

Measurement involves naming an attribute of the participants or their responses.

Objectivity

Judgement based on observable phenomena and without the influence of personal opinion, emotion or bias.

Operational definition

Describes exactly what your variables are and how they are measured in your study.

Operationalisation

This is the process of devising an operational definition.

Order effects

A term used to describe the influence that performing one task may have on performing another task, and therefore a consideration for any experiment with a within-participants design.

Ordinal level

Measurement on a scale that allows data to be put in an order, but differences between the points on the scale are not the same.

Population validity

A type of external validity that indicates how well a study's findings can be applied to the wider population.

Principle of localisation

The principle that psychological functions can be associated with particular regions of the brain.

Pseudo-sciences

The appearance of scientific methods but lacking in proper application of those methods.

Psychological constructs

Psychological processes that are believed to occur but cannot be directly observed or measured.

Qualitative methods

Methods which generate data that are not in numerical form, for instance interviews, written text such as newspaper articles or diaries, visual materials such as photographic records, or detailed observations of behaviour and practices.

Quantitative methods

Methods which generate data that can be measured, counted or expressed in numerical terms; for example, scores, ratings or percentages.

Quasi-experimental design

A design where the experimenter assigns people to a condition based on naturally occurring characteristics, such as sex, age, height, IQ or a personality trait.

Random allocation

A feature of between-participants design where participants are randomly assigned to different conditions.

Range

A measure of dispersion representing the difference between the smallest and the largest score in a data set.

Reliability

Reliability refers to the consistency, or stability, of a measure or study. In other words, it is the extent to which it can produce the same results under similar circumstances.

Replication

When a result from a research study is found again in a subsequent study. Replication is important to establishing the reliability of a finding.

Representative extracts

(or excerpts, or exemplars) from interviews can be included in the text to provide an example of what participants actually said.

Research question

A research question is a carefully worded question stating precisely what a researcher is trying to find out in a study.

Rigour

A careful and thorough approach to methods and argument; to work rigorously is to work with systematic integrity.

Sample

Subset of the population of interest that is studied in a piece of research.

Sampling

The process of selecting participants for a study.

Sampling error

This refers to the fact that any sample, however chosen, is unlikely to represent exactly the population from which it was drawn.

Self-report

Any method of collecting data that asks participants to supply information about themselves, such as their beliefs, attitudes or feelings. Common examples are questionnaires and interviews.

Semi-structured interviews

Questions are prepared in advance but the interviewer may ask additional questions during the interview in response to the interviewee's comments.

Social desirability bias

The tendency for people to respond to questions in a way they believe would meet the approval of others.

Standard deviation

A descriptive statistic that represents the average amount by which individual values in the data differ (or deviate) from the mean.

Standardisation

The process of ensuring that all participants undergo the same treatment and that all data are recorded in the same way.

Standardised test

A test that is designed to capture a specific psychological construct and is administered, scored and interpreted in a standard manner. Standardised tests have usually been rigorously tested for reliability and validity on a large number of individuals in an array of different situations and contexts.

Structured coding scheme

This is a set of pre-specified categories that is used to code behaviour.

Structured interviews

These entail asking the same questions of all the participants, in the same order.

Subjectivity

Knowledge and understanding arising from personal involvement and experience.

Subthemes

The individual components of a theme.

Thematic analysis

A qualitative method used to identify, analyse and report patterns (themes) in qualitative data.

Universalism

The assumption that phenomena observed in a study can be generalised to other contexts.

Unstructured interviews

These are the most flexible interviews, beginning with a provisional list of questions which will be adapted to suit the details that unfold in the interview.

Validity

Validity is the extent to which a measure or study is measuring what it set out to measure.

Variables

In psychological research these are any thing that can vary and be measured, controlled or manipulated.

Variance

A measure of dispersion which involves subtracting the mean from each score and squaring the result, and then arriving at an average of these values. By taking the square root of the variance, the standard deviation can be calculated.

Within-participants design

Also referred to as a repeated measures design. This is a term used to describe the design of an experiment where participants complete all conditions.

Acknowledgements

Grateful acknowledgement is made to the following sources:

Every effort has been made to contact copyright holders. If any have been inadvertently overlooked the publishers will be pleased to make the necessary arrangements at the first opportunity.

Text

Chapter 2: Burger, J.M. (2009) 'Replicating Milgram: would people still obey today?' *American Psychologist*, vol. 64, no. 1, pp. 1–11. Copyright © 2009 by the American Psychological Association. Reproduced with permission.

Chapter 4: Chen, C.-Y., Lin, Y.-H. and Hsiao, C.-L. (2012) 'Celebrity endorsement for sporting events using classical conditioning', *International Journal of Sports Marketing & Sponsorship*, April, pp. 209–19. Copyright © International Marketing Reports Ltd, UK.

Chapter 9: Loftus, E.F. and Palmer, J.C. (1974) 'Reconstruction of automobile destruction: an example of the interaction between language and memory', *Journal of Verbal Learning and Verbal Behavior*, vol. 13, no. 5, pp. 585–9. Copyright © 2013 Elsevier Inc. All rights reserved.

Figures

Figure 1.1: Copyright © Lightspring/Shutterstock; Figure 1.2: Copyright © Everett Collection/Shutterstock; Figure 1.3: Copyright © iStockPhoto/FeralMartian; Figure 1.4: Copyright © Leremy/Shutterstock; Figure 1.8: Copyright © iStockPhoto.com/pixelparticle; Figure 1.9: Courtesy of Revathy Kumar; Figure 1.10a: Copyright © dboystudio/Shutterstock; Figure 1.10b: Copyright © iStockPhoto.com/MBI_Images; Figure 2.1: Copyright © iStockPhoto.com/apomares; Figure 2.2: Copyright © Monkey Business Images/Shutterstock; Figure 2.3: Copyright © Hasloo Group Production Studio; Figure 2.5 top left and bottom left: Milgram, S. (1974) *Obedience to Authority*, Harper & Row. Copyright © 1974 by Stanley Milgram; Figure 2.5 top right: Image used with permission from Prof. Jerry Burger, Santa Clara University, USA; Figure 2.5 bottom right: Courtesy of Prof. Jerry Burger, Santa Clara University, USA; Figure 2.6: Copyright © by Stanley Milgram; Figure 3.1: Copyright © iStockPhoto.com/RobertHarness; Figure 3.2: Copyright © Philipp Hympendahl /Alamy; Figure 3.3: Copyright © MarchCattle/Shutterstock; Figure 3.5: Copyright ©

Herbert, J. and Hayne, H. (2000) 'Memory retrieval by 18–30-month-olds: age-related changes in representational flexibility', *Developmental Psychology*, vol. 36, no. 4, pp. 475–6. Reproduced by permission of the American Psychological Association Inc.; Figure 3.6: Copyright © iStockPhoto.com/iqoncept; Figure 4.1: Copyright © Erik Lam/ Shutterstock; Figure 4.6: Copyright © Eric Isselee/Shutterstock; Figure 4.8: Copyright © iStockPhoto.com/leaf; Figure 4.9 left: Copyright © iStockPhoto.com/Matt_Brown; Figure 4.9 right: Copyright © iStockPhoto.com/peepo; Figure 4.11: Copyright © pirita/ Shutterstock; Figure 5.7: Copyright © iStockPhoto.com/vgajic; Figure 5.8: Images used with permission from Prato-Previde et al. (2003) 'Is the dog–human relationship an attachment bond? An observational study using Ainsworth's Strange Situation', *Behaviour*, vol. 140, no. 2, p. 233. Copyright © Koninklijke Brill NV, Leiden, 2003; Figure 5.10: Copyright © iStockPhoto.com/winterling; Figure 6.1 top left: Copyright © iStockPhoto.com/benandlens; Figure 6.1 top right: Copyright © iStockPhoto.com/AAR Studio; Figure 6.1 bottom left: Copyright © Peteri /Shutterstock; Figure 6.1 bottom right: Copyright © xamnesiacx/Shutterstock; Figure 6.2: Copyright © XiXinXing/ Shutterstock; Figure 6.3 left: Copyright © Elnur/Shutterstock; Figure 6.3 right: Copyright © Pressmaster/Shutterstock; Figure 6.4: Copyright © Nomad_Soul / Shutterstock; Figure 6.5: Copyright © Dasha Petrenko/Shutterstock; Figure 6.10: Copyright © iStockPhoto. com/tungstenblue; Figure 7.4: Courtesy of Wonderlic at www.wonderlic. com; Figure 8.1: Copyright © imagetaker1; Figure 8.2 left: Copyright © iStockPhoto.com/ranplett; Figure 8.2 right: Copyright © iStockPhoto. com/Squaredpixels; Figure 8.3: Copyright © iStockPhoto.com/ ManuelBurgos; Figure 8.4: Copyright © Everett Collection/Shutterstock; Figure 8.5: Reproduced by kind permission of Daniel J. Simons and Daniel R. Levin; Figure 8.6: Image reproduced with permission from Simons, D. J., & Chabris, C. F. (1999). Gorillas in our midst: Sustained inattentional blindness for dynamic events. Perception, 28, 1059-1074. www.theinvisiblegorilla.com; Figure 8.9: Copyright © Junial Enterprises/ Shutterstock; Figure 9.1: Copyright © shironosov/iStockPhoto.com; Figure 9.2: Copyright © Timo Schenke/Shutterstock; Figure 9.3: Copyright © National Media Museum/Science & Society Picture Library; Figure 9.4: Copyright © Graham Pike.

Index